STRESS AND TRAUMA

Stress and trauma

Patricia A. Resick, PhD
*Center for Trauma Recovery and Department of Psychology,
University of Missouri – St. Louis, USA*

First published 2001 by Psychology Press Ltd
27 Church Road, Hove, East Sussex, BN3 2FA, UK

www.psypress.co.uk

Simultaneously published in the USA and Canada
by Taylor & Francis Inc
325 Chestnut Street, Suite 800, Philadelphia, PA 19106, USA

Psychology Press is part of the Taylor & Francis Group

Reprinted 2001

British Library Cataloguing in Publication Data
A catalogue record for this book is available from the British Library

Library of Congress Cataloging-in-Publication Data
Resick, Patricia A.
    Stress and trauma / Patricia A. Resick.
        p. cm. — (Clinical psychology, a modular course, ISSN 1368-454X)
    Includes bibliographical references and index.
    ISBN 1-84169-163-1 (alk. paper) – ISBN 1-84169-190-9
    1. Post-traumatic stress disorder. 2. Psychic trauma. 3. Stress (Psychology)
    I. Title. II. Series

    RC552.P67 R47 2000
    616.85'21–dc21
                                                            00-055381
    ISBN 1-84169-163-1 (Hbk)
    ISBN 1-84169-190-9 (Pbk)
    ISSN 1368-454X (Clinical Psychology: A Modular Course)

Cover Illustration:
Before the Storm by Carol Carter.
www.carol-carter.com
The painting depicts the evacuation in southern Florida before Hurricane Andrew
Cover design by Joyce Chester
Typeset in Palatino by Mayhew Typesetting, Rhayader, Powys
Printed and bound in the UK by TJ International Ltd, Padstow, Cornwall

Contents

Acknowledgments

I would like to express my appreciation for the support I have received from my colleagues at the Center for Trauma Recovery at the University of Missouri – St. Louis and my family Keith, Marty, and Matt Shaw. I would also like to thank Shenika Harris for her assistance with references and Michael Griffin for his thoughtful comments on early drafts of Chapter 4. Finally, I would like to thank Chris Brewin for his patience.

Series preface

Clinical Psychology: A Modular Course was designed to overcome the problems faced by the traditional textbook in conveying what psychological disorders are really like. All the books in the series, written by leading scholars and practitioners in the field, can be read as stand-alone texts, but they will also integrate with the other modules to form a comprehensive resource in clinical psychology. Students of psychology, medicine, nursing, and social work, as well as busy practitioners in many professions, often need an accessible but thorough introduction to how people experience anxiety, depression, addiction, or other disorders, how common they are, and who is most likely to suffer from them, as well as up-to-date research evidence on the causes and available treatments. The series will appeal to those who want to go deeper into the subject than the traditional textbook will allow, and base their examination answers, research, projects, assignments, or practical decisions on a clearer and more rounded appreciation of the clinical and research evidence.

Chris R. Brewin

Other titles in this series:

Depression
Constance Hammen

Anxiety
S. Rachman

Childhood Disorders
Philip C. Kendall

Classifying reactions to stress and trauma 1

Example 1: You are driving down a busy highway on a rainy day and your tire has a blowout. Your first response is one of action, pulling the car over to the side of the road while avoiding a collision with other cars. Once safely stopped, you realize that your heart is pounding, you feel like you have been kicked in the stomach and you are sweating and trembling.

Example 2: You are barely making ends meet with a part-time job and college bills to pay. You have too much to do and are worrying about an upcoming exam that is very important for your future career. You haven't been sleeping well for the past month and are constantly worrying about completing all your work. You rush into your job about 10 minutes late and the boss says, "That's one time too many. I just can't have you coming into work late. I'm going to have to let you go." You feel the blood leave your face and panic rise in your chest.

Example 3: You and your partner have been planning your wedding. Although you want an event that is special, all of the planning is beginning to feel a bit out of control with all of your other responsibilities. The caterer just went out of business and some of the bridesmaids' dresses came back in the wrong sizes. All of the invitations still need to be addressed but your boss just asked you to take on a project at work that will have you working in the evenings for the next two weeks. You have been experiencing headaches every afternoon and now you feel like you are coming down with a cold.

Example 4: You moved to a new town, don't know anyone, and have gotten lost several times trying to find your way around. You are feeling lonely and disconnected from your old friends. Although you think the move might turn out well eventually, all of the usual routines have changed and even getting a haircut or a dentist appointment is stressful because you don't know where to go or whom to choose. You feel irritable and your stomach has been bothering you.

Example 5: You are peacefully asleep in your bed when suddenly you are awakened by a voice that says, "I have a knife, so don't make any noise." You wonder if you are having a nightmare but as you awaken more fully, you feel the point of the knife at your throat. You begin to hyperventilate as you experience complete terror. You feel frozen both mentally and physically.

All of these are examples of stress, negative reactions to environmental stressors. Stressors may be positive (a promotion at work, a new baby) as well as negative. The stress response is a combination of physical reactions, thoughts (cognitions), emotions, and behaviors. In recent years, the study of stress has focused on the effects of stress on health, and a whole branch of psychology has emerged as health psychology. In the previous examples, only the first and fifth examples might represent traumatic stress. In the first example, the flat tire, some people might not consider the event traumatic because disaster was averted. Someone else might consider the event traumatic because of memories of a prior experience with a car accident, or an appraisal of imminent danger, and accompanying fear. In other words, stress and trauma may depend on how a person appraises the situation and on her or his own emotional reactions. The fifth example is an event that nearly everyone would find traumatic—a sudden, unexpected, life-threatening assault.

The primary focus of this book will be on traumatic stress, those events beyond daily hassles, beyond normal developmental life challenges, beyond more stressful and challenging circumstances such as divorce, losing a job, serious illness, or financial problems. This book will focus on events that are life threatening (and/or threatening to "self" as is the case with incest or other intimate assaults) and that are accompanied by intense fear, helplessness, or horror. Traumatic stressors frequently result in psychological symptoms of a more significant nature than more common stressors and may result in psychological disorders for many people who experience traumatic stress. This chapter will focus on the various psychological disorders that may result from traumatic stress. The next chapter will examine the prevalence of these most serious types of stressors. The remaining chapters will focus on theories of traumatic stress response, variables that affect symptoms and recovery, and treatment.

Reactions to stressful and traumatic events: Symptoms and diagnoses

Immediate reactions

Life stressors can be minor (irritating daily hassles such as waiting in line or commuting in traffic) or major (divorce, death of a loved one); they can be acute (physical injury, moving to a new home) or chronic (living in a dangerous environment, poverty). In response to stressors, people typically have emotions, thoughts (cognitions), physical reactions, and behaviors that correspond to the severity and chronicity of the stressors. For example, while anticipating or giving a speech in front of an audience, many people will experience physical symptoms such as dry mouth, "butterflies" in the stomach, or racing heartbeat. They may have trouble focusing their thoughts or have ruminative or catastrophizing thoughts ("I'm going to sound stupid"). Behaviorally, people who are anxious about performance may stammer or engage in nervous mannerisms. Emotions may include anxiety, irritability, or fear. However, shortly after the speech is finished, most people return to normal very quickly. The stress is over.

In response to chronic or cumulative stressors, people also exhibit a range of physical, behavioral, cognitive, and emotional responses that lessen when the stressful situation(s) have stopped. However, the reactions may be much more pronounced and may have lingering effects. As an example, people living in a chronically stressful situation may develop more generalized thoughts about their own helplessness, or may ruminate about the causes of the situation in a nonproductive manner. They may develop more serious emotional responses that could be diagnosable as depression, anxiety disorders, or chronic anger. They may attempt to cope behaviorally with the situation by abusing substances or withdrawing from others. Chronic stress reactions may contribute to illness and physical disorders. When the stressful situation abates, the reactions lessen, but poor coping styles and rigid or faulty thinking patterns may have evolved that will be used and abused in future stressful situations. On the other hand, if someone develops new, healthy coping strategies, they may be left stronger and more resilient to face future stressors.

Although the onset and duration of traumatic effects is typically brief, traumatic stress may result in much more dramatic reactions and continuing symptoms. Traumatic or catastrophic events are by their nature, sudden, unexpected, and threatening. At the moment the victim perceives danger, his or her body and mind immediately shift into "survival mode". Our bodies are hard-wired for emergencies through a million years of evolution to respond effectively in the face of imminent danger. When a threat is first perceived, the person responds with an alarm reaction that triggers a number of biological, cognitive, and emotional responses. The autonomic nervous system activates a cascade of biological reactions that produce increases in heart rate, respiration, blood pressure, release of stored sugar, increase in muscle tone, heightened awareness, and narrowing of focus away from unimportant information. The body is preparing for fight or flight. However, it is not always adaptive or even possible to flee or fight. An alternative response is freezing and/or dissociating as a means of survival when escape isn't possible. Freezing may function to avoid the attention of the predator, while dissociation may be the defense of last resort, surrender. Dissociation is an alteration of consciousness in which a person experiences a sense of unreality and detachment from the experience or from her/himself. The biological reaction associated with dissociation and numbing appears to have a different function: the reduction of pain and terror (Perry, Pollard, Blakley, Baker, & Vigilante, 1995).

In a study of rape victims (Veronen, Kilpatrick, & Resick, 1979), participants in the research described how they were feeling during the assault. Almost all of the participants reported experiencing multiple emotional reactions during the event (Table 1.1). These victims described a range of reactions including confusion, feelings of unreality, and numbing. In the first few hours after the assault, some reactions increased, particularly cognitive reactions like humiliation and guilt, while others decreased.

Recovery and chronicity

Once the danger has past, the traumatized person now begins the process of recovery. Those who are in pain from injuries or who have dissociated during the event may continue to be shut down emotionally. Some people continue to be emotionally numb for extended periods of time, but most people are flooded with images and

TABLE 1.1

Reactions during and shortly after rape (Veronen et al., 1979). Copyright © 1979 by Sage Publications Inc. Reprinted by permission of Sage Publications Inc.

Symptom	During rape (%)	2–3 hours post-rape (%)
Cognitive/emotional symptoms:		
Anger	80	80
Ashamed/humiliated	72	80
Confused	92	80
Depressed	48	84
Exhausted	52	96
Feelings of unreality	64	60
Guilty	48	52
Helpless	88	76
Jumpy/restless	na	88
Racing thoughts	80	80
Ruminating	64	68
Scared	96	88
Terrified	92	80
Withdrawn	24	76
Worried	96	96
Physiological symptoms:		
Dry mouth	44	52
Felt physically relaxed	4	12
Headache	16	60
Heart racing	84	48
Numbness	72	68
Rapid breathing	64	44
Shaking or trembling	96	96
Tight muscles	68	68

emotions in the aftermath of the event. As they attempt to cope with these strong memories, the victims may begin making efforts to shut off the images and feelings. Too much avoidance, either effortful or dissociative, may lead to prolonged reactions that can evolve into psychological disorders.

The normal course of recovery has been examined with prospective studies, studies of trauma victims beginning at the time of the event and moving forward in time. In the late 1970s, the earliest studies of rape victims were conducted as prospective studies to determine whether and what the psychological reactions were to being sexually assaulted (Atkeson, Calhoun, Resick, & Ellis, 1982; Calhoun, Atkeson, & Resick, 1982; Kilpatrick, Veronen, & Resick, 1979a, 1979b). Rape victims' fear, anxiety, depressive symptoms, sexual functioning, self-

Figure 1.1.
Percentage of rape
victims with PTSD (from
Rothbaum et al., 1992,
*Journal of Traumatic
Stress*, Vol. 5, with
permission from
Plenum Publishing
Corporation).

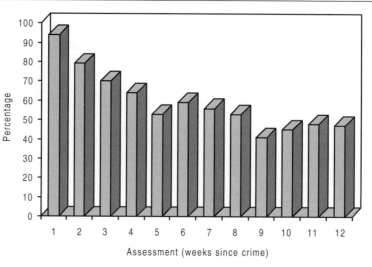

esteem, and social adjustment were examined regularly over at least a 1-year period in groups of rape victims and women who had not been raped. The rape victims reported significantly greater problems in all of these domains compared to the nonvictims although it appeared that the depressive symptoms abated more quickly than the fear and anxiety symptoms. The researchers found that the bulk of recovery occurred within the first 3 months after the event and then little occurred after that.

In the late 1980s and 1990s there were more longitudinal studies that focused specifically on post-traumatic stress disorder of crime victims, motor vehicle accidents or disasters. Rothbaum, Foa, Riggs, Murdock, and Walsh (1992) assessed rape victims weekly for 3 months following their assaults. They found that, similar to the earlier studies, there are very strong reactions initially and gradual recovery over the months that follow. In fact, at 1 week post-rape, 94% of the women assessed met all of the symptom requirements for post-traumatic stress disorder (PTSD), which will be described in detail later in the chapter. At 3 months post-crime, 47% were diagnosed with PTSD (Figure 1.1). When they examined the women who would eventually be diagnosed with PTSD, Rothbaum et al. (1992) found that these women had more severe reactions initially, and that after 1 month they stopped improving. Those who would eventually recover continued to improve throughout the entire study period.

Resick (1988) also compared the reactions of female robbery and rape victims and compared female with male robbery victims over an 18-month period. She found similar patterns although the rape victims had more severe reactions than the female robbery victims did. On the other hand, the female robbery victims had more severe reactions initially than the male robbery victims did, but these differences diminished over time.

Riggs, Rothbaum, and Foa (1995) examined the course of reactions of assault victims and found that, while similar to rape victims, the reactions did not appear as severe. Norris and Kaniasty (1994) examined the recovery of violent crime victims and property crime victims with nonvictims at three time periods: 3, 9, and 15 months post-crime. They assessed a range of emotional reactions and found that while the crime victims showed substantial improvement between 3 and 9 months post-crime, there was no improvement after that. As expected, the violent crime victims reported more distress than the property crime victims, who reported more distress than the nonvictims at each assessment point.

There have been a handful of studies that have prospectively examined reactions to serious motor vehicle accidents or natural disasters (e.g., Blanchard et al., 1996; Green, Grace, Lindy, Glesser, & Leonard, 1990; Mayou, Bryant, & Duthie, 1993; McFarlane, 1988). Generally, these studies have found that people continued to recover over the course of a year. Typically, symptoms are most severe at the earliest time point and the rates of PTSD decrease over time. However, several studies have found a small percentage of people have a delayed onset of PTSD (typically 3–5%). In these cases, those with a delayed onset of full diagnosis did not start with no symptoms; they had a partial diagnosis and then worsened over time until they reached criteria for diagnosis. Blanchard et al. (1996) tracked 132 victims of motor vehicle accidents for 18 months and found that, of the 48 who met criteria for PTSD at 1–4 months post-crime (36%), half had improved at least somewhat by 6 months post-accident, and two-thirds by the 1-year follow-up. There was no significant improvement from 1 year to 18 months post-accident.

While prospective studies are able to show recovery in the early post-trauma period, it is important to remember that the people who participate in these studies may not be representative of all trauma survivors, even those who have experienced the same event. It must be noted that to participate in a study on crime trauma, the victim must have reported the crime to some agency for them to come to the attention of the researchers. People who do not report their crimes to the police, or who suffer in silence for some other reason, may have a different pattern of recovery. In fact, the majority of rape victims do not report their crimes to the police. Also, most of the prospective studies have examined participants for relatively short periods of time, a few months to a few years. There is little research to indicate recovery patterns over a longer period of time.

In one large study of PTSD and other disorders, Kessler, Sonnega, Bromet, Hughes, and Nelson (1995) attempted to examine recovery over a much longer period of time with a retrospective study rather than a prospective study. They asked 5877 people how long it took them to recover from the worst event they had experienced (any of 12 types of events including crime, combat, disasters, etc.) at any time in their lives. These data appear to indicate that recovery occurs beyond the initial 3 months. It also appears from the reports of the participants, that counseling and therapy did not improve the rate of recovery (the number of people who eventually recovered) but those who got therapy recovered sooner. However, this study did not attempt to examine different types of counseling and therapy or even if the therapy was trauma-focused, but merely lumped them altogether.

While advantages of the Kessler et al. (1995) study include the large sample size, the representative sampling of men and women, and the range of traumas examined, because it is retrospective research, it is subject to the vagaries of people's memories. People may not remember accurately how long it took them to recover, especially for events that may have occurred years or even decades earlier. Such research may also pull for recall of specific types of symptoms over others. For example nightmares and flashbacks may be easier to recall than numbing and avoidance. It also must be remembered that when researchers are studying particular disorders and diagnoses, they are engaging in dichotomous thinking—someone is either recovered or they have a full-blown disorder. It is quite possible that someone could be partially recovered. They could have fewer symptoms or less frequent or severe symptoms. It is possible that someone who meets the diagnosis of PTSD (see later in this chapter for specific information on diagnostic criteria), at one point in time and who does not at a later time, might not be recovered. If a person becomes emotionally numb or dissociative and avoids all reminders of the incident, he or she may not have enough re-experiencing symptoms to meet the diagnostic criteria. That person might have partial PTSD, which could be triggered or reactivated at a later point in time.

In spite of these caveats, the prospective longitudinal studies and the larger prevalence studies indicate that some people recover in a reasonable amount of time, usually a few months. Other people stall out, probably early in the recovery process, and develop chronic disorders. The factors that may influence whether and how well someone recovers from trauma will be explored throughout the book. Chapter 2 will examine the prevalence of trauma and the prevalence of chronic disorder in the aftermath of particular stressors. However, first these disorders and other problematic symptoms will be described.

Description of clinical disorders

Although a range of symptoms are considered to be quite normal after a serious traumatic event, when recovery does not occur in a reasonable length of time or if the symptoms grow worse over time, then these symptoms are no longer considered normal. When the psychological symptoms persist following a traumatic stressor and cluster into particular patterns, then it is time to consider whether these reactions have evolved into one or another psychopathological conditions. The remainder of this section will describe various psychological disorders that are frequently observed following trauma. Although almost any disorder might follow in the wake of traumatic experience, there are particular disorders that are more frequent and will be focused on in this chapter. Some disorders, although frequent, will not be described here but can be found in other volumes in this series. They are: mood disorders, substance abuse/dependence, and other anxiety disorders.

Adjustment disorder

Adjustment disorder is a diagnosis that may be appropriate to apply to short-term reactions to a stressor. In this case, the stressor does not need to be unusual or life threatening, but the emotional or behavioral reaction must be in excess of what is typically observed in others who experience the same stressor. The diagnosis of adjustment disorder is not given if the criteria for another disorder (such as major depressive disorder or post-traumatic stress disorder) are met. In *Diagnostic and statistical manual of mental disorders*, 4th edition

(*DSM-IV*; APA, 1994), the first criterion, called the stressor criterion or Criterion A, is that the emotional or behavioral symptoms are in response to an identifiable stressor and begin within 3 months of the onset of the stressor. Criterion B does not specify specific symptoms but merely states that there has to be clinically significant reactions evidenced by distress in excess of what would be expected or that there is significant impairment in the person's functioning. Criterion C and Criterion D state that an adjustment disorder diagnosis should not be given if there is another diagnosable Axis I disorder or bereavement. Criterion E requires that the symptoms do not persist for more than 6 months after the stressor (or its consequences) have ended. Adjustment disorder is also coded with regard to the symptoms which are most apparent: depressed mood, anxiety, mixed anxiety and depressed mood, disturbance of conduct, mixed disturbance of emotions and conduct, or unspecified.

> Marcus, aged 9, returned home from school one day to find his mother crying. She informed him that his father had left and she didn't know how they would get money to live. For the first few days, he didn't react very much, but as it became clear to him that his father wasn't returning, he began to react in a variety of ways. Every time his mother needed to leave him with his grandmother, Marcus became tearful and clingy. This separation fear evolved into temper tantrums within a few weeks as his mother found a job that required her to be gone until 5:30 in the evening. He cried easily, lost his temper frequently and had trouble getting along with his friends. His grades at school dropped. Marcus' mother sought counseling and Marcus met with a school psychologist on a number of occasions. Within 4 or 5 months, Marcus began to adapt to the new situation, his reactions abated, and his behavior improved.

Bereavement

As everyone knows, the death of a loved one is a great stressor that most people must deal with at some time in their lives. Bereavement, the process of mourning the loss of the loved one, is a natural process and is not considered a psychological disorder. Bereavement is only listed in the *DSM-IV* as a condition that may be the focus of clinical attention. The process of grieving and the expected course of bereavement varies from culture to culture. In modern western culture, people are expected to recover from the death of a loved one far quicker than in the past. A century ago, people were expected to wear particular clothing indicative of mourning for a least a year, a tangible reminder that would serve to elicit the support of others. Queen Victoria was not considered pathological even though she opted for widow's garb for the remainder of her life. However, under the *DSM-IV* guidelines, a mental health professional may wish to consider a diagnosis of major depression if the symptoms persist for more than 2 months, especially if the survivor has strong feelings of guilt, preoccupation with worthlessness, suicidal thoughts, or other symptoms of severe depression.

A special case of bereavement may be found with the family members of homicide victims. Although there is not a great deal of research on the topic, it appears that a fair proportion of family members studied also have post-traumatic stress disorder in addition to the normal bereavement pattern. The shock of unexpected, violent death is a traumatic stressor which may result in more severe intrusive, numbing, and arousal symptoms than is usually found following natural or accidental death.

> Jim received a telephone call at 11 o'clock one Thursday night. He assumed that it was his wife calling to say that she was running late from her job at a nearby liquor store. Jim was eager to talk to his wife because they had fought right before she left for work. He was startled by a male voice who said "Mr Sojack could you please come to Mercy Hospital. Your wife is here." He refused to say anything more in response to Jim's questions. When Jim arrived at the emergency room, he was met by two police officers who informed him that his wife had been killed during a robbery of the store.
>
> Eight months later, Jim sought out therapy at the urging of his grown children. He had lost 40 pounds, had problems sleeping, and was barely functioning at work. He had moved out of their bedroom and had left all of his wife's clothing and possessions just as they had been on the night of her death. In one corner of the living room, there was a sort of shrine with a large photograph of his wife, candles, flowers, and a favorite object, a crystal polar bear. Jim informed the therapist that he couldn't really believe she

was gone and that he had great guilt over the fight they had the last time he had seen her. He was convinced that she died thinking that he didn't love her. Every time the telephone rang, Jim startled, his heart raced, and he had images of his wife as she had appeared when he identified her body.

He was also distressed and angry because the prosecuting attorney was unsure whether the case would ever make it to trial. The evidence was not particularly strong against the two young men who had been arrested and one of them had withdrawn his confession, which he now said was made under duress. Jim was obsessed with finding out every detail of the crime and often imagined how his wife's last moments must have been for her. After a careful assessment, the therapist diagnosed Jim with both major depressive disorder and post-traumatic stress disorder and began therapy with him.

Post-traumatic stress disorder

Post-traumatic stress disorder (PTSD) was first labeled as such in the APA's 1980 *DSM-III*, following the Vietnam War. Prior to that time, there had been periodic interest in traumatic stress, usually in times of war, and known under various names such as combat fatigue or shell shock. Simultaneous to the return of Vietnam veterans and efforts to better assess their trauma symptoms, were other new converging areas of information and study on other related topics. The 1970s also brought the women's rights movement with speak-outs and consciousness-raising groups by women. As women began to talk together of their lives, they began to share their experiences with rape and domestic violence. Child abuse and incest were also coming to light as they never had before and child abuse hotlines, rape crisis centers, battered women's shelters, and victim assistance programs were being developed as grass-roots efforts. During the mid-1970s, professionals were beginning to describe trauma symptoms in their constituent groups that were very similar but carried specific labels such as "rape trauma syndrome" or "battered women's syndrome". By the close of the decade, research on these topics was well under way. The *DSM-III* diagnosis of PTSD wisely included a variety of stressors, not just combat, and although researchers tended to focus on one population or another, they began to share their findings and the commonalties and prevalence of PTSD symptoms in the aftermath of many serious traumatic stressors.

The *DSM* was revised in 1987 (*DSM-III-R*) and again in 1994 (*DSM-IV*). The changes introduced in the *DSM-III-R* included classifying the symptoms into three clusters of which specific numbers of symptoms would be needed to reach criterion. Prior to the *DSM-IV* revision, a field trial was conducted at a number of sites to examine the stressor criterion (Criterion A) and to examine whether there was a separate disorder of complex symptoms (Disorders of extreme stress, not otherwise specified: DESNOS) apart from PTSD. The results were that, for the most part, events that are stressful but more normative, such as the natural death of loved ones, divorce, or the loss of a job, do not result in PTSD; whereas, life-endangering events (or self-endangering, as in the case of child sexual abuse) which are met with helplessness or horror, are more likely to precipitate PTSD. The field trial data also indicated that whereas almost everyone who had significant symptoms of DESNOS also had PTSD, or that PTSD could occur without DESNOS, DESNOS did not occur in the absence of PTSD. In other words, DESNOS symptoms appear to reflect a subset or more complex form of PTSD. These symptoms are described as associated features but are not listed as a separate diagnosis at this time. The stressor criterion was rewritten to reflect the seriousness of the event and its impact on the person at the time of the event. Under the *DSM-III-R*, the description of the stressor was that the event was outside the normal range of events. This statement of course does not reflect the reality of the prevalence of traumatic events in people's lives. Although they are not normal events, if at least half of the population has experienced at least one major traumatic event in their lives and some people have experienced many such events, then the statement is not an accurate guideline for making the diagnosis.

According to the *DSM-IV*, there are six criteria that must be met before a diagnosis of post-traumatic stress disorder can be made (see Box 1.1). The first criterion is the stressor criterion. It now states that the person had to have experienced, witnessed, or was confronted with an event that involved actual or threatened death or serious injury, or a threat to the physical integrity of the person or others. This definition allows a diagnosis not just for the direct victims themselves, but also for affected family members such as the families of homicide victims, or those who are not directly victimized such as those who work in the aftermath of violence or disaster. It also allows for a diagnosis in cases where no life threat is made but where

A. The person has been exposed to a traumatic event in which both of the following were present:

   (1) the person experienced, witnessed, or was confronted with an event or events that involved actual or threatened death or serious injury, or a threat to the physical integrity of self or others.

   (2) the person's response involved intense fear, helplessness, or horror. Note: In children, this may be expressed instead by disorganized or agitated behavior.

B. The traumatic event is persistently re-experienced in one (or more) of the following ways:

   (1) recurrent and intrusive distressing recollections of the event, including images, thoughts, or perceptions. Note: In young children, repetitive play may occur in which themes or aspects of the trauma are expressed.

   (2) recurrent distressing dreams of the event. Note: In children, there may be frightening dreams without recognizable content.

   (3) acting or feeling as if the traumatic event were recurring (includes a sense of reliving the experience, illusions, hallucinations, and dissociative flashback episodes, including those that occur on awakening or when intoxicated). Note: In young children, trauma-specific re-enactment may occur.

   (4) intense psychological distress at exposure to internal or external cues that symbolize or resemble an aspect of the traumatic event.

   (5) physiological reactivity on exposure to internal or external cues that symbolize or resemble an aspect of the traumatic event.

C. Persistent avoidance of stimuli associated with the trauma and numbing of general responsiveness (not present before the trauma), as indicated by three (or more) of the following:

   (1) efforts to avoid thoughts, feelings, or conversations associated with the trauma

   (2) efforts to avoid activities, places, or people that arouse recollections of the trauma

   (3) inability to recall an important aspect of the trauma

   (4) markedly diminished interest or participation in significant activities

   (5) feeling of detachment or estrangement from others

   (6) restricted range of affect (e.g., unable to have loving feelings)

   (7) sense of a foreshortened future (e.g., does not expect to have a career, marriage, children, or a normal life span)

D. Persistent symptoms of increased arousal (not present before the trauma), as indicated by two (or more) of the following:

   (1) difficulty falling or staying asleep

   (2) irritability or outbursts of anger

   (3) difficulty concentrating

   (4) hypervigilance

   (5) exaggerated startle response

continued

physical integrity is compromised such as the case of some rapes or child sexual abuse. However, the event must indeed be traumatic. The second part of the stressor criterion is that the person's response to the event was intense fear, helplessness, or horror. Because children may not be old enough to clearly define these reactions, the criterion may be met if the child exhibits disordered or agitated behavior.

The second criterion, Criterion B, reflects re-experiencing symptoms. A person can meet this criterion if they have recurrent and distressing recollections of the traumatic event. The recollections may take the form of intrusive images or thoughts, flashbacks, nightmares, or strong emotional or physical reactions when the person encounters reminders of the event. The person only needs one type of re-experiencing symptom to meet the criterion as long as this is recurrent and distressing. The random thought or occasional dream would not be of sufficient severity to be considered a problem.

Avoidance symptoms comprise the third criterion (Criterion C). The affected person must exhibit significant avoidance in at least three ways to meet the criterion. Although the *DSM* does not subdivide the avoidance symptoms, it is probably better to construe them as being of two types: effortful avoidance and numbing/ dissociation (Foa, Riggs, & Gershuny, 1995; Taylor, Kuch, Koch, Crockett, & Passey, 1998). In fact, on a large sample of crime victims, Foa, Riggs, and Gershuny (1995) found that the symptoms did cluster into these two types. The symptoms of effortful avoidance are: attempts to avoid thoughts, feelings, or conversations about the trauma and attempts to avoid activities, places, or people that remind the person of the trauma. Numbing or dissociation are reflected by the inability to recall important aspects of the event(s); diminished interest or participation in significant activities; feelings of detachment or estrangement from others; or a restricted range of affect. Although some of these latter items could be mistaken for depression symptoms, the intent is to tap into a sense of numbed emotions rather than sadness. And although people may feel detached or estranged from others for many reasons, here again the intent is to look for numbing or dissociation.

There is an additional item that doesn't fall cleanly into either type of avoidance symptom: foreshortened future. It has been observed that some traumatized people possess a belief that they do not expect to have a normal life with the usual milestones of career, family, or even a normal life span. Although there may be no clear reason for this belief ("Something bad is going to happen to me"), sometimes these beliefs may, in fact, be realistic. If a rape victim with PTSD is afraid of men, she is less likely to marry and have children. Problems with attention and concentration interfere with academic and career goals. The combat veterans who are angry and socially isolated will have problems in both family and work settings. Battered women and abused children, who exhibit chronic health problems, may indeed have shorter lives.

Symptoms of physiological arousal are represented in the D Criterion. They include pervasive arousal that is reflected by difficulties in concentration, hypervigilance, or irritability, and problems falling and staying asleep. Also included are exaggerated startle responses in response to stimuli. There is evidence that many of those with PTSD not only have pronounced startle reactions, but they do not appear to habituate to repeated presentations of stimuli as do non-PTSD people.

The fifth criterion for diagnosis is that the B, C, and D symptoms persist for at least a month. In other words, someone would not meet criteria if they had avoidance symptoms at one period of time and nightmares and flashbacks at another or if the symptoms lasted just a week or two. The symptoms must co-occur together for at least 1 month. The sixth criterion is that this combination of symptoms causes significant distress for the person or causes impairment in the person's social or occupational functioning. This last criterion, present for all disorders, specifies that a diagnosis of psychopathology should not be made if the symptoms are mild or do not really interfere with a person's life. Diagnosis of psychological disorders should not be made frivolously and should indicate the need for treatment. Mild or occasional symptoms fall within the range of normal reactions to stressful events.

Greg called Maggie on the phone and asked her if she would like to go for a drive. Maggie was very flattered. Greg was 2 years older and was very good looking. Maggie's mother had known Greg's parents through school activities and thought they seemed like a nice family. She told Maggie and Greg to be back by 10 o'clock because it was a school night. After driving past all the usual teen haunts and not running into any of their mutual friends, Greg began to drive the car out into the country. Maggie told Greg she was not interested in making out after he stopped the car. He pushed her back against the door and began to kiss her. Maggie grew alarmed and tried to push him off. Greg said, "You know you want this", and began pulling at her clothing. Maggie screamed "stop it", and Greg slapped her across the face. He pulled her arms behind her back and said, "you might as well do this, because if you don't cooperate, I'm going to tell everyone at school what a slut you are. Everyone will believe me." Maggie began to cry, shut her eyes, and tried to pretend she was somewhere else, as Greg proceeded to rape her. Maggie's parents were back in their bedroom when she got home. She slipped upstairs, got into the shower and scrubbed herself until the water ran cold and her skin was raw.

It was 2 years before Maggie told her mother about the rape. During that time her grades suffered and she withdrew from all of her social activities. Whenever her parents asked her what was wrong, she said "nothing" and walked away. She had regular nightmares and fear reactions whenever she saw Greg at school; she avoided places where she knew he might be and avoided his friends; she tried to put the event out of her mind. Maggie had strong startle reactions whenever someone walked up behind her and fear reactions whenever she felt closed in or if someone grabbed her wrist. She felt like she was always looking over her shoulder. Probably hardest for Maggie was the self-blame. She didn't have a name for what had happened to her. In her mind, rapists were strangers who jumped out of bushes. All she knew was that she must have done something for Greg to have treated her this way. Maggie finally told her mother when they were watching a television program that talked about date rape. Maggie began to cry and the story finally came out.

Acute stress disorder

Acute stress disorder (ASD) is a new diagnosis introduced with the *DSM-IV* following research findings that those people who dissociate more during or immediately after a traumatic stressor are more likely to develop chronic PTSD (Spiegel, Koopman, Cardeña, & Classen, 1996). The introduction of this disorder allows for a diagnosis in the first month after an event without including those who would recover naturally during that interval. Acute stress disorder requires the same Criterion A definition of a traumatic stressor as post-traumatic stress disorder (see earlier), but then Criterion B requires three or more dissociative symptoms experienced during or after the event. The five symptoms that qualify for this criterion are: (1) numbing or detachment, (2) reduced awareness of surroundings (being in a daze), (3) derealization, (4) depersonalization, or (5) dissociative amnesia (inability to recall an important aspect of the trauma). Derealization is a sense of unreality that either the situation or the person is not real. The person who says repeatedly, "I couldn't believe it was really happening", or "It felt like a dream", or "Everything seemed distorted and unreal", is expressing a sense of derealization. Depersonalization is more a sense that the person himself or herself is not real. The person may experience the traumatic event as if he/she is floating above their body or from somewhere else outside their bodies.

In addition to the dissociative symptoms, the affected person must experience symptoms from each of the PTSD symptom clusters. However, the complete criteria for PTSD do not need to be met. Only one symptom from each criteria are required. Criterion C is that the person persistently re-experiences the event through recurrent images, thoughts, dreams, illusions, flashbacks, or distress upon exposure to reminders of the traumatic event. Criterion D includes marked avoidance of reminders or thoughts of the event. Criterion E is symptoms of anxiety or increased physiological arousal such as difficulties with sleep, irritability, poor concentration, hypervigilance, exaggerated startle response, or motor restlessness.

The symptoms must cause clinically significant distress or impairment in social or work functioning or impairs the person from pursuing some necessary task such as obtaining assistance or mobilizing social support (Criterion F). The symptoms must last a minimum of 2 days and a maximum of 4 weeks and must occur within 4 weeks of the event (Criterion G). The symptoms also must not be caused by some substance such as drugs or medication or a medical condition (Criterion H).

There have been a number of studies suggesting that: (1) some people dissociate during traumatic events, (2) peri-traumatic dissociation (dissociation during the trauma) may even fall on a normal distribution like most other traits, and (3) there is a relationship between peri-traumatic dissociation and PTSD (Griffin, Resick, & Mechanic, 1997; Marmar et al., 1994; Shalev, Peri, Canetti, & Schreiber, 1996; Spiegel, 1991). However, there is little research other than one study conducted by Spiegel et al. (1996) to examine the notion that people have to experience three types of dissociative symptoms in concert with PTSD symptoms is the best way to diagnose ASD. In fact, a recent study by Brewin, Andrews, Rose, and Kirk (1999) found that, although acute stress disorder symptoms did predict subsequent PTSD, the researchers were unable to detect a unique role for the dissociative symptoms. The presence of re-experiencing and arousal symptoms in the first month after the traumatic event was an equally good predictor of PTSD 6 months later.

The inclusion of ASD in the *DSM-IV* has been controversial because so little research had been conducted to warrant this new diagnostic category. Some psychiatrists and psychologists have argued that such an addition to the diagnostic system was premature given the lack of evidence that ASD symptoms represents a unique syndrome, that it predicts later PTSD diagnosis better than a simple examination of early PTSD symptoms, or that initial reactions following trauma represent psychopathology at all. However, the addition of ASD to the *DSM-IV* is likely to spur research in the future regarding early detection and predictors of PTSD.

> Sylvia was alone in her second-story apartment when the earthquake struck. She felt the floor beneath her give way and she had nothing to grab onto as furniture, objects, and walls fell around her. An hour later, emergency workers found her walking in a daze with her dead cat in her arms. She had cuts and bruises but did not appear to be in pain and she did not respond when the emergency workers asked her if anyone else was inside her apartment. A week later, she had strong panic attacks whenever there were aftershocks or if she heard a loud truck rumbling. She had nightmares about falling and had no memory of the hour after the earthquake, how she got outside, or of finding her cat. She described herself as numb and "just going through the motions".

Dissociative disorders

Dissociation reflects a disruption in the normal flow of information processing and a disruption in functions that are usually integrated: consciousness, memory, identity, or perception of the environment. Although dissociation can occur as part of PTSD, and peri-traumatic dissociation (dissociation during or immediately after the trauma) must occur as part of ASD, there are other disorders that are primarily dissociative in nature. They are: dissociative amnesia, dissociative fugue, dissociative identity disorder, depersonalization disorder, and dissociative disorder, not otherwise specified.

Dissociative amnesia is defined as reversible memory impairment, an inability to recall important personal events that is too extensive to be explained away as normal forgetting. The amnesia is usually thought to result from a traumatic stressor. The diagnosis of dissociative amnesia is not given if the amnesia occurs exclusively during the course of one of the other post-traumatic or dissociative disorders. Problems that sometimes accompany this disorder include problems with work and interpersonal functioning, sexual dysfunction, self-mutilation, and aggressive or suicidal behavior. The person may also be diagnosed with a mood disorder or a personality disorder.

The amnesia may take several different forms. A localized amnesia is one in which the person has no memory of events during a particular period of time. In selective amnesia the person fails to remember only part of an event or events. There are three other types of amnesia that are more rare: generalized, continuous, or systematized amnesia. In generalized amnesia, there is no memory of the person's entire life. Continuous amnesia begins at some specific time and continues up into the present. Systematized amnesia refers to a loss of memory for certain categories of information, such as a particular person or one's family.

> During an intake for therapy, the therapist was reviewing a client's history. The client, Jamie, aged 32, could remember her kindergarten teacher, her best friend, and the house they lived in when she was 5–7 years of age. However, she had no memories prior to the age of 5 and said she remembered nothing between the ages of 9 and 12. Her high school years were remembered as a very troubled time in which she felt like an outsider, got drunk frequently, and skipped school. She had always had trouble forming and maintaining relationships and described them

as stormy. She had never held down a job for an extended period of time.

Jamie's more serious symptoms included cutting herself on her arms and legs, which her therapist later learned coincided with phone calls from her mother; suicidal thoughts, and occasional drinking binges. Jamie had been raped twice in adulthood, both times surrounding excessive alcohol use. Jamie's goal for therapy was to be a person. When asked what she meant, Jamie stated, "When I look in the mirror, nobody is there. I can't stand being alone because then I don't know how to be." The therapist diagnosed Jamie with borderline personality disorder on Axis II and dissociative amnesia on Axis I. Although she had some of the symptoms of PTSD, such as nightmares and some distressing flashes of images, at the time she began therapy she did not have enough of the symptoms of PTSD to warrant that diagnosis. Much later in therapy she was to recall that during the missing 2 years, her mother's brother, her Uncle Hank, had sexually abused her while he was living with her family. She also remembered and a sister confirmed that he had molested her at a much earlier age.

Dissociative fugue refers to sudden flight away from home accompanied by amnesia for one's past. People in a fugue state may have amnesia of their own identity and may adopt a new identity. Travel may occur for a few hours in a nearby location to complex travel over months and thousands of miles. People in a fugue state do not act bizarrely and may only be identified because of their amnesia. The person in a fugue state who assumes a new identity is likely to exhibit a more outgoing personality than before, and may adopt a whole new life with a new name, residence, and social life. Although it is a rare disorder, the incidence increases during times of major stressful events such as natural disasters or war.

Following the death of his wife and child in a car accident in which he was the driver, Mark wandered away from the accident in a daze. Five days later, he was stopped by a policeman in a nearby city who had seen a bulletin about Mark with his photograph. Mark did not know who he was or how he came to the city. He had no identification on him but did have a few dollars in his pocket. He said that for the last few days he had been wandering around and sleeping in the park.

Depersonalization disorder is a persistent or recurrent feeling of detachment or estrangement from one's self. The person has the feeling of being an observer of his or her own thoughts or body and depersonalization has a dreamlike quality about it. However, during the depersonalization episode the person, although he/she may feel like an automaton, has good reality testing, and knows that it is just a feeling. The depersonalization must cause significant distress or impairment of functioning to warrant a diagnosis.

Dissociative identity disorder (DID) was formerly called multiple personality disorder. The name change reflects a change in perspective on the disorder. Rather than viewing the person as having more than one personality, the disorder may be better understood as a single personality that has split off memories, experiences, or mood states into separate identities or personality states, in other words, a dissociation of identity. The criteria for DID are: (A) that the person has two or more separate identities or personality state with their own distinctive patterns of perceiving their experiences and themselves, relating to and interacting with others. These personality states must be enduring rather than momentary; (B) At least two of these identities or personality states must take control of the person's behavior recurrently; (C) The person has amnesia for personal information that is too pervasive to be ascribed to ordinary forgetfulness; and (D). The symptoms are not due to substance abuse or a general medical condition such as complex seizures. Although dissociative amnesia is part of the diagnosis and dissociative fugue or depersonalization may occur as well, the diagnosis of DID takes precedence such that the other diagnoses would not be made once a diagnosis of DID is given. However, other diagnoses may co-occur, such as PTSD, mood disorders, substance abuse, or eating, sleeping, or sexual disorders. The person with DID may exhibit enough symptoms to also warrant a diagnosis of borderline personality disorder, such as self-mutilation, impulsivity, and sudden and intense changes in relationships.

Most people diagnosed with DID report having experienced severe abuse during childhood, at which time the disorder appears to have emerged. DID reflects an inability to integrate memories and aspects of identity into an autobiographical whole. Each personality state may be experienced as though he or she had their own distinct history, self-image, mannerisms, and moods. The personality states may be given separate names or labels (e.g., Mad, Baby, Nobody). Most often, there is a primary identity who has the person's given name (often referred to as the host) who presents in therapy as depressed and dependent. Other identities may be quite different and appear to be angry, hostile, and controlling; childlike and playful with childish language and behaviors; or sophisticated and sexual. The number of personality states reported in the psychological literature varies from two to over a hundred. There can also be a great range in the perceived identities with regard to age, gender, race, vocabulary, knowledge, or predominant mood. Furthermore, there may be marked differences in physiological functioning across personality states including visual acuity, allergies, pain tolerance, and even response of blood glucose to insulin.

The diagnosis of DID (and multiple personality disorder) has always been controversial. Some mental health professionals do not believe that the disorder exists and is instead just the by-product of poor diagnosis. Others believe that it is not a rare disorder at all, but has been under-diagnosed because those with DID attempt to hide their condition from others, or do not realize they have it because of extensive periods of amnesia. It does appear, however, that therapists who become fascinated with the disorder in their clients may over-focus on the separateness of the personalities and inadvertently encourage the creation of new and more identities.

> Sharon sought treatment for her chronic depression at the urging of her physician. For several months the therapist attempted to help the client challenge her pervasive negative self-image, a profound belief that she was bad and that bad things would happen to her. When asked about her history, Sharon was vague and said that she couldn't remember most of her childhood. Slowly, Sharon began to describe troubling experiences. One day she found an army fatigue jacket on her bed which she didn't own. She wondered if someone was playing tricks on her. However, she admitted there were other items in her closet that she didn't remember buying or being given— they just appeared there. She described recent amnesia, periods of time up to half a day during the week that she couldn't remember. She reported nightmares and times just before going to sleep or waking up when someone was talking to her. Sharon expressed fears that she was going crazy.

During one session Sharon became particularly upset when describing what she called a nightmare; someone had his hands around her throat and she couldn't breathe. When the therapist asked her whether she had trouble falling back asleep, Sharon replied that she hadn't been sleeping at the time; she had been driving her car. Confused, the therapist probed further and realized that what Sharon was labeling nightmares were probably flashbacks.

The next session, Sharon bounced into the room and began talking in an outgoing, cheerful manner about some friends with whom she had spent the previous evening. The therapist noted the change in her mood compared to their previous sessions and happened to use her name. At that point, the client, looking disdainful, said, "I'm not Sharon. I'm Margot. I just thought I would come in here and see what all this therapy stuff is about." She proceeded to tell the therapist that there were two others, "a sniveling, whining kid who's always crying" and "Jean, the one you don't want to tangle with". Unbeknownst to Margot, there were two other parts of her personality that she was unaware of, which explained the times when she had amnesia. She was usually aware of what was going on when either Sharon or Jean were "out", and only took over herself in social situations "when it was time for some fun". She said that the little kid never came out; she just cried when she was scared.

Adjustment problems/functional impairment

As was mentioned earlier, none of the diagnoses listed previously are given unless there is a serious impact on the person's life with regard to either distress or functioning. In fact, the disorders just described usually do have a major impact on functioning. Whereas some people can continue with their education, hold down jobs, or raise families, others are unable to function successfully in one or more spheres of their life. Avoidance plays a prominent role in ASD, PTSD, and the dissociative disorders. Effortful avoidance is an overt, conscious decision to stay away from reminders of the event (or from overgeneralized reminders). Spontaneous avoidance reflects more the process of avoiding memories or shutting down affect such as is found with dissociation or numbing. Both types of avoidance can wreak havoc on functioning in an adaptive manner.

Crime victims may avoid certain environments, which remind them of the crime. If a young woman is raped at college, or by another student, she may drop out of school or avoid social situations or dating. Problems with intrusive imagery, strong emotional reactions, or problems with concentration may interfere with learning or job performance. Anger and irritability affect relationships. A Vietnam veteran with PTSD may have sufficient anger and irritability that he has difficulty maintaining employment and has relationship problems. Chronic numbing of emotions not only interferes with intimacy but also may preclude empathy, allowing the person with PTSD to become abusive or violent with others. Dissociation interferes with learning and with performance because knowledge may not be accessed when needed. The mother who was abused as a child herself, may dissociate rather than recognize that her own child is being abused. The distress of PTSD symptoms may spur attempts at numbing through substance abuse. Once addicted to drugs or alcohol, the trauma sufferer now has two major problems that interact to interfere with functioning, the symptoms that developed as a result of the trauma and the problems that are associated with alcohol or drug abuse.

Research has indicated that people with severe trauma reactions exhibit problems in normal functioning. In a prospective study of rape victims compared to nonvictims, Resick, Calhoun, Atkeson, and Ellis (1981) found that the rape victims reported more problems with work adjustment for 8 months following the rape and other areas of social and economic adjustment for a few months following the incident. A study by Kilpatrick, Acierno, Resnick, Saunders, and Best (1997), found a dangerous cycle among sexual assault victims. Women who were sexually assaulted were more likely to abuse alcohol and drugs. However, increasing drug consumption put the women at greater risk for further victimization. The long-term effects of childhood sexual abuse not only include psychological symptoms and disorders, but also multiple adjustment problems including substance abuse, learning difficulties, running away, prostitution, revictimization, impaired relationships and trust, self-abusive behavior, and poor parenting (see Schetky, 1990 for a review).

Relationship problems and domestic violence have both been found to be disproportionately high among Vietnam veterans with PTSD (Byrne & Riggs, 1996; Kulka et al., 1990; Stretch, 1991). Vietnam veterans with PTSD were also more likely to be divorced and report parenting problems (Kulka et al., 1990). Chronic anger has also been associated with PTSD (Chemtob, Hamada, Roitblat, & Muraoka, 1994) and may contribute to relationship problems and domestic violence. With regard to employment, Vietnam veterans with PTSD are more likely to be unemployed (Kulka et al., 1990) Underemployment is harder to estimate. It is not known how many people do not reach their full potential because their education was curtailed or because their symptoms interfered with job performance or promotions. Alcohol and drug abuse are particularly serious problems among combat veterans with PTSD. In a large national study of Vietnam veterans, Kulka et al. (1990) found that almost three-fourths of the veterans with PTSD had an alcohol abuse or dependence disorder and 22% had a current disorder at the time they were assessed, over a decade after the end of the war.

Finally, being a victim is associated with being an offender. Although many people who have experienced severe trauma do not become violent themselves, there is a disproportionately high rate of trauma in the histories of violent offenders. Vietnam combat veterans with PTSD are reported to have more problems with crime, interpersonal violence, and antisocial behavior than men who have not been exposed to combat trauma (Barrett et al., 1996; Beckham, Feldman, Kirby, Hertzberg, & Moore, 1997; Kulka et al., 1990). Although one might argue that some of these people are just making excuses or are trying for leniency, it is also possible that trauma begets trauma. Beating all of the humanity out of someone may pave the way for him or her to return the favor on others.

The intergenerational transmission of violence, abuse across generations within a family, is a well-established phenomenon that has been studied by both psychology and sociology. Recent theorists have been examining attachment theory (that is, the failure to emotionally attach at an appropriate level to others) to explain why and how people commit physical and sexual abuse upon their own family members.

Stress-related illness or physical disorders

The original work on stress by Hans Selye conceptualized stress in terms of physical reactions to external stressors. The focus of that research and much of the stress research that followed was more on the chronic nature of the daily hassles of living and its impact on the body than on single or multiple, but infrequent, severe traumatic stressors. There is a great deal of research connecting psychological stress with physical illness, particularly on the effects of stress on the immune system. However, there is less research on severe acute stressors, the traumatic stressors, and subsequent illness. As might be predicted, of those studies that have examined trauma and physical health, there is a connection between the two, especially among those with PTSD or depression (Friedman & Schnurr, 1995). Four types of health outcomes associated with trauma have been examined: self-reported health problems, utilization of medical services, morbidity as indicated by physician diagnosis or tests, and mortality.

The large study of Vietnam veterans, the NVVRS, found that there was poorer perceived health status and greater numbers of reported chronic health problems among Vietnam veterans with high levels of war zone stress than among era veterans who did not serve in Vietnam or civilian counterparts (Kulka et al., 1990). Those with either current PTSD or substance abuse problems rated their physical health as significantly worse than those without the disorders. Female rape and incest survivors report more somatic symptoms and lower perceived health status (Felitti, 1991; Kimerling & Calhoun, 1994; Rimsza & Berg, 1988; Waigandt, Wallace, Phelps, & Miller, 1990).

Koss, Koss, and Woodruff (1991) studied the relationship between sexual assault and health care utilization and found that those women who had a history of rape had more health problems and more visits to their primary care physicians. In fact, they found that raped and sexually assaulted women made twice the number of visits to their primary care physicians than nonvictimized women. Battered women are subjected to not only acute incidents of violence that result in injuries, but are under chronic stress and threat of violence. Not surprisingly, there is an association between domestic violence, illness, and medical utilization (Drossman et al., 1990; Jaffe, Wolfe, Wilson, & Zak, 1986; Weaver & Chard, 1997). Increased medical utilization has also been found among World War II and Korean War veterans and among victims of disasters in England and Australia (Abrahams, Price, Whitlock, & Williams, 1976; Beebe, 1975; Bennet, 1968).

With regard to morbidity, or diagnosable disorders, there has been a range of studies throughout the world that have found associations between trauma and physical illness or disorders. For example, 8 years after a North Sea oil rig disaster, Norwegian survivors were found to have greater incidence of cardiovascular disease, lower back pain, musculo-skeletal problems, and dermatological problems than controls (Holen, 1989).

Hopefully, as the links between psychological trauma and physical illness and disorders are more fully recognized, psychological treatment will become a more integral part of health care. Physicians and nurses need to be aware of the association not just between trauma and injuries (abused children and battered women are often first identified in emergency rooms), but also between chronic or repeated physical illness and a history of victimization.

Summary

Although everyone experiences stress during life, traumatic stress is caused by life-threatening or self-threatening events that are accompanied by fear, helplessness, or horror. A range of disorders may result from traumatic stressors including adjustment disorder, acute stress disorder, post-traumatic stress disorder, and the dissociative disorders. Associated disorders may include depression, other anxiety disorders, and substance abuse. Aside from psychological disorders, traumatic stress may affect some or many areas of a person's functioning as well as health.

Prevalence of traumatic stress and related disorders 2

A century or two ago, life expectancies were lower than they are now, infant and maternal mortality was higher, antibiotics had not been discovered, bad weather could not be predicted with any accuracy, and workplace safety practices (much less child labor laws) had not been established. People did not recognize the problem with family violence, sexual assault, or incest. Pioneers crossing America in covered wagons were not surprised to lose loved ones or all of their possessions. People did not work in offices behind computers, but in factories, mines, and farms. Life was hard and traumas were prevalent. At the turn of the millennium, people in industrialized countries do not expect that sudden catastrophic events can or will happen to them. The purpose of this chapter will be to examine the prevalence of traumatic events and the frequency with which people develop psychological disorders such as PTSD in response to these events.

Within the topic of stress and trauma, prevalence can be examined on several different levels. First, it is possible to examine how frequently stressful/traumatic events occur to people within a given period of time, or across their lifetime. On a national and international level, the most frequently studied stressors are the incidence and prevalence of criminal victimization. However, there are other important events that do not fall under the category of crime such as the trauma of war, natural or technological disasters, or accidents. A few studies have examined the prevalence of trauma in general.

Aside from determining the frequency of traumatic stressors in people's lives, it is also possible to determine the frequency of various psychological outcomes, the prevalence of psychological problems in the aftermath of trauma. These outcomes could be examined singly or in combination. The co-occurrence of more than one diagnosable disorder is referred to as comorbidity. This chapter will overview the prevalence of traumatic stressors in people's lives and will then examine the prevalence of diagnosable disorders following particular stressors. Finally, the combination of disorders, comorbidity, will be discussed.

Prevalence of trauma

Although most people do not live without a certain level of stress and daily hassles, serious trauma is, by its very nature, unexpected and more rare. That is to say, traumatic events are not common daily experiences in most people's lives. Some people never experience the most serious levels of trauma in their lifetimes. However, the majority of people do experience at least one traumatic stressor and a large number experience more than one of these major events.

Rate of victimization is calculated as the number of victimizations divided by the number of persons/households in a specific category of interest. It is a measure of the incidence of victimization. For example, according to the US National Crime Victimization Survey (NCVS) in 1995, for every 1000 people aged 12 and older, there were two rapes, two assaults with serious injury, and five robberies. Prevalence, on the other hand, is the number of persons or households who have been victimized one or more times in a given time period divided by the population of interest. It is, therefore, the percentage of people who have experienced trauma in the population. The period of time could be a single year or it could be across the course of a lifetime. When the prevalence of disorders is examined, it can also be presented as the percentage of people who experience the disorder at some point in their lives or the percentage of people who are currently experiencing the disorder.

In the United States, two of the major criminal victimization surveys, which are conducted annually, are the National Crime Victimization Survey (NCVS) and the Uniform Crime Reports (UCR). The NCVS is a survey of 100,000 households and considers a range of crimes that may or may not have been reported to the police. The UCR considers only those crimes that were reported to police. Both of these surveys break down crime rates by a variety of demographic variables. Until recently, some researchers criticized the NCVS because the survey did not conduct a very thorough assessment of crimes committed against women (Koss, Gidycz, & Wisniewski, 1987; Resnick, Kilpatrick, Dansky, Saunders, & Best, 1993). The item regarding rape was merely "Did someone try to attack you in some other way?" In response to this criticism, the survey was revised in

1992 and subsequent years. The UCR has also been criticized as a source of prevalence data because so few people report crimes to the police. For example, it is frequently found that only 10–15% of rape victims report their crimes to the authorities. It should also be remembered that criminal victimization is only one type of traumatic stressor that could affect people. Combat trauma, accidents, natural disasters, and political terrorism/war are all significant traumas that may contribute to psychological problems. The next subsection will consider overall population prevalence followed by estimates of prevalence of specific stressors.

Overall population prevalence

The prevalence of trauma has been estimated based on surveys that have been conducted either in local areas or as national surveys. Although some studies focus exclusively on particular traumatic events such as rape or disaster, there have been a few studies that have examined the rates and prevalence of trauma more generally. For example, Breslau, Davis, Andreski, and Peterson (1991) conducted a survey of 1007 young adults who were patients in a health maintenance organization in Detroit, Michigan. They found that 39% of the people surveyed had experienced a traumatic event. Norris (1992) conducted a study of 1000 people (age 18–60+) from four Southern US cities. She found a higher rate of trauma but she also studied a wider age span. In her study, 69% experienced at least one of nine major traumatic stressors over their lifetime, and 21% reported experiencing at least one event in the past year.

A survey of 1000 people was conducted in Winnipeg, in Canada, to determine rates of trauma and current PTSD (Stein, Walker, Hazen, & Forde, 1997). Stein et al. found that 74% of women and 81% of men reported at least one traumatic event. Forty-six percent of the women and 55% of the men experience more than one event. Resnick et al. (1993) conducted a national study of women in the US, which included 4008 women (2008 national probability sample, 2000 oversampling of women 18–34 years). They oversampled the younger age group because they were particularly interested in determining the prevalence of rape, which is most likely in the younger group of adults. They too found a very high rate of trauma (69%). When they extrapolated their results to the US population based on census statistics for 1989, they estimated that 66 million women in the US had experienced at least one major traumatic event.

In the largest prevalence study of multiple traumas, Kessler et al. (1995) surveyed a representative national sample of 5877 persons (2812 men and 3065 women) in the United States. This study, which included both men and women, assessed 12 categories of traumatic stressor. They found that a majority of people had experienced at least one major traumatic event. It is important to recognize that people are not limited to just one experience. This study found that of those who had experienced trauma, only a bit over a quarter of the sample reported only one major trauma; 15% of the men and 14% of the women reported experiencing two; 10% of the men and 5% of the women had experienced three; and another 10% of men and 6% of women reported four major traumas. So, overall, 35% of the men and 25% of the women reported more than one major traumatic event in their lives thus far.

Particular populations/stressors

Table 2.1 shows the breakdown for the different traumas assessed in the Kessler et al. study. While the majority of people in that study reported experiencing at least one traumatic event, there is a great deal of variability in what types of events are experienced. The most common events are witnessing someone seriously injured or killed, disasters, and accidents. Experience with these events was reported by 19–36% of the men and 14–15% of the women. Less commonly reported were rapes, physical assaults, and child abuse. However, there have been other studies that have focused on these latter topics in particular and have found higher rates, perhaps because these more sensitive topics need special attention during survey questioning.

The Kessler et al. study merely asked "Did any of these events ever happen to you" and then presented 12 more prompts including "You were raped (someone had sexual intercourse with you when you did not want to by threatening you or using some degree of force)". The assault prompt was "You were seriously physically attacked or assaulted" and the child abuse prompt was "You were physically abused as a child". Furthermore, another item collapsed being threatened with a weapon, held captive, or kidnapped, which could reflect stranger crimes or domestic violence. While the rape question is an improvement over the old national crime victimization survey question, it is quite possible that people don't apply the words "rape", "assault", or "abuse" to themselves, especially when these events are perpetrated by acquaintances or family.

TABLE 2.1

Kessler et al. (1995) National Comorbidity Study, percentage of people experiencing various traumas

Trauma	Men (%)	Women (%)
Rape	1**	9**
Molestation	3	12*
Physical attack	11	7*
Combat	6*	0
Shock (trauma to significant other)	11	12
Threat with weapon	19	7*
Accident	25	14
Disaster	19	15
Witness	36	15
Neglect	2*	3
Physical abuse	3*	5*
Other trauma	2	3*

* traumas more likely to be associated with PTSD; ** most likely to be associated with PTSD.

In the Resnick et al. (1993) national study of women, a series of screening questions were used that behaviorally described the legal definitions of rape but did not use the word rape. They found that 13% of the women reported completed rapes, and they estimated this to represent 12 million women in the US using 1989 census statistics. Another 14% (14 million women) reported attempted rape or molestation. Koss et al. (1987) studied sexual assault on US college campuses nationally and found 15% of the women had experienced rape and another 12% experienced attempted rape. That study also used a series of behavioral questions called the Sexual Experiences Survey. Similar studies have been conducted at universities in Canada and New Zealand (DeKeseredy, Schwartz, & Tait, 1993; Gavey, 1991) that found prevalence data almost identical to those of Koss et al. using the same survey instrument. Russell (1984) studied 930 adult women in San Francisco using in-person interviews and found that 24% had been raped but only 9.5% had reported the crime to the police. It is evident that studies that included more extensive questioning resulted in higher prevalence rates for rape.

Domestic violence is another trauma that has major impact but has probably been given short shrift in the major prevalence studies. The Kessler et al. (1995) study asked about serious attack or assault but did not specify that the attacker could be an acquaintance or family member. This could have left the subjects responding to their stereotypes about what constitutes an assault. The researchers puzzled over the fact that men were twice as likely to experience assault (and threats with weapons), while women were fifteen times more likely to develop PTSD as a result of physical assaults. It did not appear to occur to them that the experiences of assault might be very different for men and women. Perhaps the men were more likely to experience assault as part of a fight or street crime, whereas women were more often being attacked at home (perhaps repeatedly) by partners who purportedly love them. While the Resnick et al. study clearly guided their respondents to consider serious physical attacks by family and friends along with strangers, they did not report their results in such a way that domestic violence could be examined separately from other types of assault. Nevertheless, 10% of the women reported being seriously assaulted and physical assaults were more likely to lead to PTSD than were rapes (39% vs. 32%).

There have been a few national probability studies of domestic violence along with a number of smaller local or regional probability or nonprobability studies (see Garner & Fagan, 1997 for a review). National Family Violence Surveys were conducted in 1975 and 1985 (Gelles & Straus, 1988; Straus, Gelles, & Steinmetz, 1980). The prevalence rates were similar across the two surveys and it was found that violence occurred in 16% of 2000 households surveyed and that 28% of the respondents reported at least one incident of violence in their current relationship. Population estimates based on the findings were that at least two million women a year are seriously abused by their partners in the United States each year.

The most serious level of crime, homicide, not only results in the death of a victim or victims, but a terrible trauma for the loved ones who are left behind. In a national US survey, Amick-McMullan, Kilpatrick, and Resnick (1991) studied the prevalence of homicide-surviving family members and friends. Although homicide rates are generally known and reported each year, this was the first study to examine the prevalence of loved ones affected by homicide. In phase one of the research, 12,500 people were screened by telephone to determine the prevalence of adult survivors of homicide victims. Two types of homicide were assessed: criminal homicide and alcohol-related vehicular homicide (death by drunk drivers). In phase two, 206 immediate family survivors were surveyed in more depth with regard to reactions. These reactions will be discussed later in the chapter.

TABLE 2.2

National prevalence estimates of adult survivors of homicide victims (Amick-McMullan et al., 1991). Copyright © 1991 by Sage Publications Inc. Reprinted by permission of Sage Publications Inc.

Survivor's relationship to victim	Type of homicide	Percentage having experienced	Estimated number of US adult survivors
Immediate family member	Criminal	1.6	2.8 million
	Alcohol-related vehicular	1.2	2.2 million
	Total	2.8	5.0 million
Other relative	Criminal	1.5	2.6 million
	Alcohol-related vehicular	2.2	4.0 million
	Total	3.7	6.6 million
Close friend	Criminal	0.7	1.3 million
	Alcohol-related vehicular	2.0	3.5 million
	Total	2.7	4.8 million
Total		9.3	16.4 million

Table 2.2 shows the percentages and population estimates of the immediate family members, other relatives, and friends who have experienced the homicidal death of a significant other. Although the percentages appear fairly small, when translated out to actual population numbers, the statistics are staggering.

On an international level there have been studies and estimates of the magnitude of traumatic stressors. With regard to crime, there has been an international effort since the late 1980s to assess crime victimization throughout the world using the same survey instrument across countries for comparison purposes (Alvazzi del Frate, Zvekic, & van Dijk, 1993). In the most recent survey, which covered a 5-year period up to 1996, a total of 134,000 people had participated from 54 countries (van Dijk, 1997). The results by global region are presented in Table 2.3 and represent the percentage of men and women who were assaulted over a 5-year period plus the percentage of people who experienced any type of crime (e.g., car theft, burglary, other theft). The overall victimization rates and the rates of contact crimes (sexual violence, assaults/threats, and robbery) are highest in Latin America and Africa, where three out of every four citizens aged 16 and older living in an urban area were victimized at least once over the period. The overall victimization rates were lowest in Asia, but even there, over 50% of the people surveyed had been a victim of crime.

While Asia is safer for men, it is not safer for women. Women are assaulted at greater rates than men in Africa, Asia, and Latin America

TABLE 2.3

Percentages of the public victimized by contact crimes, violence against women and men, and any crime over 5 years in urban areas of six global regions—results of the International Crime Victims Survey, 1988–1996 (van Dijk, 1997)

	All	W. Europe	New World	Latin America	Central & E. Europe	Asia	Africa
Number of countries	52	15	4	5	16	6	6
Number of respondents	64,239	12,729	5,951	7,015	17,300	13,037	8,180
Contact crime (%)	20.2	15.8	20.2	33.2	17.5	15.5	31.8
Violence							
Females (%)	7.4	5.0	8.0	13.9	5.9	6.3	12.6
Males (%)	6.2	5.0	8.4	7.9	6.5	4.5	7.9
Any crime (%)	63.4	61.2	65.3	74.5	62.2	51.4	74.0

than other parts of the world. Although the rates of assault are fairly high in the New World countries (Canada, USA, Australia, and New Zealand), there are no overall sex differences. However, because women are more likely to be sexually assaulted than men throughout the world, the similar rates between men and women in Western Europe, Eastern Europe, and the New World countries probably mean that men are more likely to be physically assaulted and women are more likely to be sexually assaulted. Furthermore, in an analysis from a previous survey, the physical assaults on women were more likely to be domestic assaults (Alvazzi del Frate & Patrignani, 1995), indicating that domestic violence is a major social problem in Latin America, Africa, and Asia.

It may be impossible to estimate the prevalence of the traumatic effects of war. War produces widespread trauma on a national and global level. Aside from the soldiers and civilians who are killed or injured in combat, family and friends of those who were killed/injured are also traumatized. Participating in combat, in and of itself, may be very traumatic. Norris (1992) found that 9% of participants in a survey of 1000 people had experienced combat. Kessler et al. (1995) found 6% (of men) in their survey had combat experience. In the Canadian study, Stein et al. (1997) found 7% of the men had experienced combat.

Prisoners of war, victims of torture and the imprisonment of soldiers and civilians are additional sources of war trauma. War causes massive social upheaval resulting in loss of homes, jobs, entire communities, and even countries. Millions of people have fled their native war-torn countries and have experienced the stress or trauma of being refugees in foreign lands. In fact, it has been estimated that over the 5-year period from 1990 to 1995, there were approximately 16,000,000 refugees and asylum seekers per year who had to leave their countries (International Federation of Red Cross and Red Crescent Societies, 1996). At the current time, Africa is the continent that generates the largest number of refugees. The Red Cross has estimated that 40 million people have been killed in wars and conflicts since World War II (International Federation of Red Cross and Red Crescent Societies, 1993). On a worldwide scope, the number of people traumatized by war is incomprehensibly large.

Natural disasters and accidents are also highly prevalent. The Red Cross also reports on the number and impact of natural disasters and disasters with a non-natural trigger (accidents, technological accidents, fire) each year (International Federation of Red Cross and Red Crescent Societies, 1996). These disasters, not including war, kill over 150,000 people per year and impact on the lives of 128 million.

In the population studies which were mentioned earlier (Kessler et al., 1995; Norris, 1992; Stein et al., 1997) the lifetime prevalence of fire or other natural disaster is in the range of 8–11% for fire, 13–14% for other natural disasters, or 15–19% combined. Norris also assessed other hazards that forced evacuations from home or posed imminent danger and found that 15% of women and men had experienced such hazards. Both Norris and Stein et al. assessed motor vehicle accidents and both found sex differences, with men more likely to have experienced a serious accident. Norris found 28% of men and 20% of women had experienced a car accident serious enough to cause injuries. Stein et al. reported almost identical prevalence with 29% of men and 20% of women having had car accidents. The Kessler et al. (1995) study reported on experience with a life-threatening accident but did not specify the cause. They also found significant sex differences with 25% of the men and 14% of the women reporting serious accidents. Clearly, a large majority of the population has experienced at least one serious traumatic stressor. However, not all people suffer from psychological disorders as a result of these traumas.

Prevalence of disorders

There are many ways in which people might be affected by their traumatic experiences. They may recover from the experience fully with no psychological, biological, or behavioral effects. They may develop a diagnosable psychological disorder that may be experienced briefly or over a long period of time. People may also experience reactions that affect their interpersonal functioning, such as marital relationships, sexual functioning, family functioning, or ability to form or maintain friendships. Trauma may affect people's relationship with themselves, that is, with regard to self-esteem, confidence, trust in their own judgement, or other beliefs about themselves. Reactions to trauma may compromise the immune system resulting in physical illnesses. Many of these common problems were listed in the first chapter. To begin the discussion of the prevalence of trauma-related problems, PTSD will be examined first and in most depth because it is the disorder that appears to develop most frequently and has been studied the most.

PTSD

There are two ways in which prevalence of PTSD can be examined. One way is to estimate the prevalence across the population as a whole. However, because PTSD requires a trauma to occur before even considering diagnosis, another way to examine the question is with regard to at-risk populations. In other words, prevalence can be estimated for only those people who experienced a traumatic stressor. Some studies have focused on the prevalence of PTSD following particular traumatic stressors such as combat or rape. At-risk populations and particular stressors will be considered after a more general consideration across the whole population.

As mentioned earlier, Breslau et al. (1991) studied 1007 young adults in Detroit, Michigan. They estimated a lifetime prevalence of PTSD of 9%. Of those who had been exposed to trauma, 24% had developed PTSD at some point. They also found sex differences regarding the development of PTSD. In the total sample, 6% of the men and 11% of the women developed PTSD, while the prevalence among those who had experienced trauma was 14% for men and 31% for women. In their national survey of 4008 women, Resnick et al. (1993) found that 12% of the entire sample had PTSD during their lifetime; of those who had experienced a traumatic event, 18% had developed PTSD during their lifetime. Resnick et al. also measured current PTSD in their study, defined as experiencing sufficient symptoms to qualify for diagnosis in the 6 months prior to the interview. They found that 5% of the total sample and 7% of the trauma-exposed sample had current PTSD.

In the largest prevalence study conducted to date, Kessler et al. (1995) surveyed 2812 men and 3065 women. They found a population prevalence of PTSD to be 8% overall with 10% of women and 5% of men to have developed PTSD during their lifetime. The PTSD rate among those exposed to trauma was 20% for women and 8% for men. This study did not examine current PTSD. In discussing the sex difference in PTSD, Kessler et al. pointed out that whereas men were more likely than women to experience at least one trauma overall, women were more likely than men to experience a trauma associated with a high probability of PTSD (e.g., sexual assault).

Although the results of these studies are not identical, they are remarkably similar given the differences in the studies. Overall, it can be estimated that 5–6% of men and 10–12% of women in the population have experienced a diagnosable post-traumatic stress disorder at some time in their lives. These percentages may appear small, but they translate to millions of people on a national or international scale.

At-risk populations

At-risk populations are particular groups of people who are known to have experienced a particular traumatic stressor. There have been a number of studies that have examined the rates of PTSD within particular groups. The groups most commonly studied are war veterans, crime victims, and disaster victims. It is clear from the existing research that all stressors are not equal. Referring back to Table 2.1, it can be seen that the more frequent stressful events are also the events least likely to be associated with PTSD. The most frequently occurring traumas, life-threatening accidents, witnessing someone being badly injured or killed, or natural disasters (including fires) result in PTSD in less than 10% of the victims, whereas somewhat less common events such as combat, child abuse, or rape are more likely to produce PTSD. Rape was the single event most likely to cause PTSD in both men and women. In the Resnick et al. (1993) national survey of women, they found that 9% of women who had experienced a disaster or accident had met the criteria for PTSD at some point and 3% had current PTSD. However, the lifetime prevalence of PTSD for rape, sexual assault, and physical assault was 32%, 31%, and 39% respectively. It appears that events that are violent and intended are much more likely to cause PTSD than events that are traumatic but natural, or at least impersonal (accidents).

War. The traumatic effects of war have been studied with two groups: combat veterans (including nurses), and civilians who are affected by war. The largest study of combat veterans was the National Vietnam Veterans Readjustment Study (NVVRS), which was conducted by a mandate from the United States Congress in 1983 (Kulka et al., 1990), to study post-traumatic stress disorder and other psychological problems following the Vietnam War. During the years of the war, over 8 million people served in the US military. Of those, 3.1 million served in Vietnam (theater veterans) and the remainder served in the US or other areas abroad (era veterans). Of the 3.1 million serving in Vietnam, only 7200 were women. There were over 255,000 women who served elsewhere during the Vietnam era. This study conducted in-depth interviews and assessments with three groups: 1632 Vietnam theater veterans, 730 Vietnam era veterans, and 668 nonveterans/civilian counterparts, for a total of 3016 interviews.

The results of the NVVRS were that the majority of Vietnam theater veterans made a successful readjustment to civilian life and did not suffer from PTSD or other problems. However, the researchers also found that 31% of male and 27% of female veterans had a full diagnosis of PTSD at some time during their lives. Furthermore, 15% of male and 9% of female veterans have PTSD currently. These rates translate to 479,000 Vietnam veterans with current PTSD in the United States. In addition, 11% of male and 8% of female veterans currently suffer from partial PTSD, which means that they have significant symptoms and distress but do not meet the full criteria for PTSD. This translates to an additional 350,000 men and women in the US alone who are still suffering in the aftermath of the Vietnam War.

A study of Vietnam veterans from New Zealand found very similar rates of PTSD (MacDonald, Chamberlain, & Long, 1997). Although PTSD was only identified by that name following the Vietnam War, there have been subsequent studies of veterans of other wars. And while the recent prevalence studies only find that 5–6% of the male population has experienced combat, in the population over the age of 65, 25% have been exposed to combat (Spiro, Schnurr, & Aldwin, 1994). Jongedijk, Carlier, Schreuder, and Gersons (1996) assessed 21 Dutch veterans of combat in World War II or in the Dutch East Indies. They ranged in age from 60 to 73 and been traumatized 45 years earlier on average. The researchers found that 67% met full criteria for PTSD and another 33% had partial PTSD. In a study of 125 non-psychiatric World War II and Korean War veterans, Hyer et al. (1996) found that 39% had full PTSD. Studies have also found PTSD rates of 47% and 50% among former prisoners of war four decades after World War II (Goldstein, van Kammen, Shelly, Miller, & van Kammen, 1987; Kluznik, Speed, van Valkenberg, & Magraw, 1986).

A range of other people affected by war has also been studied with regard to PTSD. For example, in 1985, a study was conducted among Vietnam nurses and it was determined that 3% had PTSD at the time of assessment (Stretch, Vail, & Maloney, 1985). Several studies have been conducted with Cambodian refugees, particularly those who were children at the time of the Pol Pot regime (Hubbard, Realmuto, Northwood, & Masten, 1995; Kinzie et al., 1990). At least half of those assessed reported significant PTSD. One study of 322 Indochinese refugees in a clinic setting found that overall 70% met the criteria for PTSD, but the rates varied among the different groups assessed. Although 54% of the Vietnamese patients had PTSD, over 90% of the Cambodians and Mien (a tribe in Laos) had PTSD and had not improved over many years (Kinzie et al., 1990). These refugees had survived many years of bloody war and some had survived concentration camps in their homelands.

Jewish survivors of the Holocaust have also been studied for the presence of PTSD. For example, 124 survivors, 63% of whom had been detained in concentration camps and 78% of whom lost first-degree relatives in the war, were assessed for PTSD (Kuch & Cox, 1992). Forty-seven percent of the total group had PTSD five decades after the war. Members of a subsample of 20 Auschwitz survivors were three times more likely to have PTSD than the other war survivors (labor camps, ghettos, or in hiding).

A study conducted in England reported on PTSD among refugees who had been tortured (Van Velsen, Gorst-Unsworth, & Turner, 1996). Sixty patients, the majority of whom were refugees from Turkey, were assessed for PTSD and other disorders. PTSD was diagnosed in 52% of the cases. Other studies of torture victims have found rates of 30% and 51% for lifetime PTSD (Basoglu et al., 1994; Ramsay, Gorst-Unsworth, & Turner 1993).

Crime. A number of the traumas assessed in the National Comorbidity Study (Kessler et al., 1995) were related to crime, either committed in childhood (child abuse, molestation, neglect) or adulthood (rape, physical assault, threat with weapon). Participants in the study were assessed for the most upsetting trauma. The rates of lifetime PTSD for men ranged from 2% for physical attack to 65% for those who had been raped. For women, the rates of PTSD ranged from 20% (child neglect) to 49% (child physical abuse). For both genders combined, rape was the event most likely to be reported as most upsetting and resulting in PTSD.

Sexual assault was also found to result in the highest rates of current PTSD (14%) among a range of traumas in a study of four cities in the Southern United States (Norris, 1992). However, physical assault resulted in rates almost as high (13%). In future research, when assessing physical assault, it will be important to determine whether the assault is a single incident event by a stranger or a series of assaults by an intimate. It is quite possible that domestic violence results in PTSD as much or more often than sexual assault. However, because sexual assault may occur within a domestic violence situation, it will also be important to sort out whether the PTSD is due to the physical violence, due to the sexual assault, or both.

There have been a few studies that have focused particularly on PTSD among battered women. These studies have not been drawn from representative community samples but have examined clinical samples, women who were seeking services through therapy clinics, battered women programs, or through shelters. PTSD rates in these studies range from a low of 31% for lifetime PTSD in a nonshelter sample of battered women (Gleason, 1993) to a high of 84% in a shelter sample of battered women assessed 3–5 days after arrival to the shelter (Kemp, Rawlings, & Green, 1991). It should be noted that, at least among battered women, depression might be even more serious than PTSD. In the Gleason study, 81% of the nonshelter women and 63% of the shelter women reported lifetime history of major depression.

The national study in the US of rape prevalence and PTSD, entitled "Rape in America: A Report to the Nation" (Kilpatrick, Edmunds, & Seymour, 1992) found that almost a third of all rape victims (31%) developed PTSD sometime after the event and that 11% still have PTSD. Given a US population of 96.3 million adult women, this translates to 3.8 million women who have had rape-related PTSD and 1.3 million women who currently have PTSD due to rape. This study was a retrospective study that did not control for the length of time since the rape. Although the sample in this study was large and representative, because some of the women in the study may have been raped decades earlier and may have forgotten the range and severity of symptoms they experienced soon after the event, it is possible that the rates of lifetime PTSD may be underestimates of the actual impact of rape on functioning. A look at prospective studies gives us another piece of the puzzle from a different angle.

Most of the studies described previously are retrospective studies. A retrospective study assesses the prevalence of trauma and/or disorders across a particular population regarding events that happened at some time in the past. Although some studies have a fairly short time frame such as events occurring in the past year, many prevalence studies ask participants to report on events or symptoms across their whole lifetime. The advantage of retrospective population studies is that the sample may be very representative of the population of interest. The disadvantage is that trauma reactions are being questioned and compiled for events that may have occurred perhaps decades apart and could be affected by memory and subsequent events.

A prospective study assesses participant's reactions from the time of a traumatic event forward for some period of time. The advantage of this type of study is that everyone is assessed at uniform times post-trauma so the reactions are not affected by time, nor are they affected as much by memory and recall as retrospective studies.

However, because the participants must have told someone about the incident in order to be identified and invited to participate in the research, these studies cannot be assumed to represent the population as a whole. For example, people who do not report their victimization to someone might have different types or severity of reactions from those who report and discuss their trauma with others.

One prospective study by Rothbaum et al. (1992), described in the previous chapter assessed PTSD weekly in 95 rape victims in after they reported their crimes to the police/hospital. They found that at the first assessment (average time was 13 days post-crime), 94% of the women met the symptom criteria for PTSD; 12 weeks later, 47% still had full PTSD. In a similar study with male and female non-sexual assault victims who were victimized by nonfamily members (robbery, simple assault, aggravated assault), the researchers found a similar but less severe pattern of recovery (Riggs et al., 1995).

At the first assessment, within a month of the crime, 71% of the women and 50% of the men met the criteria for PTSD. At the final assessment, 12 weeks later, 21% of the 38 women but none of the 22 men who completed the study still had PTSD. Riggs et al. pointed out that although many of the participants did not have full PTSD at the final assessment, many of them still had component symptoms. More than 50% of the non-PTSD participants met the re-experiencing and arousal criteria, although few reported sufficient avoidance/numbing symptoms to meet the avoidance criteria or the overall diagnostic criteria. They also found that those who dropped out of the study (i.e., they did not complete all of the assessments) reported more severe assaults than those who completed the study. The authors concluded that their rates of PTSD might be an underestimate of the true level of reactions following assault.

Aside from being a crime victim directly, it is also possible to develop PTSD as a secondary victim. The loved ones of a homicide victim are particularly at risk for developing PTSD in addition to their grief reactions. In the random survey of the US population mentioned earlier in the chapter (Amick-McMullan et al., 1991), after ascertaining the percentage of family and friends who are affected by homicide, the researchers examined PTSD. Immediate family survivors of either criminal homicide or alcohol-related vehicular homicide included grandparents and grandchildren, along with parents, spouses, children, and siblings. Overall, it was found that 23% reported meeting full PTSD criteria at some point after the homicide (19% for criminal and 28% for vehicular homicide). Current PTSD was assessed in 5% of the sample. Higher percentages of survey participants reported partial PTSD. There were no statistical differences regarding whether the loved one was killed in a car crash or by criminal homicide. Although the homicides occurred on average 17 years earlier, the researchers found no relationship between length of time since the crime and the number of PTSD symptoms. This indicates that the PTSD had become a chronic condition with little change over time.

Disasters. There have been a number of studies that have examined the rates of PTSD following disaster. Two decades after a devastating flood, Green et al. (1990) found that 25% of their sample still had PTSD. However, in a more general population study comparing rates of PTSD across different stressors, exposure to fires, disasters, and other hazards were only associated with current PTSD in 5–8% of cases. Disasters were less likely to cause PTSD than crimes (especially sexual assault at 14%) or motor vehicle crashes (12%). McFarlane and Papay (1992) studied 147 firefighters who were exposed to Australian bushfires 42 months after the disaster. They found that 13% still had PTSD.

Motor vehicle accidents. Norris (1992) has pointed out that although motor vehicle accidents (MVAs) are less frequent than some traumas (e.g., tragic death or robbery) and less traumatic than some events (sexual or physical assault), when both frequency and impact are considered together, MVAs may be the single most significant event. The lifetime frequency of MVAs is 23% and the PTSD rate is 12%, which results in a rate of 28 seriously distressed people for every 1000 adults in the United States, just from one type of event.

Other disorders

Unlike PTSD, which has a particular identifiable precipitant, most other disorders may occur without any identifiable stressor. However, it is possible to determine how many new cases of a disorder occur after a particular traumatic stressor or to compare the rates of disorders among those who have or have not experienced a traumatic stressor. For example, Smith, Robins, Przybeck, Goldring, and Solomon (1986) examined new cases of psychiatric disorders in the year after dioxin exposure and/or a flood in St. Louis, Missouri. They found that there were new cases in only four of twelve diagnoses that were assessed: depression, alcoholism, generalized anxiety, and post-traumatic stress disorder. The rates of new cases among those

TABLE 2.4

Percentages of mental disorders among sexually assaulted and nonassaulted people in a community survey (Burnam et al., 1988). Copyright © 1988 by the American Psychological Association. Reprinted with permission

	Percentage with disorder	
Disorder	Sexually assaulted (%)	Non-assaulted (%)
Major depression	17.9	4.7**
Mania	2.5	0.3*
Schizophrenia	1.6	0.4
Alcohol abuse or dependence	18.4	13.8
Drug abuse or dependence	20.4	5.5**
Antisocial personality	4.6	2.4
Phobia	22.2	9.7**
Panic disorder	4.6	0.8**
Obsessive-compulsive disorder	5.3	1.4**

* $p < .01$, ** $p < .001$.

who were exposed ranged from 1% (depression) to 6% (generalized anxiety disorder). In addition, in examining those who had a diagnosis both before and after the disaster, there were significant differences in those who were directly exposed versus those from the area who were not exposed to the disaster. Those who were exposed had significantly greater persistence of symptoms of alcohol abuse and generalized anxiety.

Another community epidemiology study compared the rates of psychological disorders among people who had or had not been sexually assaulted (Burnam et al., 1988). This study, which was conducted in Los Angeles, included 3132 adults, 53% of whom were female. Overall, 13% of the population interviewed had been the victim of at least one sexual assault, with more women (17%) than men (9%) reporting sexual assaults, and a staggering 80% of first assaults occurring before the age of 25. Burnam et al. compared 432 people who had been sexually assaulted with 432 matched nonvictim comparison participants. The rates of psychological disorders other than PTSD, which was not assessed, are listed in Table 2.4. There were large differences between those who had and had not been sexually assaulted in major depression, drug abuse or dependence, phobias, panic disorder, and obsessive-compulsive disorder. There were no differences in the rates of schizophrenia, alcohol abuse/dependence, or antisocial personality disorder.

In order to examine the onset of disorders since the assault, Burnam et al. (1988) examined the onset of disorders each year for 5 years after the first assault for the victim group and an equivalent 5-year period for the nonvictim group. The nonvictim group developed psychological disorders at a fairly even rate over the 5 years. However, the victim group was more likely to develop alcohol abuse/dependence, depression, panic disorder and obsessive-compulsive disorder in the first year or two after the assault, indicated that the assault may have played some role in these disorders.

Comorbidity of trauma-related disorders

Because other disorders resulting from trauma have been studied less, most research has attended to the prevalence of other disorders only in relationship to PTSD. Comorbidity is the co-occurrence of more than one diagnosable disorder (see the case study on bereavement in Chapter 1 for an example). It is possible that other disorders develop independently of PTSD. However, it is also quite possible that the other disorders develop as maladaptive coping attempts and then become full-blown problems in and of themselves. For example, if someone has severe PTSD symptoms including nightmares, sleep disruption, flashbacks, hypervigilance, and other physiological arousal symptoms, that person may attempt to reduce his/her symptomotology by consuming alcohol. If the person consumes enough alcohol to become addicted or to cause serious problems in his/her life, then he/she would also have a substance abuse or dependence diagnosis secondary to the PTSD. If the person had a substance abuse problem prior to the trauma, then both the substance abuse and PTSD would be considered primary diagnoses.

There have been three types of studies that have examined the comorbidity of disorders in traumatized populations: epidemiological studies with community samples, studies of particular at-risk populations, and studies with clinical populations. Epidemiological studies examine the rates of disorders found in the general population and then typically examine the comorbidity of secondary disorders among those who have been diagnosed with a particular primary disorder. In the case of PTSD, most studies have started by looking at secondary disorders among those who are known to have PTSD. Very few studies have examined the rates of PTSD among those who are known to have another diagnosis such as substance abuse or depression. Studies of at-risk populations are studies that examine people who are identified as having been exposed to a traumatic stressor, usually the same stressor, and then examining the rates of comorbidity among those who have been diagnosed with PTSD. Examples of at-risk populations are combat veterans, rape victims, or survivors of particular natural disasters. Finally, clinical studies are those that examine the comorbidity of disorders among treatment-seekers. These studies could reflect a particular traumatic stressor such as combat or rape victim treatment seekers or they could be more general studies of clinics or inpatient settings. All three types of studies provide important information that converges to form a more complete picture of the disorders that may emerge in the aftermath of traumatic events.

Community surveys: Epidemiological studies

An example of an epidemiological study is the National Comorbidity Study in which Kessler et al. (1995) conducted a national survey of 5877 people. They found that, of those with PTSD, 88% of the men and 79% of the women also had comorbid disorders. Table 2.5 lists the most common comorbid disorders for men and women.

In an attempt to determine whether PTSD was primary (the chief disorder caused by the trauma) or secondary (caused not by the trauma, but by another disorder) to other comorbid disorders, Kessler et al. (1995) examined whether the PTSD had an earlier age at onset than other comorbid disorders. This attempt was limited by the fact that they assessed PTSD for only the most distressing event each person was exposed to rather than the first event. They placed as an upper bound the percentage of people with comorbidity who had no other disorder as of the age at their earliest lifetime trauma. The lower bound was the percentage of people with comorbidity who had no other disorder as of the age of their most upsetting trauma. Using this method they determined that PTSD was primary more often than not with respect to comorbid depression (range 53–78%) and substance use disorders (53–84%) and somewhat less likely to be primary with respect to comorbid anxiety disorders (30–56%). In other words, there is evidence that PTSD developed as a result of the trauma and the comorbid depression and substance abuse may have developed as a result of having PTSD. The anxiety disorders were more likely to be independent diagnoses, and not caused by having PTSD.

In thinking about the meaning of these findings, it is clear that the rates of comorbid disorders are very high. Relatively few people

TABLE 2.5

**Percentages of disorders comorbid with PTSD in the
National Comorbidity Study (Kessler et al., 1995)**

	Men (%)	Women (%)
MDD	48	49
Dysthymia	21	23
Mania	12	6
GAD	17	15
Panic	7	13
Simple phobia	31	29
Social phobia	28	28
Agoraphobia	16	22
Alcohol	52	28
Drugs	35	27
Conduct disorder	43	15

suffer from only one disorder such as PTSD. Most of those with PTSD also develop one or more other diagnosable disorders. Epidemiological studies do a good job describing prevalence of comorbid disorders across the population and over one's lifetime. However, it should be noted again that community surveys are retrospective studies in which some participants are reporting about events and symptoms that may have occurred years or even decades earlier, whereas other participants may have experienced traumatic events more recently. These studies also report across a range of potential traumatic events that could vary a great deal in their likelihood of producing PTSD or other comorbid disorders. Given that the epidemiological studies are examining disorders across a lifetime, it is possible that the rates of comorbidity are higher than one would find if they examined participants cross-sectionally, that is, at a specific time after a traumatic event happens. The studies of at-risk populations tend to study homogeneous samples of people (they all were exposed to the same or similar traumatic stressors) at a specific point in time post-trauma.

At-risk populations

Studies of at-risk populations examine people at one or more points in time post-trauma. As discussed earlier in the chapter, the most famous at-risk study is the National Vietnam Veterans Readjustment Study (NVVRS; Kulka et al., 1990). This was the national study of

3016 Vietnam veterans, era veterans (who did not serve in Vietnam), and civilian controls. They found that 15% of the Vietnam veterans had current PTSD at the time of assessment. The rates of comorbidity were 99% for lifetime comorbidity and 50% for current comorbidity. The most prominent coexisting problem was substance abuse (73%), followed by major depression (26%) and dysthymia (21%).

Hubbard et al. (1995) studied 59 Cambodian American adolescents who were traumatized during Pol Pot's regime (1975–79). They found that 24% of them had current PTSD and 59% met the criteria for a lifetime diagnosis. The overall comorbidity was 57% with the rates fairly evenly distributed across disorders: 21% met the criteria for current major depression, 21% for generalized anxiety disorder, 21% for social phobia, and 29% for somatoform pain disorder. The authors noted that the somatoform pain was found only among female respondents. Social phobia was found equally in the PTSD and no PTSD groups, leading the authors to suggest that the social phobia reflected acculturation issues rather than a disorder comorbid to PTSD. It should also be noted that in this group substance abuse was a comorbid problem for no one.

Green, Lindy, Grace, and Leonard (1992) interviewed 193 victims of the Buffalo Creek dam collapse 14 years later. They found that of the 25% of people studied who still had PTSD, the most frequent comorbid disorders were major depression (42%), generalized anxiety disorder (42%), and simple phobia (29%). Substance abuse was not prevalent and was comorbid in only 8% of those with PTSD. McFarlane and Papay (1992) studied a population of firefighters 42 months after a severe bushfire in Australia. As with the Green et al. study, they found that 51% of those with PTSD also had major depression, 39% had generalized anxiety disorder, 37% had panic disorder, and 33% had phobias. However, it should be noted that among those without PTSD, 50% had a phobic disorder, 37% had generalized anxiety disorder, and 26% had major depressive disorder. Therefore, it appears that the only disorder that was more often associated with PTSD was depression.

The results of these studies indicate that even with homogeneous samples, the comorbidity rates are quite high. Depression is the most common co-occurring problem. Comorbid substance abuse rates varied widely depending upon the population studied. It is very frequent among Vietnam veterans but virtually nonexistent among the young adults who immigrated from Cambodia, and infrequent among middle-aged adults who experienced a flood. So, rather than being a highly frequent concurrent disorder, substance abuse appears to reflect maladaptive coping style within particular groups or ages. It is also possible that substance abuse and dependence develop slowly as secondary disorders when other coping mechanisms fail to comfort or reduce distress or when support systems are no longer available.

Personality disorders

Most studies have focused on the clinical disorders that are classified as Axis I disorders. Very few studies have examined the comorbidity of PTSD with the more pervasive personality disorders (Axis II). A personality disorder, according to the *DSM-IV* (APA, 1994), is "an enduring pattern of inner experience and behavior that deviates markedly from the expectations of the individual's culture" (p. 633). The maladaptive pattern must be expressed in at least two of the following domains: cognition, affect, interpersonal functioning, or impulse control. The pattern is (1) inflexible and pervasive across a broad range of personal and social situations; (2) is distressing or causes impairment in work or social functioning; (3) is stable and of long duration; (4) can be traced to at least adolescence or early adulthood; (5) is not better accounted for by the diagnosis of another mental disorder; and (6) cannot be accounted for by the effects of a substance or general medical condition.

Several studies have examined one personality disorder in particular, antisocial personality disorder (ASPD). A pervasive pattern of disregard for and violation of the rights of others characterize antisocial personality disorder. This disorder begins in childhood and continues into adulthood. The antisocial person repeatedly engages in at least three of the following: acts which violate the law, deceitfulness, impulsivity, irritability and aggressiveness, reckless disregard for self or others, consistent irresponsibility, or lack of remorse. In the first study to examine comorbid ASPD, Sierles, Chen, McFarland, and Taylor (1983) found that, among Vietnam veterans, 12% of those with PTSD also met criteria for antisocial personality disorder with onset prior to age 15. If they included those with onset at age 15, the number jumped to 36%. Helzer, Robins, and McEvoy (1987) also examined antisocial personality disorders but found a very low rate in a community sample (3%).

The large NVVRS study of Vietnam veterans (Kulka et al., 1990) found a rate of 31% among those with PTSD. More recently, in the National Comorbidity Study with a large community sample, Kessler

TABLE 2.6

Percentage of comorbidity of personality disorders among veterans and female assault victims with PTSD

	Southwick, Yehuda, and Giller (1993)	Cashman et al. (1995)
Cluster A: Odd-eccentric		
Paranoid	38	27
Schizoid	6	4
Schizotypal	26	4
Cluster B: Dramatic-emotional		
Antisocial	15	4
Borderline	76	15
Histrionic	9	7
Narcissistic	21	5
Cluster C: Anxious-fearful		
Avoidant	41	14
Dependent	21	7
Obsessive-compulsive	44	9
Passive-aggressive	35	11
Self-defeating	32	16

et al. (1995) found a comorbidity rate of 43% for men and 15% for women. These findings should be compared to the general population in which 3% of men and 1% of women are found to have antisocial personality disorder (*DSM-IV*, APA, 1994). In the Cooperative Study on Psychophysiology of PTSD, both ASD and borderline personality disorder (BPD) were examined (Keane et al., 1998). There were more cases of current PTSD with BPD (18%) than with ASD (11%).

Three studies have examined a greater range of comorbid personality disorders. Keane and Wolfe (1990) found that 26% of the Vietnam veterans they assessed with PTSD also met the criteria for a personality disorder, but virtually all of them were diagnosed with antisocial personality disorder or mixed personality disorder with antisocial features. On the other hand, Southwick, Yehuda, and Giller (1993) found other disorders to be much more likely than ASPD with a sample of Vietnam veterans, as did Cashman, Molnar, and Foa (1995) with a sample of female rape and assault victims. Table 2.6 describes the results of these two studies. However, it should be noted that these studies are describing very different samples. The Southwick, Yehuda, and Giller (1993) study was reporting on 34 treatment-seeking male Vietnam veterans, obviously many years post-combat, whereas Cashman et al. (1995) were examining 64 female rape and assault victims with PTSD 3 months after their crime who were participating in an assessment study.

There is a big difference between the recent sample of rape and assault victims and the very chronic group of veterans in treatment. The only disorder in which there were similar findings was paranoid personality disorder. Paranoid personality disorder is diagnosed when someone (1) has a pervasive distrust and suspiciousness of others such that he/she suspects that others are exploiting or harming him/her, (2) is preoccupied with doubts regarding the trustworthiness of others, (3) is reluctant to confide in others because of the unwarranted fear that the information will be used against him or her, and so forth. It could be that the higher rates of the other disorders noted in the Vietnam veterans reflect the generalization of symptoms and maladaptive coping patterns that slowly emerge over time. For example, in borderline personality, among other symptoms, the person exhibits a pattern of unstable and intense interpersonal relationships, engages in impulsive and potentially self-damaging behaviors, has intense reactive moods or inappropriate intense anger, stress-related paranoid ideation, or severe dissociative symptoms. Any of these symptoms could reflect difficulties in coping with traumatic memories that have become pervasive. In fact, it is not unusual for adults with a history of child sexual abuse to receive a diagnosis of borderline personality disorder.

It has been proposed by Herman (1992a) that, instead of viewing trauma survivors as having comorbid personality disorders, perhaps a more parsimonious way to view their symptoms is that they have a complex form of PTSD. Herman suggested that when violence has been repeated over a prolonged period of time, particularly starting in childhood, the effects may be so wide ranging that the person appears to have a personality disorder, and that the symptoms reflected in the PTSD diagnosis do not capture this range of effects. In the PTSD field trial for the development of the *DSM-IV*, the issue of complex PTSD, then called Disorders of extreme stress, not otherwise specified (DESNOS) was examined (Pelcovitz et al., 1997; Roth, Newman, Pelcovitz, van der Kolk, & Mandel, 1997). The results of the field trial were that complex DESNOS symptoms occur comorbid with PTSD in many cases and do not occur in the absence of PTSD, reflecting a complex form of PTSD. Complex PTSD was most likely to occur with people who had been sexually and physically abused in childhood. These symptoms/characteristics of complex PTSD are now listed in the *DSM-IV* as associated features of PTSD. It is unknown what the exact relationship is between these complex PTSD symptoms and various personality disorders.

Areas of functioning that have been observed to be associated with complex PTSD are: impaired affect modulation; self-destructive and impulsive behavior; dissociative symptoms; somatic complaints; feelings of ineffectiveness, shame, despair, or hopelessness; feeling permanently damaged; a loss of previously sustained beliefs; hostility; social withdrawal; feeling constantly threatened; impaired relationships with others; or a change from the individual's previous personality characteristics (*DSM-IV*, APA, 1994, p. 425). Affect modulation is the ability to regulate the level of emotional expression. Someone with poor affect regulation will fly into rages or become extremely emotional with little provocation. By the same token, the person with poor impulse control might act rashly without considering consequences. Both behaviors and emotions appear to be extreme, and rather than falling onto a continuum as most people experience, appear to be either completely on or completely off. Dissociation, which has been discussed in the prior chapter, appears to be a splitting off of memory and emotion so that the person shuts down physically and emotionally when reminded of traumatic events or cues. Somatic complaints are the development of physical problems in response to stress. The remainder of the associated symptoms pertain to negative emotions, beliefs, and impaired interpersonal relationships.

Summary

Although not frequent in individual lives, most people experience at least one severe event over the course of their lives that would be considered a traumatic stressor—most studies indicate that approximately 70% of the population experience at least one traumatic stressor during their lifetime. In the general population, 8–12% have suffered from diagnosable post-traumatic stress disorder and there are typically sex differences reported with women having higher rates than men. Of those people who have experienced a traumatic event, 8–24% report diagnosable PTSD during their lifetimes. There is a great deal of variability in rates of PTSD depending upon the type of trauma. War and interpersonal violence are the events most likely to lead to PTSD. PTSD occurs very frequently associated with other disorders, most commonly major depression. Comorbid substance abuse rates vary widely and it appears that comorbid substance abuse is more frequently found in Vietnam veterans than in non-veteran samples. There are a number of symptoms and reactions that may co-occur with PTSD that may contribute to a complex form of PTSD.

Psychological theories of stress and trauma 3

Theories are the skeletons upon which we build our facts to produce an understanding of the phenomenon under consideration. A good theory should explain and account for the findings from research. In fact, if research findings contradict or do not support a theory, then the theory should be modified or discarded. A good theory of trauma response should be able to describe the reactions that have been observed clinically, should increase our ability to predict who will develop problems (or not), and should point to the elements of effective treatment. A good theory should be testable and should lead to a logical series of studies to examine the topic of interest.

Throughout the history of psychology, there have been large periods of time in which trauma was largely ignored and no research was being conducted. There have been times of increased attention, particularly in times of war, during which theories, clinical attention, and research increased dramatically, only to be neglected once the war ceased. However, in the late 1970s and 1980s, attention increased from several different arenas (the Vietnam war, the women's movement, the victim assistance movement, disaster work) and research interests have converged and expanded beyond what had ever existed previously. As a result, research has proliferated and theories have been offered to explain these findings. This chapter will begin with a brief discussion of stress theory, and in particular, a recent stress theory, Conservation of Resources Theory. Then, before moving to the modern theories of trauma response, this chapter will focus on the first trauma theories, beginning with Freud.

Stress theory: Conservation of resources

Modern stress theories evolved from studies of the effects of the environment on body and mind. Work on stress was initially conducted from a biological model (see Chapter 4). Stress was viewed as a physical response to environmental stressors and if these stressors were chronic or severe, the organism would break down. Psychological factors were introduced in the 1960s and 1970s such that the focus also included psychological upset as a response, and perception of threat was introduced as a concept to explain individual differences in the stress response. Spielberger (1966) proposed that events are stressful if they are perceived to be threats either physically or psychologically. Some researchers proposed that change, whether for the positive or negative, was stressful (Holmes & Rahe, 1967). In the 1980s Lazarus and Folkman (1984) defined stress as "a particular relationship between the person and the environment that is appraised by the person as taxing or exceeding his or her resources and endangering his or her well-being" (p. 19). These models focused on balance, or homeostasis, and assumed that if the person were returned to homeostasis, then the psychological distress would decrease. These models supported crisis intervention as a form of treatment.

More recently, Hobfoll (1989) moved away from a view of stress as an imbalance between physical or psychological demands on a person and that person's perceived or actual capability to cope. In the Conservation of Resources (COR) theory, Hobfoll has proposed that psychological stress is simply a reaction to losses (or threatened losses) in resources. Hobfoll begins with an assumption that people are motivated to obtain, retain, and protect important resources, those things they value. Resources are defined broadly to include four basic categories: objects (i.e., car, belongings), conditions (good marriage, seniority), personal characteristics (self-esteem, skills), and energies (knowledge, money, time).

Stress responses occur when these resources are threatened or lost. Hobfoll also proposes that distress can also occur when someone unsuccessfully invests a great deal to obtain a resource. All that someone has to prevent losses are other resources. Coping itself is stressful because it requires the expenditure of existing resources and, if coping efforts fail, positive beliefs about oneself are likely to decrease. Expenditures of resources in coping with losses leaves people vulnerable to further losses because their resources become depleted, a process called a loss spiral. By the same token, gaining resources makes future gains more likely, producing gain spirals.

COR theory does not view positive changes or transitions as stressful; they are viewed as challenges that have positive outcomes. Only when a transition or change results in loss is it viewed as stressful. Furthermore, COR theory proposes that resource loss is more powerful than resource gain and that it is more difficult to prevent loss than to obtain gains (Hobfoll & Lilly, 1993). In COR theory, minor daily hassles are only viewed as stressful inasmuch as they result in threat or loss of important resources such as time or role fulfillment.

In applying this theory to traumatic stress, Hobfoll (1991) proposed that trauma represents a sudden loss of resources. The resources lost during and following traumatic events are likely to be those with the highest value for people such as safety, self-esteem, trust, or a perception of control. Hobfoll (1991) suggested that resources are lost rapidly in traumatic stress situations because traumatic stressors attack people's most basic values, often occur unexpectedly, make excessive demands, are outside the realm of typical coping strategies, and leave powerful mental images that can be easily evoked. Hobfoll suggested that many traumatic stressors are of sufficient magnitude that no amount of resources is sufficient to prevent a strong initial negative reaction.

Some research has been conducted to support COR theory. For example, Freedy, Shaw, Jarrell, and Masters (1992) studied people who were exposed to Hurricane Hugo in Charleston, South Carolina. As predicted by COR theory, those who experienced the greatest resource losses were the most likely to experience the greatest distress and PTSD symptoms. Those who experienced the greatest losses were also more likely to report more coping efforts. In a study of pregnant women, Wells, Hobfoll, and Lavin (1997) found that women's resource losses predicted distress better than either their resource gains or their employment status (greater employment reflecting more role strain). In a study over time in Israel, Hobfoll, Lomranz, Eyal, Bridges, and Tzemach (1989) found that a national event that represented an attack on important values produced more depression than did a period of war, which produced more depression than quiet periods.

The Conservation of Resources theory appears to be a promising model of general stress responses. Although there is mention of heightened imagery with regard to traumatic events, there is no real explanation of how this fits with the rest of the theory and no explanation of the other specific symptoms or disorders that develop as a result of trauma. In other words, although the COR theory explains stress responses generally, it does not explain why some people develop chronic psychopathology such as PTSD in reaction to traumatic events. Psychodynamic, behavioral, and cognitive theories have focused less on general distress and more on the specific symptoms of PTSD.

Psychodynamic theories

Freud had an ambivalent relationship with trauma. Early in his career, Freud (1896) presented a paper "The Aetiology of Hysteria" in which he presented a revolutionary theory of mental illness. Based on his first 18 cases, Freud proposed that hysteria (the term that was used to describe somatic symptoms without a physical cause) was, in fact, caused by the sexual abuse of children. Although the theory came to be known as the seduction theory, in his lecture and subsequent publication, Freud used words that are properly translated as "rape", "abuse", "attack", and "aggression", clearly indicating that he did not view the child's participation as voluntary (Masson, 1985). Freud proposed that as a result of the threat to the ego, the traumatic memory and emotions would be repressed.

Freud's theory was met with stony silence. In letters he wrote in the weeks following his delivery of the paper, he stated "A lecture on the aetiology of hysteria at the Psychiatric Society met with an icy reception from the asses, and from Krafft-Ebing the strange comment: It sounds like a scientific fairy tale" (p. 9), and "I am isolated as you could wish me to be: the word has been given out to abandon me, and a void is forming around me." (p. 10) (cited in Masson, 1985). Within a year, Freud abandoned the seduction theory and began to espouse the idea that sexual abuse by the patients' fathers was a fantasy of the patients born of an intrapsychic conflict: the Oedipal Complex (see Box 3.1).

Although subsequent psychoanalytic theory served to de-emphasize the impact of external events in the development of psychological problems, Freud was clearly aware of the impact of trauma, particularly during and after World War I. He differentiated traumatic neurosis from spontaneous neurosis and identified some of the symptoms that would be recognized today as PTSD symptoms. For example, in *The Introductory Lectures on Psychoanalysis* (1917, pp. 274–275), Freud wrote:

> The traumatic neuroses give a clear indication that a fixation to the traumatic accident lies at their root. These patients regularly repeat the traumatic situation in their

Freud in 1896

"Whatever case and whatever symptom we take as our point of departure, in the end we infallibly come to the field of sexual experience. So here for the first time we seem to have discovered an aetiological precondition for hysterical symptoms."

"I therefore put forward the thesis that at the bottom of every case of hysteria there are one or more occurrences of premature sexual experience, occurrences which belong to the earliest years of childhood but which can be reproduced through the work of psycho-analysis in spite of the intervening decades."

"Whatever you may think about the conclusions I have come to, I must ask you not to regard them as the fruit of idle speculation. They are based on a laborious individual examination of patients which has in most cases taken up a hundred or more hours of work."

—from "The Aetiology of Hysteria" (reprinted in Masson, 1985, pp. 267, 271, & 289)

Freud in 1925

"I believed these stories, and consequently supposed that I had discovered the roots of the subsequent neurosis in these experiences of sexual seduction in childhood . . . If the reader feels inclined to shake his head at my credulity, I cannot altogether blame him."

". . . I was at last obliged to recognize that these scenes of seduction had never taken place, and that they were only fantasies which my patients had made up."

"I had in fact stumbled for the first time upon the Oedipus complex, which was later to assume such an overwhelming importance but which I did not recognize as yet in its disguise of phantasy."

—from "An Autobiographical Study" (these quotes reprinted in Masson, 1985, p. 198)

dreams; where hysteriform attacks occur that admit of an analysis, we find that the attack corresponds to a complete transplanting of the patient into the traumatic situation, as though they were still faced by it as an immediate task which has not been dealt with; and we take this view quite seriously.

This passage indicates that Freud was aware of intrusive, re-experiencing symptoms such as flashbacks (a complete transplanting of the patient into the traumatic situation) and physiological reactivity (hysteriform attacks). Freud continued to believe that conflict was the source of neurosis but the conflict in this case might be between the peacetime ego versus a war-affected ego or between the superego (the horror of war) and the id (fear, aggression). As in his earlier theory, the primary defense mechanism was repression. It appears that Freud was able to recognize the more socially acceptable traumas such as war or accidents even while he found it necessary to deny the existence or impact of incest.

A colleague and friend of Freud, Sandor Ferenczi, also attempted to bring to light the traumatic effects of sexual abuse even though it caused a falling out with Freud at the end of their lives. In 1932, Ferenczi opened the 12th International Psycho-Analytic Congress with a paper describing the traumatic effects of sexual abuse on children (reprinted in Masson, 1985, pp. 291–303). Again, the response of the psychoanalytic community was negative and, after his death a year later, the matter was dropped once again. Ferenczi's paper was not even translated into English for another 17 years.

Because Freud's psychoanalytic theory of intrapsychic conflict and repressed infantile sexuality came to dominate the field, some of the other theories that actually reflect more modern thinking were ignored. Charcot, who influenced Freud greatly at the beginning of his career, was the first to propose that trauma was implicated in the symptoms of his hysterical patients. Pierre Janet, also practicing therapy and developing theories in the late 1800s, developed a theory of trauma response that has held up very well a century later. Rather than focusing on repression, Janet attended more to dissociative processes and the need to integrate the traumatic event.

Janet was the first to use the term "subconscious" in reference to memories that form mental schemes that guide people's interactions with the environment. These mental schemes depend upon appropriate categorization and integration of memories in order to guide the person to cope with subsequent events. Traumatic events cause "vehement emotions" which prevent the person from matching the event with existing mental schemes. Because the memories of the event cannot be integrated into personal awareness, they are split off, or dissociated from consciousness. In other words, strong emotional arousal prevents the memory of the event from being integrated into the person's experience. In fact, Janet (1919) referred to the result as "a phobia of memory". He also proposed that when people fail to integrate the traumatic experience into their conscious awareness, they become "attached" to the trauma and cannot assimilate other new experiences either. Their personality stops developing at that point (Janet, 1911). Janet proposed that the dissociated memories are not translated into a personal narrative but continue to intrude as terrifying perceptions, obsessional preoccupations, and somatic re-experiences (anxiety reactions) (van der Kolk & van der Hart, 1989).

Although some current theories of PTSD are very reminiscent of Janet's work, the whole area of trauma studies was overshadowed by Freud and the development of psychoanalytic thought. In fact, the Oedipal theory was so dominant that prevailing thought was that women secretly desired rape (and that it was not traumatic). In 1945, Helene Deutsch, a disciple of Freud wrote an extensive work called *The Psychology of Women*. According to thinking at the time, women suffer from a sexual overendowment, the possession of two genital organs, the clitoris and the vagina. Early psychoanalytic thought was that clitoris represented an immature form of sexual arousal and that, as a woman matured, her sexual pleasure would transfer from the clitoris to the vagina, thereby rendering the clitoris unnecessary. Deutsch noted that for most women, this transfer is never completely successful. She then went on to say (Deutsch, 1945, pp. 79–80):

> The "undiscovered" vagina is—in normal, favorable instances—eroticized by an act of rape. By "rape" I do not refer here to the puberal fantasy in which the young girl realistically desires and fears the sexual act as a rape. That fantasy is only a psychologic preparation for a real, milder, but dynamically identical process. This process manifests itself in man's aggressive penetration on the one hand and in the "overpowering" of the vagina and its transformation into an errogenous sexual zone on the other.

The only other mention of rape in Deutsch's two volumes on the psychology of women was in a chapter on feminine passivity and masochistic longings. So, not only was trauma theory slowed down, but also the very identification of rape as a traumatic experience was denied. This belief that women unconsciously desire rape and are basically masochistic is a myth that is still perpetuated today among some people, in spite of evidence that rape is indeed traumatic and frequently leads to psychological and sexual dysfunction.

Modern psychodynamic theories share some theoretical components with social-cognitive theories but also contain components of earlier psychoanalytic theories (Marmar, Weiss, & Pynos, 1995). Like the social-cognitive theories, which will be reviewed later in the chapter, psychodynamic theory emphasizes the impact of the traumatic event on a person's view of self or others. Unlike the social-cognitive theorists, psychodynamic theories also include an emphasis on earlier psychological conflicts including the Oedipal stage of development, and developmental issues more generally.

Marmar et al. (1995) theorize that strong affect results when conscious or unconscious representations of ones' self or others spurred by the trauma are in conflict with the person's usual views of self and others. The person then mobilizes his/her psychological defenses to cope with these discrepant meanings and emotions. As the trauma reactions continue over time, the person may begin using more primitive defenses including splitting (either/or thinking, e.g., people are either all bad or all good) and dissociation. The trauma victim may lose a coherent sense of self or others and may become disillusioned. He or she may have more difficulty controlling affective states and may behave more impulsively.

The themes that emerge after the trauma may also reactivate conflicts from earlier development periods in the person's life. Themes from various developmental periods that had been left unresolved may become dominant. For example, the trauma may reactivate early issues with attachment, danger, and protection. From the Oedipal period, there may be issues regarding maternal protection and nurturance, control of emotions, bodily functions and fears of retaliation. From adolescence there may be issues regarding trust, moral development, dependency, or autonomy. Marmar et al. propose that as the person's psychological functioning regresses, the trauma victim will have a tendency to repeat early maladaptive relationship patterns. These patterns will feature shifting views of self and others as victims, victimizers, or rescuers. These shifting relationship views will result in tumultuous interpersonal relationships and will be re-enacted within the therapeutic relationship (see Chapter 7 on treatment).

Learning theory

Behavior therapy has its roots in experimental psychology. As researchers and behavioral therapists began to study and treat rape victims and Vietnam veterans in the 1970s, they began to draw upon learning theory as an explanation for the symptoms that they were observing. Mowrer's two-factor theory (1947) of classical and operant conditioning was first proposed to account for post-trauma symptoms (Becker, Skinner, Abel, Axelrod, & Cichon, 1984; Holmes & St. Lawrence, 1983; Keane, Zimering, & Caddell, 1985; Kilpatrick, Veronen, & Best, 1985; Kilpatrick, Veronen, & Resick, 1982). Classical conditioning was used to explain the high levels of distress and fear which were observed in trauma victims. In this model, the traumatic event is the unconditioned stimulus (UCS) which evokes extreme fear, the unconditioned response (UCR). The trauma (UCS) becomes associated with cues, previously neutral stimuli, which happen to be present during the event, which then become conditioned stimuli (CS). For example, at the time of an assault, a victim is alone, in the dark, and in the parking lot of a grocery store. Thereafter, thinking about or being alone, in the dark, or seeing a parking lot would be conditioned stimuli that could elicit a conditioned emotional response (CER). A combination of two or three stimuli would prompt a stronger response than any one alone. Thus, any time these cues are present in the environment, the CSs evoke fear, which has now become the conditioned response (CER). Then, via stimulus generalization and higher order conditioning, other related stimuli are conditioned, as well as the memory and thoughts about the event. For example, the person might come to fear all parking lots or even going outside after dark at all.

Normally, in a classical conditioning model, one would expect that this link between the CS and CER would extinguish over time if the original UCS is not repeated. Operant conditioning is used to explain the development of PTSD avoidance symptoms and maintenance of fear over time despite the fact that the UCS, the traumatic stressor, does not recur. Because the trauma memory and other cues (CS) elicit fear and anxiety (CER), these cues are avoided (or escaped from) and the result is a reduction in fear and anxiety. In this manner, avoidance of the CSs are negatively reinforced which prevents extinction of the link between the trauma cues (CS) and anxiety (CER) which would normally be expected without repetition of the trauma itself (UCS). Using the previous example, the person who was assaulted may become highly anxious whenever it is dark, he/she is alone, or when expected to go out, particularly alone or at night. The victim leaves lights on at night and avoids parking lots. Therefore, he/she avoids places and activities that feel dangerous whenever possible. He or she would also attempt to avoid thinking about the assault, because the memory of the event is paired with distress. This, unfortunately, prevents him/her from learning that these situations and even the memory of the assault are not truly dangerous, and PTSD symptoms may become chronic.

Recently, Wagner and Linehan (1998) tackled dissociative responses from a behavioral perspective. Because dissociation may include amnesia, depersonalization, derealization, and/or identity disturbance, their theory focuses on each aspect separately as learned behaviors. However, overall, their theory proposes that the primary function of dissociative behavior is to regulate exposure to cues that are related to traumatic experiences. Dissociation occurring during the trauma (peri-traumatic dissociation) reduces exposure to aspects of the trauma while it is occurring. Dissociative behaviors after the trauma regulate the extent of exposure to reminder cues. Dissociation can then generalize as an operant to reduce exposure to negative affect generally. Amnesia, or forgetting, may result from being punished for remembering or rewarded for forgetting or for diverting attention away from the event. Depersonalization (a lack of connection with one's body) and derealization (a lack of connection to the situation) can result from a lack of awareness of one's emotional reactions and other internal states.

Wagner and Linehan (1998) have focused particularly on the implications of an invalidating environment for the development of dissociative responses as well as borderline personality disorder, more generally (Linehan, 1993). An invalidating environment is one in which children are punished or ignored for communicating about their emotional experiences ("You are not sad", "It didn't happen", "Mommy is not drunk, she is sick"). As a result, the child grows up unable to label internal emotional states, use self-referent language, or self-soothe. Consistent failure to reinforce or punishment for communication of internal experiences can lead to disruptions in normal development. A traumatic event and subsequent invalidation would then reinforce the use of dissociative behaviors as a means of reducing physical and emotional reactions to trauma cues. Wagner and Linehan point out that while dissociative behaviors could be used consciously to avoid trauma cues, they may be largely outside a person's awareness.

Cognitive theories

Information processing theory

Although learning theory accounts for much of the development and maintenance of the fear and avoidance of PTSD, it does not really explain intrusion symptoms, i.e., the repetitive memories of the trauma that intrude into the victim's thoughts in both conscious and unconscious states. Based on Lang's (1977) concept of anxiety development, Foa, Steketee, and Rothbaum (1989) have suggested that PTSD emerges due to the development of a fear network in memory that elicits escape and avoidance behavior. Mental fear structures include stimuli, responses, and meaning elements. Anything associated with the trauma may elicit the fear structure or schema and subsequent avoidance behavior. The fear network in people with PTSD is thought to be stable and broadly generalized so that it is easily accessed. Chemtob, Roitblat, Hamada, Carlson, and Twentyman (1988) proposed that these structures are always at least weakly activated in individuals with PTSD and guide their interpretation of events as potentially dangerous.

When reminders of the trauma activate the fear network, the information in the network enters consciousness (intrusive symptoms). Attempts to avoid this activation result in the avoidance symptoms of PTSD. According to information processing theory, repetitive and sufficiently prolonged exposure to the traumatic memory in a safe environment will result in habituation of the fear and subsequent change in the fear structure. As emotion decreases, clients with PTSD will begin to modify their meaning elements spontaneously and will change their self-statements and reduce their generalization. However, brief exposures to stimuli will only activate and enhance the avoidance and will actually help maintain the disorder.

There have been a number of studies that provide support for the idea that people with PTSD have a greater underlying tendency to attend to danger cues (an activated trauma network) than people without PTSD. Rather than relying on subjective reports of participants, these experiments demonstrated that people with PTSD have an attentional bias for verbal information that is trauma related. The most common method for studying attentional bias is a modified Stroop color-naming paradigm (Stroop, 1935). In this task, research participants are asked to name, as fast as they can, the color of print in which words are written, while ignoring the content of the words themselves. The words may be positive, neutral, or negative and are matched for their reading level and commonality. In the case of PTSD studies, the negative words may be generally negative or specifically trauma related. In studies with Vietnam veterans, rape victims, and disaster survivors, it has been found that participants with PTSD were slower to name the colors of words that were trauma related compared to either control subjects or those who had experienced trauma but did not have PTSD (Cassiday, McNally, & Zeitlin, 1992; Foa, Feske, Murdock, Kozak, & McCarthy, 1991; McNally, Kaspi, Riemann, & Zeitlin, 1990; Thrasher, Dalgleish, & Yule, 1994; Vrana, Roodman, & Beckham, 1995).

Social-cognitive theories

The social-cognitive theories are also concerned with information processing but they focus on the impact of the trauma on a person's belief system and the adjustment that is necessary to reconcile the traumatic event with prior beliefs and expectations. So while the information processing theories focus more on the structure of cognitive processing and mechanism of fear maintenance, social-cognitive theories attend more to the content of cognitions, the meaning of trauma in a social context. The first and most influential social-cognitive theorist was Horowitz who moved from a more psychodynamic to a cognitive processing theory.

Horowitz (1986) has proposed that processing is driven by a "completion tendency", the psychological need for new, incompatible information to be integrated with existing beliefs. The completion tendency keeps the trauma information in active memory until the processing is complete and the event is resolved. Horowitz also theorized that there is a basic conflict between the need to resolve and reconcile the event into the person's history with the desire to avoid emotional pain. When the images of the event (flashbacks, nightmares, intrusive recollections), thoughts about the meanings of the trauma, and emotions associated with the trauma become overwhelming, psychological defense mechanisms take over and the person exhibits numbing or avoidance. He suggested a person with PTSD oscillates between phases of intrusion and avoidance and that if successfully processed, the oscillations become less frequent and less intense. Chronic PTSD would mean that the event stays in active memory without becoming fully integrated and still able to stimulate intrusive and avoidant reactions.

Several other researchers and theorists have focused more on the actual content of the cognitions and that basic assumptions about the world and oneself are shattered. Constructivist theories are based on the idea that people actively create their own internal representations of the world (and themselves). New experiences are assigned meaning based on people's personal model of the world (Janoff-Bulman, 1985, 1992; Mahoney & Lyddon, 1988; McCann & Pearlman, 1990). Janoff-Bulman has paid particular attention three major assumptions which may be shattered in the face of traumatic events: a belief in personal invulnerability ("I am less likely than others to experience misfortune"), the assumption that the world is meaningful (predictable, controllable, and fair), and a perception of one's self as positive or worthy. In research, Janoff-Bulman has found that trauma victims had significantly more negative beliefs in those realms than nonvictims did. She proposes that traumatic events shatter these assumptions and that, as a result, intense psychological crisis ensues. Because prior assumptions are no longer adequate guides for experience, the result is cognitive disintegration and anxiety.

The task for recovery is to reconstruct fundamental schemas (core beliefs) and the establishment of equilibrium. Janoff-Bulman suggested that this process is accomplished by reinterpreting the event to reduce the distance between the prior beliefs and the new beliefs. She pointed out several possible mechanisms such as downward comparison ("It could have been worse. Others have had more devastating traumas"), re-evaluating the trauma in terms of benefits or purpose ("This event has made me stronger. I have learned an important lesson"), or self-blame ("It is my fault that it happened. I shouldn't have been there").

Janoff-Bulman went on to postulate two different types of self-blame: behavioral self blame and characterological self-blame. Behavioral self-blame is saying the trauma happened because of the victim's behavior; she/he made a mistake. In characterological self-blame, the person blames him/herself because of who she/he is ("It happened because I am bad"). In an initial study, Janoff-Bulman and Wortman (1977) found that among motorcycle accident victims, behavioral self-blame was associated with better recovery, whereas characterological self-blame was associated with poor outcome. In later studies with rape victims, this finding was not upheld (Frasier, 1990; Meyer & Taylor, 1986; see Weaver & Clum, 1995 for a meta-analysis of 10 studies). In other studies both types of self-blame were evidenced, but both types of self-blame were associated with poorer recovery. Perhaps, in the case of crime, when there is clearly someone else who should be blamed, any type of self-blame is maladaptive.

One of the problems of examining only shattered positive assumptions is that it is possible for someone to have negative assumptions prior to the traumatic event. In that case, the traumatic event might actually serve to confirm negative beliefs about one's self and the world. For example, if a person had poor self-esteem prior to the trauma, the event might be viewed as confirmatory evidence that the victim is worthless or bad. Another problem with Janoff-

Bulman's theory is evidence that having a history of traumatic events
prior to a particular traumatic event is associated with more PTSD
(Kilpatrick et al., 1985; Nishith, Mechanic, & Resick, 2000). In those
cases, the pre-existing trauma should have already shattered positive
assumptions and the later event would have been schema-congruent.

Other theorists have proposed that if pre-existing beliefs were
particularly positive or particularly negative, then greater PTSD
symptoms would result (Foa, 1996; McCann & Pearlman, 1990; Resick
& Schnicke, 1992). Foa focused particularly on beliefs regarding
the predictability and controllability of the trauma, whereas
McCann and Pearlman proposed that several areas of cognition
might be either disrupted or seemingly confirmed: beliefs regarding
safety, trust, control/power, esteem, and intimacy. In a constructivist
self-development theory, McCann and Pearlman (1990) propose that
psychological needs form the basis for core schemas about self and
world (see Box 3.2) and that disruptions in schemas are most dis-
turbing when they occur in need areas that are most central to them. In
a research study with rape victims, Mechanic, Resick, and Griffin
(1994) found support for cognitive disruptions following rape. They
found at 2 weeks post-crime, victims who met symptom criteria for
PTSD (minus the time criterion) had greater disruptions in beliefs
regarding esteem, intimacy, safety, and trust than rape victims
who did not meet symptom criteria for PTSD. At 3 months post-
crime, those with PTSD reported greater disruptions in safety, trust,
and intimacy. Mechanic, Resick, and Griffin (1998) also found that,

following successful treatment of PTSD, rape victims reported improvement in cognitive disruptions.

One might wonder why someone would develop PTSD if a traumatic event is schema congruent (matching negative beliefs about self and world). After all, if someone had prior negative beliefs about themselves or the world and then something terrible happens, this confirmation should not result in conflict or symptoms. However, it is important to remember that traumatic events are not daily occurrences. A trauma, by its very nature, is sudden, unexpected, and shocking. The addition of a new trauma does not answer the questions "why me?" or "why now?" and the trauma is still incongruent with daily events.

It is also possible that the conflict may not be between what has happened now and prior experience, but what has happened and how things *should* be. For example, even if a parent is consistently abusive and cruel, it would not take very long for a child to observe other parents (of friends or in the media) who are not cruel when their children behave in the same way. Parents *should be* loving and kind. The child would left wondering why he/she is being abused when other children are not, for doing the same things. Attempting to predict and control inconsistent or cruel parent behavior might result in very distorted beliefs about oneself and the world. The traumatic event haunts him/her as he/she attempts to determine how the event could have been prevented.

Resick and Schnicke (1992, 1993; Resick, 1995) have argued that post-trauma affect is not limited to fear and that individuals with PTSD may be just as likely to experience a range of other strong emotions, such as shame, anger, or sadness. Some emotions such as fear, anger, or sadness may emanate directly from the trauma (natural emotions), because the event is interpreted as dangerous and/or abusive, resulting in losses. It is possible that manufactured emotions can also result from faulty interpretations made by the victim. For example, if someone is intentionally attacked by another person, the danger of the situation would lead to a fight–flight response and the attending emotions might be anger or fear. However, if in the aftermath, the person encountered other people who blamed him/her for the attack or made other demeaning statements, the person might experience shame or embarrassment. These secondary, or manufactured, emotions would have resulted from thoughts and interpretations about the event, rather than the event itself. Kubany and Manke (1995) have provided other examples of Vietnam veterans who made decisions during combat, often the lesser of two bad choices, only to develop great shame and guilt (and PTSD) afterwards because they reappraised their choices as wrong or bad.

New information which is congruent with prior beliefs about self or world is assimilated quickly and without effort because the information matches the schema and little attention is needed to incorporate it. On the other hand, when something happens that is schema discrepant, individuals must reconcile this event with their beliefs about themselves and the world. Their belief systems, or their schemas, must be altered, accommodated, to incorporate this new information. However, this process is often avoided because of the strong affect associated with the trauma and frequently, because altering beliefs may in fact leave people feeling more vulnerable to future traumatic events. For example, many people believe that bad things happen to bad people and good things happen to good people. This just-world belief would need to be altered after something traumatic happened. However, even when victims accept that bad things can happen to them that they aren't responsible for, they may be more anxious about the possibility of future harm. Thus, rather than accommodating their beliefs to incorporate the trauma, victims may distort (assimilate) the trauma to keep their beliefs intact.

In the case of strong affect, it may be that cognitive processing does not occur because trauma victims avoid the strong affect and subsequently never accommodate the information because they do not ever completely remember what happened or think through what it means (i.e., process the event). Some people are raised believing that emotions are a sign of weakness or that they should be avoided. While people may be able to distract themselves or deflect normal affective experience, traumatic events are associated with much greater emotion that cannot be avoided entirely. Individuals with PTSD may have to work hard to shut down their affective response. Moreover, because the information about the traumatic event has not been processed, categorized, and accommodated, the trauma memories continue to emerge during the day as flashbacks or intrusive reminders or at night in the form of nightmares. The emotional responses and arousal that are part of the trauma memory emerge as well, which triggers further avoidance.

An alternative to assimilation or accommodation, is over-accommodation. In this case, trauma victims alter their belief structure to the extreme in an attempt to prevent future traumas. These overgeneralized beliefs may take the form of extreme distrust and poor regard for self and others. Prior traumatic events or negative pre-existing beliefs would contribute to "the evidence" that these extreme statements are true. For example, a rape victim may believe that no one can be trusted or that she is damaged and worthless because of the rape. A Vietnam veteran might state that anyone who is associated with the government (even a therapist at a Veterans Administration Hospital) is bad or is trying to "mess" with him. These over-accommodated beliefs interfere with the natural emotions that emanated from the event (e.g., fear, sadness) and therefore prevent appropriate processing of the emotions and beliefs. Furthermore, overgeneralized negative statements can produce a different set of emotions that might not have originally been associated with the event (e.g., shame, guilt).

Given this social-cognitive model, affective expression is needed, not for habituation, but in order for the trauma memory to be processed fully. It is assumed that the natural affect, once accessed, will dissipate rather quickly, and that the work of accommodating the memory with schemas can begin. Once faulty beliefs regarding the event (self-blame, guilt) and over-accommodated beliefs about oneself and the world (e.g., safety, trust, control esteem, intimacy) are challenged, then the secondary emotions will also vanish along with the intrusive reminders.

Dual representation theory

In an attempt to reconcile the cognitive theories of PTSD, Brewin, Dalgleish, and Joseph (1996) have proposed a dual representation theory that incorporates both the information processing and social-cognitive theories. Brewin et al. have suggested that the concept of a single emotional memory is too narrow to describe the full range of memory that has been observed in research and clinical observations. Based on prior research, they proposed that sensory input is subject to both conscious and nonconscious processing. The memories that are conscious can be deliberately retrieved and are termed verbally accessible memories. These verbally accessible memories (VAMs) contain some sensory information, information about emotional and physical reactions and the personal meaning of the event. Although VAMs might be reasonably detailed, they may also be very selective because attention is narrowed under conditions of stress and short-term memory capacity may be decreased.

The other type of memory is nonconscious and is situationally accessed memory (SAMs). This type of information, which is probably much more extensive than the autobiographical memories of the event, cannot be deliberately accessed and is not as easily altered or edited as the more verbally accessible memories. The situationally accessed memories are composed of sensory information (auditory, visual, tactile, etc.), physiological, and motoric information which may be accessed automatically when a person is exposed to a stimulus situation that is similar in some fashion to the trauma or when he/she consciously thinks about the trauma. The SAM is then experienced as an intrusive sensory image or flashback accompanied by physiological arousal.

Dual representation theory has two types of emotional reactions. One type of emotional reaction is conditioned during the event (e.g., fear, anger), is recorded in the SAMs, and is activated along with re-experienced sensory and physiological information. The other emotions, secondary emotions, result from the consequences and implications (meaning) of the trauma. These secondary emotions may also include fear and anger, but could also include guilt, shame, and sadness.

Brewin et al. propose that emotional processing of the trauma has two elements. One element of the processing is the activation of SAMS (as suggested by the information processing theories) the purpose of which is to aid in cognitive readjustment by supplying the detailed sensory and physiological information concerning the trauma. The activation of SAMs may eventually diminish in frequency when they are blocked by the creation of new SAMs or when they are altered by the incorporation of new information. When the SAMs are brought into consciousness they can be altered by being paired with different bodily states (e.g., relaxation or habituation) or different conscious thoughts. Eventually, if the SAMs are replaced or altered sufficiently, there will be a reduction in negative emotions and a subsequent reduction in attentional bias and accessibility of the memory.

The second element (as proposed by the social-cognitive theorists) is the conscious attempt to search for meaning, ascribe cause or blame, and to resolve conflicts between the event and prior expectations and beliefs. The goal of this process is to reduce the negative emotions and to restore a sense of relative safety and control in one's environment. In order to obtain this second goal, the traumatized person may have to edit his/her autobiographical memory (VAMs) in order to reconcile conflicts between the event and the person's belief system. The traumatized person may alter her/his memory of the event in some way in order to re-establish the pre-existing belief system or may alter pre-existing beliefs and expectations to accommodate this new information.

TABLE 3.1

Outcomes of emotional processing: Brewin's dual representational theory of PTSD

Outcome	Description
Completion/integration	No memory bias
	No attentional bias
	No symptoms
Chronic emotional processing	Memory bias
	Attentional bias
	Phobic state
	Depression
	Panic
	Anxiety
	Substance abuse
Premature inhibition of processing	Attentional biases
	Avoidance schema
	Impaired memory
	Phobic state
	Dissociation
	Somatization

Brewin et al. propose that there are three possible endpoints to the emotional processing: completion/integration, chronic emotional processing, and premature inhibition of processing (see Table 3.1). Completion/integration is a successful resolution of the traumatic event. In this case, the trauma has been fully processed, conflicts between the trauma and the person's prior belief system have been resolved, if SAMs are activated, they do not lead to strong negative affect, and there is no memory or attentional bias toward trauma-related cues.

Chronic emotional processing may occur when the event has not been integrated for any of a number of reasons. Repeated and severe trauma, especially at a young age, may repeatedly trigger SAMs and VAMs, lack of support, avoidant coping style, or negative secondary emotions (e.g., guilt and shame) may all prevent successful processing. If the SAMs and VAMs about the trauma(s) are chronically processed, the person is preoccupied with the consequences of the trauma and with the intrusive memories. The processing is repetitive with little change occurring to the SAMs or VAMs. Brewin et al. suggest that the comorbid disorders that are frequently observed in those with PTSD (depression, substance abuse, and anxiety) are indicative of those with chronic processing.

Brewin et al. also suggest a third option, which has not yet been identified in the research or clinical literature. They suggest that emotional processing can be prematurely inhibited as a result of pronounced efforts to avoid reactivation of the aversive SAMs and VAMs. If the avoidance strategies are successful, the process becomes automatic and the person may be able to direct his/her conscious attention away from reminders of the event. However, even though there is no active emotional processing, SAMs regarding the trauma are still accessible under some circumstances. This may account for the delayed PTSD that is occasionally observed or the activation of PTSD intrusion for an earlier event later in life when another trauma occurs. Brewin et al. predict that although the person with premature inhibition may not have conscious intrusions regarding the trauma, he/she will still have attentional bias, memory impairment for the trauma, phobic avoidance of trauma-related stimuli, and may show somatization (physical symptoms). Further research will be needed to determine if there are in fact, three possible outcomes.

Summary

This chapter focused on a range of theories of stress and traumatic stress. The earliest theory, proposed by Freud, focused primarily on intrapsychic conflict and tended to reduce or ignore the role of external stressful events. Modern psychoanalytic thinking acknowledges the role of environmental stressors but still focuses on intrapsychic conflicts as being activated by the traumatic event. The conservation of resources model of stress focuses extensively on the external stressor and its depletion of a person's coping resources. This theory explains psychological distress following traumatic stress as resulting from the sudden and extreme loss of very important personal resources. Behavioral theories first focused on two-factor theory of classical conditioning and operant avoidance. Then, in order to explain the more cognitive symptoms of flashbacks and nightmares in intrusive recollections, this theory was modified into information processing theories that include stimuli, responses, and meaning elements as a fear network in memory to escape and avoid perceived danger.

The social-cognitive theories widened the focus beyond fear reactions and emphasize more the meaning elements and conflicts between the traumatic event and prior beliefs about self and world.

The memory of the traumatic event needs to be integrated into the person's basic belief system and symptoms occur when this cannot be accomplished successfully. Dual representation theory has attempted to integrate information processing theory with the social-cognitive theories by proposing that memory exists on two levels and is processed somewhat differently on each level. Less attention has been paid to dissociation and dissociative disorders. Psychoanalytic theories regarding dissociation have been the predominant viewpoint in understanding dissociation although there has been a behavioral model proposed recently that may be useful to consider. In the future, theories will need to integrate information on the biological responses with psychological responses to trauma. The next chapter will describe the biology of stress and trauma.

Biological bases of stress and trauma reactions

4

Before describing the physiological and biochemical reactions that have been observed in trauma survivors with PTSD or dissociative reactions, it is important to understand the normal response to acute stress. While the chemicals of the body have normal diurnal (daily) variations, in response to stressors, these chemicals, neurotransmitters and hormones, will spur changes to allow the body to adapt and cope with the stressor. The two major divisions of the nervous system are the peripheral and central nervous systems. The peripheral nervous system is composed of nerves, which communicate information throughout the body. The central nervous system (CNS) is composed of the brain and spinal cord. Although we typically think of the autonomic nervous system as functioning within the peripheral nervous system, it also has cell bodies within the CNS. The autonomic nervous system (ANS) functions to serve the internal organs of the body. The ANS is divided into two divisions, the sympathetic and the parasympathetic divisions. The sympathetic division is activated when the body needs to be aroused. The parasympathetic division takes over during periods of rest and functions to restore the body. It is the sympathetic division that we attend to most in the study of the stress response along with the neuroendocrine system, which is needed to send chemical messages to start or stop responses.

The endocrine system consists of a group of glands, controlled by the hypothalamus, that secrete chemicals called hormones. Endocrine glands secrete their hormones into the bloodstream where they are carried to the point they are used. Just below the hypothalamus in the brain is the pituitary, the master gland that regulates the secretion of the endocrine glands. The endocrine glands, which are most relevant to the study of stress, are the adrenal glands that sit on top of the kidneys. The central portion of the adrenals, the adrenal medulla, secretes the hormones adrenaline and noradrenaline (also called epinephrine and norepinephrine) which act on the internal organs.

The outer portion of the adrenals, the adrenal cortex, produces glucocorticoids, which are released during stress and which act on all cells of the body.

The stress response

Peripheral nervous system

In the twentieth century, one of the most prominent influences in the study of stress was the work of Hans Selye (1956/1976). Selye proposed a "general adaptation syndrome" in response to stress, which included three stages: alarm and mobilization, resistance, and exhaustion. The alarm stage is the initial reaction to a stressor and may last up to a few hours. In this stage the stress hormones are mobilized. In the resistance stage, response systems are activated to return the body to homeostasis. The resistance stage may last for days or weeks. However, if the stressor is prolonged or repeated, then the exhaustion stage sets in, having important implications for physical and psychological health. The autonomic nervous system (ANS) and the endocrine system are implicated most broadly in the first stage as the person undergoing acute stress experiences a fight–flight reaction. Although the ANS continues to be involved in the next two stages, these later stages are heavily influenced by the neuroendocrine system. Selye did not focus on particular stressors or distinguish between normative and traumatic stressors. Rather, his focus was more on the universal nature of the stress response and how continued stress would sap a person's adaptational energy. As research has focused more on the most serious stressors, it is clear that even if the stressor is of a very brief duration, if it is perceived as severe, then chronic and perhaps permanent changes in biology may occur.

In the face of an acute stressor, the person who is exposed to the stressor experiences a strong autonomic nervous system reaction to face the emergency. This sympathetic reaction, first called a "fight or fight" response by Cannon (1914), is intended to be a short-term protective reaction to move blood into the major muscle groups for motor response, rapidly increase energy supply to the muscles by mobilizing blood glucose, increase heart rate and respiration, constrict the blood vessels in the skin to limit blood loss, and stop unnecessary biological processes during the emergency. In order to accomplish these tasks, important hormones are activated.

When exposed to stress, the brain responds with a cascade of neurochemicals intended to respond to the threat. Among them, epinephrine (adrenaline) and norepinephrine (noradrenaline) play a major role. These hormones, the catecholamines, act to increase heart rate, blood pressure, respiration, oxygen consumption, and blood sugar. Epinephrine and norepinephrine are secreted by the adrenal glands, the locus coeruleus, and by sympathetic nerve fibers and are received by adrenergic receptors. The coordinated response between these hormones and nerves allow the proper emergency reaction to maximize a fight or flight response. Norepinephrine is associated with the "flight response" and result in hypervigilance, autonomic arousal, fear, and exaggerated startle (Davis, Suris, Lambert, Heimberg, & Petty, 1997).

Serotonin also appears to modulate norepinephrine. In both animals and humans, low levels of serotonin are associated with exaggerated emotional arousal (high levels of irritability, excitability, and impulsivity). Serotonin may help inhibit behaviors that are elicited by emergency situations and may be more associated with the "fight response" including symptoms of rage, impulsivity, aggression, depression, and anxiety (Davis et al., 1997). Serotonin is also implicated with sleep. Low levels of serotonin disrupt both slow wave sleep (SWS) and rapid eye-movement sleep (REM). Norepinephrine also has an inhibitory role in sleep, REM in particular.

In an acute stress situation, glucocorticoids are also released by the adrenals. Cortisol, a glucocorticoid that has received the most attention, is believed to help regulate the stress response. Yehuda, Southwick, Mason, and Giller (1990) have proposed that cortisol is an "antistress hormone". Cortisol, which is a steroid, helps the body to adapt to prolonged stress by releasing more nutrients into the bloodstream (elevated blood sugar), increasing the tone of muscles in the heart and blood vessels, decreasing inflammation, and enhancing metabolism. Cortisol also acts through a negative feedback loop whereby when the level of cortisol rises and high levels of cortisol are received in the hypothalamus and pituitary, it signals the brain to shut off the stress hormones.

Increased cortisol has been observed in both anxious and depressed persons. Although not harmful in short bursts as in the case of acute stress, with prolonged stress, the continued elevated blood sugar and metabolism spurred by cortisol will have an effect on the immune system because there is a shift away from the synthesis of proteins which are necessary for the immune system. In fact, cortisol may have a direct inhibiting effect on the immune system.

Selye (1956/1976) suggested that the prolonged secretion of the glucocorticoids produces most of the harmful effects of stress. Therefore, although the short-term effects of cortisol are essential, prolonged hyperactivation can be damaging to one's health.

Finally, endogenous opiates are thought to increase in response to stress, particularly when there is injury and pain, as a natural analgesia. There are many examples of people who did not realize they had been injured or who did not experience pain until the emergency situation was finished. There is some evidence that when endorphines (endogenous morphines) are released, they suppress immune functioning. Although it has not been established yet with humans, it is possible that chronic dissociation, as is found with those with dissociative disorders, may place the person at greater risk for physical disorders and illnesses, including immune disorders. As was discussed in Chapter 1, there is an association between stress (and particularly PTSD) and both immune suppression and physical disorders and diseases.

Central nervous system

The brain is organized into complex systems that perceive, store, process, and react to information from the external (worldly) and internal (bodily) environments. The systems of the brain are composed of billions of neurons organized into networks that respond to signals from other parts of the brain, body, or environment. Different parts of the brain store information specific to the function of that part of the brain, resulting in different types of memories (e.g., motor: driving a car; cognitive: memorizing facts for an exam; affective: smell of Christmas tree). The brain is also organized in a hierarchical top-down fashion, such that the systems in the cortex (the outer most part of the brain) are responsible for abstract thought and language. The limbic areas (central region) are responsible for affect regulation and emotion, while the brainstem (innermost region) is responsible for heart rate, blood pressure, and arousal states (Perry et al., 1995; van der Kolk, 1994).

The areas of the brain most likely to be involved in the stress response are the locus coeruleus, hippocampus, amygdala, and neocortex. The locus coeruleus, which is located in the brain stem, has an important role in mediating the fight–flight reaction. When exposed to stress, the neurons of the locus coeruleus begin firing and sending norepinephrine throughout the brain. With repeated or chronic stress, the system becomes sensitized and reacts more with less stimulation.

This sensitization of the fight–flight reaction has led some researchers to suggest that PTSD may reflect a hyperactive central noradrenergic system (Zigmond, Finlay, & Sved, 1995).

The hippocampus and amygdala form one of the circuits in the limbic system, which affects behaviors related to self-preservation, learning and memory, and emotion. The hippocampus receives information from all regions of the sensory association cortex, the motor association cortex, and the amygdala and appears to have a coordinating or mapping function that puts the information into context. The hippocampus is also involved in short-term memory such that memories are held temporarily, after which they are either stored in long-term memory or forgotten.

The hippocampus is believed to be essential in declarative memory. Declarative memory is memory that a person can state in words, the retelling of things or events previously experienced (as opposed to procedural memory, which reflects motor skills). It appears that the hippocampus is involved in tying together the different perceptions involved in an event. Therefore, the hippo-campus enables relational learning between stimuli. Damage to the hippocampus results in disruption of the formation of new memories.

There is evidence that high levels of circulating corticosteroids (glucocorticoids) may cause damage to the hippocampus (Sapolsky, Uno, Rebert, & Finch, 1990). People with Cushing's disease (caused by tumors in the adrenal or pituitary glands) have higher levels of circulating corticosteroids. These people develop short-term memory problems and have decreased hippocampal volume indi-cating atrophy or shrinkage of the hippocampus proportional to the amount of cortisol (Starkman, Gebarski, Berent, & Schteingart, 1992). Problems with short-term memory have also been observed in people who have abused corticosteroid drugs for a long time (e.g., athletes).

The amygdala, located in the temporal lobes, is the most important part of the brain for the expression of emotional responses that are provoked by negative stimuli. The amygdala receives input directly from the sensory cortex. The amygdala is important in learning the emotional significance of external events, particularly social actions. Damage to the central nucleus of the amygdala reduces or eliminates emotions and physiological responses. The central nucleus is necessary for the learning of conditioned emotional responses. LeDoux (1987) has demonstrated in rats that, if the central nucleus of the amygdala is destroyed, then emotional conditioning does not occur. Furthermore, the amygdala contains high concentrations of benzodiazepines and opiate receptors. If either opiates or benzo-diazepines are introduced into the amygdala, learning and the expression of conditioned emotional reactions are decreased.

The neocortex is involved in the interpretation of incoming stimuli. Different regions of the cerebral cortex have different functions. The frontal lobes are involved in the planning, execution, and control of movements. The posterior lobes of the brain, the parietal, temporal and occipital lobes, are involved in perceptions. The rest of the neo-cortex is called the association cortex and is involved with planning of movements, perception, memory, and speech. Most emotional reactions in humans are generated from complex stimuli (sights, sounds, smells, meanings) that have to be coordinated and inter-preted. The analysis of social situations requires experiences, memories, and judgments. All of this is coordinated through input from the various structures of the cortex to the amygdala (emotional memory), and the hippocampus (relational memory).

Post-traumatic stress disorder

When researchers began studying traumatic stress, and in particular, PTSD, they made the assumption that the biological processes would reflect the normal responses to stress. However, while the normal stress response is an acute reaction that quickly returns to homeo-stasis, the biological responses to PTSD reflect chronic and even increasing reactivity over time. Even when stress is chronic, the results are different than those of traumatic stress. The effects of chronic stress develop slowly over time (and include perceptions of being overwhelmed), whereas the effects of traumatic stress are sudden and dramatic (and are marked by fear, terror, or horror) (Yehuda, 1998). This section will begin with studies that have examined physiological reactivity among those with PTSD and will then move to a discussion of neurobiology and its effects on arousal, attention, and memory.

Psychophysiological reactivity

Because one of the major symptom clusters associated with PTSD is concerned with physiological reactivity, especially hypervigilance and startle, there have been a number of studies on physiological arousal as a marker for PTSD. The vast majority of modern studies have been conducted with Vietnam veterans with PTSD. This is probably due to the fact that the VA hospitals have been responsible for determining if someone has developed PTSD as a result of combat and may be entitled to compensation. It was hoped that psychophysiological assessment could be used as an objective indicator of PTSD and would be able to differentiate those with the disorder from those who were malingering in order to collect compensation.

The study of psychophysiological reactivity is not new. Meakins and Wilson (1918) found that World War I veterans with "shell-shock" had greater increases in respiration and heart rate upon exposure to sulfuric flames and sounds of gunfire than healthy comparison subjects. Also in 1918, Fraser and Wilson found that when war veterans were administered epinephrine, they had exaggerated psychophysiological arousal. In 1941, Abraham Kardiner labeled traumatic stress "physioneurosis", recognizing the connection between physiological and psychological reactions to traumatic stress.

Most studies of autonomic nervous system activity (ANS) have focused on skin conductance and heart rate, although some studies have also measured blood pressure or muscle response through electromylographic activity (EMG). Research on psychophysiological assessment usually compares a group of people with PTSD with a healthy nontrauma sample, a trauma sample without PTSD, or a sample with other psychological disorders. The typical research design is to examine the psychophysiological reactivity during a resting baseline period and then to examine reactions to neutral, generic stressful, or trauma-related stimuli. The generic stressful stimuli may be stressors such as mental arithmetic or a public-speaking fear script, which most people react to with increased arousal. Trauma-related stimuli may include sounds or visual images such as slides or film depicting combat accompanied by combat noises on tape; they may be generic trauma scripts that are presented to all the research participants, or they may be individualized scripts. When individualized scripts are used, the researcher meets with the participant in advance and develops a short vignette which describes the actual event the participant experienced, including sensory details, emotions, and physical reactions. Typically, the participant is presented with the script orally and then he or she is instructed to imagine the scene as vividly as possible. Box 4.1 gives an example of an individualized combat script.

There have been a number of studies that have examined whether those with PTSD have greater overall arousal due to their reported hypervigilance. In early research on baseline arousal (heart rate at rest), a number of studies did find that PTSD subjects had higher resting heart rate than non-PTSD participants. However, some more recent studies have not found this to be the case. In reviewing studies of baseline arousal, Prins, Kaloupek, and Keane (1995) observed that there were a number of methodological differences that could account for these findings. Among them were the comparison samples selected. There appear to be differences in resting baseline when PTSD subjects are compared to healthy controls. However, compared to others with anxiety disorders, there were no differences (Pitman, Orr, Forgue, Altman, & deJong, 1990). Prins et al. concluded that, rather than a biological difference in resting heart rate, these studies were picking up on greater anticipatory anxiety of those with PTSD or other anxiety disorders than healthy comparison subjects.

Another explanation of whether resting heart rate is different between groups with and without PTSD may be concerned with when the assessment takes place. In a more recent prospective study, Shalev et al. (1998) examined the resting heart rate of trauma victims in the emergency room immediately after the trauma and then at 1 week, 1 month, and 4 months later. They found those with PTSD to have higher heart rates immediately after and 1 week after traumas, but not 1 month and 4 months post-trauma. When they examined a number of variables (sex, age, trauma history, event severity, immediate response, dissociation, and initial heart rate) to predict 4-month PTSD status, they found that only event severity and initial heart rate were predictive. Perhaps the immediate elevation of heart rate (and other fight–flight reactions) play a role in conditioning trauma responses initially, but are not necessary to maintain the PTSD symptoms over time in all trauma victims.

The findings regarding trauma-related stimuli and PTSD are more compelling. Although generic stressors such as mental arithmetic do not prompt differential psychophysiological responding across PTSD and nonPTSD groups, combat-related stimuli consistently produce differences between PTSD groups and various comparison groups. Vietnam veterans with PTSD were consistently more reactive to combat imagery, particularly personally relevant scripts, than combat veterans without PTSD even when the comparison samples had other anxiety disorders or other psychological problems (Keane et al., 1998; Pitman et al., 1987, 1990). Similar results have been found with people suffering from PTSD as a result of motor vehicle accidents and child sexual abuse (Blanchard et al., 1996; Orr et al., 1998).

Although there were overall group differences in psychophysiological studies of PTSD, that does not mean that every person in the PTSD group exhibited such reactivity. In fact, Prins et al. (1995) estimate that as many as 40% of PTSD subjects do not exhibit the expected reactivity. While they speculated that this nonreactivity could be due to methodological reasons or subject variables (use of caffeine or other nonreported medications), a recent study may have found an alternative explanation, at least for some nonresponders.

Griffin, Resick, and Mechanic (1997) have studied psychophysiological reactivity among recent rape victims using a somewhat different methodology than prior studies. Rather than listening to scripts, participants were asked to talk for 5 minutes on a neutral recall topic or to describe their rapes. These neutral and trauma phases were interspersed with baseline conditions. Rather than looking at the PTSD group as a whole, Griffin et al. examined skin conductance and heart rate with regard to peri-traumatic dissociation. Peri-traumatic dissociation (PD) is the extent to which someone dissociated during the traumatic event (see Box 4.2 for the list of questions).

They found a small group of highly dissociative women who responded in a very different manner than the other women with PTSD. Although the skin conductance and heart rate of those with low PD scores increased as expected while they were talking about the rape, those with high PD scores showed a decrease in the physiological measures. Figure 4.1 shows heart rate responses of the high and low dissociative groups across the five phases of the study. When they examined the participants' subjective distress during each of the phases, the high PD group reported the same level of distress as the low PD group. Therefore, while they were experiencing distress, their physiological responses were suppressed. Griffin et al. speculated that there may be a dissociative subtype of PTSD that responds quite differently than the more phobic type of PTSD. This might explain why some studies have found a proportion of PTSD nonresponders.

BOX 4.2 Peri-traumatic dissociation questions

During the assault

1. Did you feel confused or disoriented?
2. Did you feel numb?
3. Did you have moments of losing track of what was going on—that is, did you "blank out" or in some other way not feel you were part of the experience?
4. Did you find yourself going on "automatic pilot"—that is, doing something that you later realized you had done but had not actively decided to?
5. Did your sense of time change during the event—that is, did things seem unusually speeded up or slowed down?
6. Did what was happening seem unreal to you, as though you were in a dream or watching a movie or a play?
7. Were there moments when you felt like you were a spectator, watching what was happening to you—that is, did you feel as if you were floating above the scene or observing it as an outsider?
8. Were there moments when your sense of your own body seemed distorted or changed—that is, did you feel yourself to be unusually large or small, or did you feel disconnected from your body?

—Griffin et al. (1997)

Figure 4.1.
Heart rate changes during a laboratory assessment in participants with PTSD.

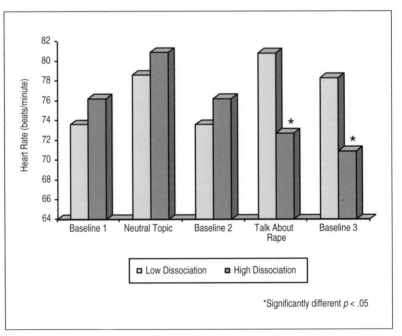

*Significantly different $p < .05$

Startle

Although exaggerated startle reactions are one of the symptoms of PTSD, there has been only a modest amount of research on startle thus far. In these studies, startle reactions are induced with a loud noise burst and, along with other psychophysiological measures, the eyeblink response is measured. The two aspects of the startle response that have usually been examined are the magnitude, or strength of the startle reaction, and the number of trials until the response is extinguished. Thus far, research has usually been conducted with combat veterans. It appears that habituation to the noise is not significantly different in those with or without PTSD. However, most studies have found a greater magnitude of response. The question remains whether this represents an overall shift in biological responding or whether the startle reactions represent a conditioned fear reaction.

In reviewing the studies on startle reactions, Prins et al. (1995) suggested that the loud bursts of noise used in these experiments sound like gunfire and that the combat veterans may be reacting with conditioned emotional reactions, not some generalized change in startle strength. Two studies support this contention. Butler et al. (1990) studied two different types of startle stimuli: acoustic startle and tactile startle. They found differences between the PTSD and non-PTSD veterans with the acoustic probe but not the tactile probe. Another group of researchers (Morgan, Grillon, Southwick, Davis, & Charney, 1996) studied eyeblink startle reflexes with acoustic stimuli under two conditions: baseline and anticipation of electric shock. They did not find exaggerated startle at baseline (absence of stress), but did find greater startle reactions among the PTSD veterans when the subjects anticipated being shocked. They concluded that the startle response was not chronically elevated but probably represents a greater conditioned emotional reaction in the PTSD group.

Neuroendocrine abnormalities in PTSD

Several types of studies of the neuroendocrine system have been conducted with people with or without PTSD. One type of study is to examine the level of circulating hormones at one time point or over the course of a day to determine if there are differences in the baseline levels of the hormones in those with or without PTSD. Another type of study introduces a challenge; however, rather than an external challenge such as a loud noise or listening to a trauma script, the person is challenged with the administration of some chemical which should have particular effects.

As would be expected in those with chronically increased sympathetic nervous system activity, there is evidence that the levels of epinephrine and norepinephrine (NE) are higher in combat veterans with PTSD than in veterans with other psychiatric disorders, or than normal controls (Kosten, Mason, Giller, Ostroff, & Harkness, 1987; Yehuda et al., 1992). These studies examined baseline 24-hour urinary excretion of NE. In addition to the levels of catecholamines, several studies have examined the number of receptor sites. For every neurotransmitter, there are very specifically shaped sites that can receive the messages. Just as the amount of chemicals being transmitted can vary, there can also be varying numbers of receptor sites. It has been found that both combat veterans and traumatized children with PTSD have fewer total alpha-2-adrenergic receptor binding sites per platelet compared to controls, probably because of the greater level of circulating catecholamines in these trauma victims (Perry, 1994; Perry, Giller, & Southwick, 1987). However, people with either depression or generalized anxiety disorder had higher levels of these binding sites than those with PTSD, indicating that PTSD differs from the other two disorders with regard to catecholamine regulation (Yehuda, Perry, Southwick, & Giller, 1990).

In another study, in which a challenge was introduced, it was found that yohimbine produced panic attacks in 70% and flashbacks in 40% of combat veterans with PTSD (Southwick, Krystal, et al., 1993). Yohimbine is an alpha-2 adrenergeric receptor antagonist, which means that it blocks the receptor sites and thereby increases the level of norepinephrine in the system. This effect of panic attacks and flashbacks was not found for any of the control subjects and has not been found for depression, schizophrenia, obsessive-compulsive disorder, or generalized anxiety disorder (Charney, Woods, & Price, 1990). However, a similar effect for increased panic attacks was found in those with panic disorder. (Charney, Woods, Goodman, & Heninger, 1987). In other words, in those people who are prone to flashbacks or panic attacks, blocking the receptor sites increases the level of norepinephrine circulating in the blood, which then triggers the PTSD symptoms.

With regard to serotonin, less research has been conducted on the effects with PTSD. The indirect suggestion of serotonin system involvement in PTSD is that selective serotonin reuptake inhibitors (SSRIs), such as Prozac or Zoloft, have been found helpful in reducing some of the symptoms of PTSD. There is a danger, however, in inferring biological mechanisms based on treatment effects. The effect could be caused by the overlap between PTSD and depression symptoms (SSRIs are normally used in the treatment of depression) or by some unknown mechanism. In one of the only studies conducted on the serotonin system, Southwick and his colleges administered a serotonin agonist to veterans with and without PTSD (Southwick et al., 1990). In the PTSD 31% experienced a panic attack and 27% had a flashback. There was almost no overlap between the subjects reacting to the serotonin agonist and those who reacted to yohimbine, suggesting that there may be different subtypes of PTSD based on neurotransmitters.

One of the most surprising findings regarding PTSD has been with regard to cortisol. While increased cortisol is an expected part of the stress response, and people with depression show elevated cortisol levels, people with PTSD appear to have low baseline levels of cortisol and the extent of cortisol suppression is related to PTSD (Mason, Giller, Kosten, Ostroff, & Podd, 1986; Yehuda, Giller, Levengood, Southwick, & Siever, 1995). In challenge studies, subjects with or without PTSD are given dexamethasone, which is a synthetic steroid. The presence of a substance similar to cortisol should stimulate a shut down of cortisol via the negative feedback loop. People with major depression are notable for "nonsuppression" of cortisol when given dexamethasone; they appear to be hypersecreting glucocorticoids. However, in PTSD, dexamethasone appears to stimulate hypersuppression. Those people with PTSD typically suppress cortisol more than the normal response. Although at first glance, these findings appear paradoxical, this hypersuppression may indicate an enhanced stress response.

In a very interesting study immediately after a trauma, Resnick, Yehuda, Pitman, and Foy (1995) examined the cortisol levels of women at the emergency room, immediately after being raped. Three months later, these women were assessed for PTSD and were interviewed about their histories of trauma. They found that the rape victims who also had a history of child sexual abuse were more likely to have PTSD after 3 months. They also found that the women with sexual abuse histories had lower cortisol levels soon after the rape than the women without such histories. This finding supports the idea that chronic trauma results in a sensitization of the stress response such that cortisol is quickly metabolized. In fact, Yehuda and her colleagues (Yehuda, Boisoneau, Lowy, & Giller, 1995; Yehuda, Boisoneau, Mason, & Giller, 1993) have found that combat veterans with PTSD have a significantly larger number of glucocorticoid receptors compared to normal groups or groups with major depression, panic disorder, mania, or schizophrenia. Yehuda, Giller et al. (1995) have suggested that in PTSD the HPA axis is showing enhanced negative feedback and reflecting a system that is maximally responsive to stress, as opposed to a system that has habituated or adapted. In fact, Yehuda (1997) has suggested that PTSD should be renamed "post-traumatic sensitization disorder".

Central nervous system abnormalities in PTSD

With the advent of various brain scanning techniques such as positron emission tomography (PET) and magnetic resonance imaging (MRI), it is now possible to map out the structures and functions of the brain more precisely than ever before. In animals, it has been shown that high levels of stress-induced glucocorticoids are toxic and result in damage to the hippocampus and impair learning and memory (Sapolsky et al., 1990). Preliminary studies with humans suggest the same types of dysfunction may occur in people with PTSD.

Several studies have found that people with PTSD have smaller hippocampal volume on one or both sides than people without PTSD. The decreases ranged from 8 to 26% in combat veterans and adult survivors of child sexual abuse (Bremner, Randall, Scott et al., 1995; Bremner, Randall, Vermetten et al., 1997; Gurvits et al., 1996). Corresponding to the findings regarding the size of the hippocampus, several researchers have found problems in short-term verbal memory in people with PTSD (Bremner, Scott et al., 1993; Sutker, Winstead, Galina, & Allain, 1991). Because the studies on the hippocampus are preliminary findings, it is unknown how stable these results are across PTSD populations, whether the smaller hippocampal volume might have preceded the trauma and contributed to the development of PTSD rather than being a reaction, or whether the effect is reversible with successful treatment. Furthermore, Nishith, Weaver, Resick, and Uhlmansiek (1999) found that after successful treatment of PTSD, the verbal memory of rape victims improved significantly compared to a waiting list group who received delayed treatment.

There has been one study thus far on the amygdala. Rauch et al. (1996) conducted a study using positron emission tomography (PET). After generating narratives of the specific traumatic experiences people experienced, as well as neutral scenes, the researchers read the accounts back to the people with PTSD. When they began to experience autonomic responses or had flashbacks, a scan was made. The researchers found that only the right hemisphere showed heightened activity, particularly the amygdala. There was also heightened activity in the right visual cortex that reflected the visual re-experiencing of the trauma. Furthermore, an area in the left hemisphere, Broca's area, showed decreased activity. Broca's area is associated with verbal activity, so the researchers concluded that the people with PTSD were experiencing the flashbacks as visual rather than verbal memories and that they would be having trouble putting their feelings and memory into words, an observation that is frequently made of people with PTSD.

Dissociation

The neurobiology of dissociation appears to be somewhat different from the fight–flight response. Although the research on this topic is new with humans, it is possible to extrapolate from what is known about the "defeat" response in animals, which Perry et al. (1995) propose matches the neurobiology and phenomenology of dissociation. Like the fight–flight response, dissociation involves central nervous system activation (brainstem). However, in dissociation, although epinephrine increases, vagal tone also increases (the major nerve serving the heart), resulting in a decrease in blood pressure and drop in heart rate. If the drop in blood pressure and heart rate are dramatic enough, fainting occurs.

Also involved in defeat and dissociation are the dopamines which trigger the endogenous opoids (opiates). The opoids are involved in pain perception and can affect one's sense of time, place, and reality. Perry et al. (1995) point out that over the long period of evolution, although the fight–flight response may have been more adaptive for adult males, the dissociative response may have had more survival value for females and children, perhaps explaining why dissociation is more frequently observed in women and children (and perhaps has been understudied thus far). It has been pointed out by van der Kolk (1996) that, in animals, both freezing and panic interfere with memory. Both excessive opoids and norepinephrine interfere with storage of explicit memory that van der Kolk proposed allows the organism not to "consciously experience" or remember the overwhelming traumatic event, resulting in symptoms of dissociation or amnesia.

Summary

This chapter reviewed biological responses to normal and traumatic stress. The stress response includes a cascade of neurochemicals that affect and are affected by various regions of the brain. Some of these, norepinephrine, serotonin, and cortisol, in particular, have been studied with regard to the development and maintenance of PTSD. Areas of the brain implicated in both stress and traumatic stress and receiving the most attention at this time are the locus coeruleus, hippocampus, and amygdala. Research on PTSD has focused on psychophysiological reactivity in responses to trauma cues, startle responses, and the study of the stress response neurochemical under both baseline and response to challenge conditions. The biology of dissociation has not been studied as extensively as PTSD at this point, but dissociation appears to have a somewhat different neurobiology including the release of endogenous opoids that may produce the emotional numbness, analgesia, and amnesia that are often observed among people who dissociate a great deal.

Psychological risk factors: Pre-trauma and peri-trauma influences

5

Because people show varying responses to similar traumatic events, it is likely that the trauma itself is not solely responsible for causing the post-trauma symptoms. This leads to a search for the variables that may affect trauma response and recovery. The previous chapter considered how trauma affects biological responses and, further, how biological responses might affect recovery from trauma. This chapter will cover how trauma responses are affected by personal variables that occur prior to or during the trauma. Some of the variables may be considered basic demographics such as the trauma victims' gender, race, their age at the time of the trauma, or their educational level. Some factors that influence recovery are much more personal, such as victims' psychological history or their prior experiences with trauma. The severity of the stressor and other factors occurring within the trauma may affect reactions and recovery. Finally, the way in which people respond cognitively and emotionally during the trauma may influence how they react and recover.

Demographic variables

Age

The age of the person being studied appears to be associated with the level of trauma symptoms. Age was the strongest risk factor for predicting global distress following traumas in a sample of 1000 adults who were surveyed in four cities in the southern United States (Norris, 1992). Ten lifetime traumatic stressors were assessed. The young group were those from 18 to 39. The middle group was 40–59 and the older group was 60+. The oldest group reported the least impact with regard to general stress and PTSD. Weaver and Clum (1995) conducted a meta-analysis, a statistical analysis of 50 studies on interpersonal violence. They found that age was not related to impact of the trauma. However, across all of these studies, the mean age was 24 and the range was age 6 to 41. Therefore, the participants in these studies would have fallen in Norris' youngest group.

On the other hand, Keane et al. (1998) examined Vietnam veterans who were receiving psychological services and found that age on arrival in Vietnam did make a difference. Men with current PTSD were more likely to be younger at the time they went to Vietnam than men who never developed PTSD. Fontana and Rosenheck (1994) examined the veterans of three different wars: World War II, Korea, and Vietnam. They found that the older veterans were less sympto- matic than the younger men, even after controlling for the effects of education, medical conditions, traumatic exposure, and in which war they served. However, it should be pointed out that it is possible that among the older populations, those with severe trauma responses had already died, leaving only the more resilient to be studied. Given the effects of trauma responses upon health discussed in Chapter 1, this possibility should not be disregarded.

In a few large population studies, the same age effect was found (Davidson, Hughes, Blazer, & George, 1991; Kessler et al., 1995). For example, in the Davidson et al. study, they found that 77% of the PTSD subjects were below the age of 45. Less than 7% were older than 65. Kessler et al. found only a modestly decreasing probability of PTSD with increasing age among those who were exposed to trauma. Amick-McMullan et al. (1991) studied 206 immediate family survivors of homicide victims. They found equal rates of PTSD among those who experienced the homicide as children, adolescents, or in adulthood, the three groups they studied.

Overall, it appears that if there is an age effect, it is with adult groups. The problem in examining this question with retrospective studies is that the age effect might just reflect the length of time since the trauma, reflecting slow natural recovery, or fading memory, rather than the effect of the age (and developmental level) of the person at the time of the trauma. As mentioned earlier, it could also reflect differential death rates.

A number of researchers have conducted studies at set points in time following particular disasters, which circumvents the problem of varying lengths of time since exposure (Bolin & Klenow, 1982–1983; Huerta & Horton, 1978; Melick & Logue, 1985–1986). All of these studies found that younger victims reported more family problems, emotional stress, and physical stress.

When age was not used as a linear variable but groups were divided into younger, middle-aged, and elderly, some studies have found that the middle aged (36–50) were at the greatest risk for symptoms (Phifer, 1990; Price, 1978; Shore, Tatum, & Vollmer, 1986; Thompson, Norris, & Hanacek, 1993). For example, in examining the effects of Hurricane Hugo, Thompson et al. found that experience with prior trauma, injuries, life threat, and personal loss did not vary by age, but the middle-aged people were most seriously affected with a range of outcomes (depression, anxiety, somatization, general stress, and traumatic stress). After examining several possible explanations, Thompson et al. proposed that the middle age groups have more burden placed upon them and hence more stress. They have greater responsibilities for both children and aging parents as well as greater societal and financial responsibilities. Community disasters increase the stress disproportionately in this group.

Race

Most studies have found that race is not associated with psychological impact of trauma (e.g., Breslau, Davis, Andreski, Peterson, & Schultz, 1997; Kessler et al., 1995). In the meta-analytic analysis of 50 studies of interpersonal violence, Weaver and Clum (1995) found that race was not associated with reactions following interpersonal trauma. However, there have been some exceptions. In a study of rape victims in Hawaii, Ruch and Chandler (1980) found that Asian victims suffered greater trauma than Caucasian victims did. In a study of a range of traumas, Norris (1992) found that, overall, there was higher stress and post-traumatic stress among white subjects. However, there was also an interaction of race and gender such that the strongest psychological reactions were found among African-American men. In the National Vietnam Veteran's Readjustment Study (Kulka et al., 1990) it was found that Hispanics had the highest rate of current PTSD (28%) followed by African-Americans (21%) and then whites/others (14%). The more recent Vietnam veterans study by Keane et al. (1998) also found that Hispanics were over-represented in the current PTSD group compared to the former PTSD or never PTSD groups. These differences may have been accounted for by differences in level of exposure. Minority veterans were exposed to greater combat trauma during the war.

In a study of 912 veterans of the Persian Gulf War, Sutker, Davis, Uddo, and Ditta (1995) indicated that minority group veterans reported more depression as well as PTSD than white veterans. However, the minorities again reported greater combat. In this study, African-Americans, Hispanic-Americans, and other minorities were grouped together.

In a study of over 550 elementary school children, three months after Hurricane Andrew in Florida, researchers found that there were no differences in post-trauma reactions among three different ethnic groups (Vernberg, La Greca, Silverman, & Prinstein, 1996). The children who were African-American, Caucasian-American, and Hispanic-American reacted in a similar manner to life threat and loss-disruption caused by the Hurricane.

Aside from PTSD, there has been a study that examined general tendencies to dissociate, peritraumatic dissociation, and race. Using data from the Vietnam Veterans Readjustment Study (NVVRS), Zatzick, Marmar, Weiss, and Metzler (1994) found that African-Americans reported significantly greater dissociation tendencies and peritraumatic dissociation. However, when they adjusted for the level of war zone stress, the authors found that there were no longer differences. They concluded, "This suggests that when individuals from diverse ethnic backgrounds are challenged with psychological trauma, the severity of the trauma rather than ethnic background is the key factor in the degree of dissociative response" (p. 579). Frueh, Brady, and de Arellano (1998), in a review of the research on race differences in PTSD, concluded that there has been too little research on the topic to draw confident conclusions.

Gender

Findings with regard to gender have been fairly consistent. Overall, women have a higher lifetime prevalence of PTSD than men (Breslau et al., 1991; Kessler et al., 1995; Weaver & Clum, 1995). One study of the effects of a plane crash into an apartment building in Amsterdam found that there were no gender effects. Another study of flooding and mudslides in Puerto Rico also found that there were no gender effects. The discrepancy in these findings may be accounted for by the fact that the latter two studies examined the effects of a single disaster upon people. In their national prevalence study of PTSD, Kessler et al. found that although women had higher rates of lifetime PTSD than men did, the results might be accounted for somewhat by the differences in their traumas. Although men were more likely than women to have experienced at least one trauma, the women were more likely to have experienced, as their worst event, an event likely to cause PTSD (e.g., rape).

In studying gender differences in PTSD, Breslau et al. (1997) found that there was a two-fold difference in PTSD between women and men primarily due to age and trauma differences. They found an interaction such that women were more likely to experience PTSD if their trauma exposure occurred in childhood before the age of 15. They also found that young girls were more likely to have as their traumas, rape, assault, or ongoing physical or sexual abuse, whereas boys were more likely to have experienced serious accidents or injury. Accidents and injuries were not as likely to lead to PTSD in victims of either gender, whereas childhood sexual and physical abuse resulted in PTSD in 63% of the participants. Therefore, they concluded that younger age at the time of the trauma and the experience of interpersonal violence may contribute to the gender differences that have been observed.

Socioeconomic status/income/education

It might be predicted that education and income might play a role in recovery from trauma inasmuch as they might reflect greater access to resources. Some studies have found socioeconomic status (SES) to be a predictor of greater reactions to trauma but others have not. In a study of 72 rape victims, lower SES was correlated with worse outcome on a range of symptom measures (Cohen & Roth, 1987). Atkeson et al. (1982) found that lower SES predicted depression at 12 months post-crime among rape victims. Also with rape victims, Burgess and Holmstrom (1978) conducted a 4- to 6-year follow-up after assessing rape victims in an emergency room. They found that less economically advantaged rape survivors had more symptoms. Breslau et al. (1991) studied 1007 young adults in Detroit, Michigan and found that those with lower education were more likely to be exposed to violence, and therefore indirectly to have greater effects. In the National Vietnam Veterans Readjustment Study (Kulka et al., 1990), there was a small but significant effect of SES during childhood, on PTSD. There was also an interaction such that men with lower education were more likely to be exposed to high war stress; they were more likely to be in combat. In the Keane et al. (1998) study of Vietnam veterans, the men with current PTSD were also more likely to have less education prior to their military service than those who never had PTSD.

On the other hand, Kilpatrick et al. (1992) and Kilpatrick, Saunders, Amick-McMullan, and Best (1989) found no relationship between SES and psychopathology in rape victims. Breslau et al. (1997) did not find education to be associated with PTSD. Weaver and Clum (1995) in their meta-analysis of 50 studies did not find that either SES or education were related to distress. Overall, it appears that if there are socioeconomic or educational differences, they may be indirect such that those with lower income and education may be exposed to more traumatic stressors. Although they did not examine the impact of demographic variables on trauma reactions, Byrne, Resnick, Kilpatrick, Best, and Saunders (1999) did examine the cyclical relationship between poverty and victimization among women. They found that women are at increased risk for victimization when they are living below the poverty level, are unmarried, or newly divorced. Moreover, women who are physically or sexually assaulted are more likely to experience increased risk for unemployment, divorce, and poverty.

Pre-trauma variables

Family environment

Several studies have found that early family environment may play a role in how people respond to traumas. Davidson et al. (1991) studied a community sample of 2985 people and found that those with PTSD were three times more likely to have experienced parental poverty, familial psychiatric illness, early parental separation and/or abuse as a child. Breslau et al. (1997) found that a family history of anxiety disorders or early separation from parents served as risk factors for PTSD. In an earlier study, Breslau et al. (1991) found that a family history of psychiatric disorders or substance use problems were risk factors for exposure to traumas and that a family history of instability and deviance, early separation from parents, or parental anxiety disorders increased their children's vulnerability to develop PTSD. Parents with psychological problems may be unable to protect their children from victimization, or support them appropriately should traumatic events occur. Such early childhood experiences, as well as generally poor modeling by the parents, may also affect one's coping abilities with stressors later in life.

Childhood trauma

One of the risk factors for adjustment problems following adult traumas is experiences with trauma early in life. The effects of early traumas might be direct inasmuch as people who were abused as children might never fully recover psychologically prior to the subsequent events; they might develop poorer coping skills with which to handle later traumas; or they might develop personality disorders or other psychological problems because of the impact on psychological development of living in family turmoil, in which childhood trauma is likely to occur. Personality disorders or other psychological disorders may affect how one responds during and after traumas. It is even possible that early trauma may effect the developing brain (Perry et al., 1995). On the other hand, the effects could be indirect such that early abuse might place someone at higher risk for subsequent traumas.

Bremner, Southwick, Johnson, Yehuda, and Charney (1993) studied Vietnam veterans with or without combat-related PTSD. Those with PTSD had higher rates of childhood physical abuse than those without PTSD (26% vs. 7%). Although childhood abuse is not a consistent predictor of becoming a battered woman, Cimino and Dutton (1991) found that in comparing battered women with or without PTSD, a history of child physical abuse was more likely in the backgrounds of those with PTSD (63% vs. 36%).

Gidycz, Coble, Latham, and Layman (1993) conducted a prospective study with college women. They found that those with a history of abuse were 1.5–2 times more likely to be victimized during their initial academic quarter of participation in their longitudinal study than women without a history of abuse. In a subsequent paper, Gidycz et al. (1997) reported that women who were victimized in adolescence were four times as likely to be victimized during one academic quarter in college. It could be that traumatic stress reactions such as PTSD and dissociation interfere with risk assessment, risk reduction, and self-defense. It could also be the case that young women who have been abused previously are at higher risk for revictimization because they have lower self-esteem and are less likely to assert their rights and needs as early in encounters as those women with good self-esteem.

Nishith et al. (2000) examined the trauma histories of 117 adult women who were assessed within a month after being raped. They examined the participants' histories of childhood sexual abuse, childhood physical abuse, and other adult sexual and physical victimizations in addition to the recent rape. The researchers found that childhood sexual abuse increased vulnerability to adulthood victimizations. Childhood sexual abuse did not directly predict the severity of recent post-rape symptoms but the extent of other adulthood victimizations did directly affect the severity of post-rape symptomatology. These findings point out the complex pattern and cumulative effects of childhood sexual trauma and adult revictimization leading to greater trauma reactions.

The effects of prior life events and trauma

Life events

Aside from child abuse, stressful life events (such as divorce, death of a loved one, or loss of income) and traumas can occur prior to the particular event being studied by researchers. These experiences may have cumulative effects that may serve as risk factors for the development of psychopathology. Ruch, Chandler, and Harter (1980) examined the presence of 11 life stressors during the year prior to a rape and found a curvilinear relationship. Women who had experienced major life changes were most traumatized, women with no changes were intermediate and those with minor changes were the least traumatized. Apparently, experience with some life stress may have an inoculating effect but too great a level of stress interferes with the development of coping methods needed to deal with an event as traumatic as rape. Looking at it somewhat differently, Kilpatrick and Veronen (1984) divided rape victims into four groups, low, moderately low, moderately high, and high distress. They found that the two more distressed groups were more likely to have suffered the loss of a spouse in the past year than the low distressed group.

Wirtz and Harrell (1987) examined the relationship of a number of nonvictimization life stress events with fear scores at 1 and 3 months post-rape. They found that those events, which could be construed as life threatening (death of a friend, major illness), were associated with greater post-rape fear, whereas other major, but non life-threatening events (birth of a child, divorce) were associated with less fear. In fact, the subjects who reported the latter type of stressor in the year prior to the rape reported less fear than subjects who reported no stressors the previous year. The authors concluded that the element of vulnerability to perceived future harm is the link between past life-threatening events and levels of fear subsequent to rape.

Prior traumas

Ruch and Leon (1983) evaluated rape victims within 48 hours post-crime and then again at 2 weeks post-crime. They found that women with no history of prior victimization showed a decrease in their trauma levels, whereas those with prior victimization exhibited an increase in trauma scores across the 2 weeks. They concluded that women who were multiple-incident victims were especially at risk for delayed responses.

In contrast, Frank and Anderson (1987) and Frank, Turner, and Stewart (1980) found that victims of more than one sexual assault did not differ significantly from single-incident rape victims on standardized measures of depression, anxiety, or fear from 1 to 4 months post-rape. However, the multiple incident victims did report poorer global social adjustment and greater disruption in social functioning in their immediate household. With regard to longer term reactions, McCahill, Meyer, and Fischman (1979) found that multiple-incident rape victims were not different from single-incident victims at 1 year post-rape except that multiple-incident victims reported more intense nightmares and a greater fear of being home alone.

Several studies on rape have examined the effect of prior victimization of any type, not just prior rapes. Burgess and Holmstrom (1979) conducted a 4- to 6-year follow-up of women originally seen at a hospital emergency room. They reported differences in recovery depending upon their history of victimization; 86% of participants with no prior history of victimization said they felt recovered, while only 53% of victims with such a history felt recovered upon follow-up. In assessing treatment-seeking rape victims, Marhoefer-Dvorak, Resick, Hutter, and Girelli (1988) found that single and multiple-incident rape victims did not differ on any of several standardized measures, but those victims with a history of major victimization did differ on assertiveness and somatization. Women who had been victims of a crime that involved the threat or presence of bodily harm prior to the sexual assault reported that they were more assertive but had greater somatic symptoms.

Rather than analyzing prior victimization as a simple presence versus absence categorization, Resick (1988) has studied the extent of prior victimization. Statistical analyses were conducted to determine how increasing levels of history of domestic violence, child physical abuse, emotional abuse, incest, observation of violence during childhood, and previous criminal victimization would affect reactions and recovery to a recent rape. Subjects' responses were examined at four points in time: 1, 6, 12, and 18 months post-crime. A history of prior victimization was associated with greater distress through 1 year post-rape.

Prior psychological functioning

In studying immediate reactions to rape, Ruch and Leon (1983) found pre-existing mental health problems one of the most influential variables affecting the level of trauma at intake, which was a maximum of 48 hours after the rapes. Although a history of psychotherapy or hospitalization was not associated with elevations in depression, fear, or anxiety, Frank, Turner, Stewart, Jacob, and West (1981) found that rape victims with a history of psychotropic medication, alcohol abuse, suicidal ideation or attempts were more distressed in the first month after the rape than victims without such histories.

In another study, Frank and Anderson (1987) found that based on clinical interviews, those rape victims with a prior diagnosis (using *DSM-III* criteria) were significantly more likely to meet criteria for a psychiatric disorder in the first month after rape than those with no diagnosable disorder in their histories. With regard to longer-term recovery, Atkeson et al. (1982) found that depression, suicidal history, and sexual adjustment problems prior to rape significantly predicted depression scores at 4 months post-assault. Prior anxiety attacks and obsessive-compulsive behaviors predicted depression at 8 months post-crime. At 12 months post-rape, prior anxiety attacks, obsessive-compulsive behaviors, and psychiatric treatment history predicted depression.

In a study of 469 firefighters in Australia, McFarlane (1989) found that a past history of treatment of psychological disorders was a better predictor of post-trauma symptoms than the degree of exposure to the disaster or the losses sustained. Prior psychiatric symptoms were also found to predict PTSD among Vietnam veterans (Kulka et al., 1990).

Alcohol and drug abuse can contribute to a particularly vicious circle of victimization and trauma reactions. Cottler, Compton, Mager, Spitznagel, and Janca (1992) found that cocaine or opiate users are three times as likely as comparison subjects to report experiencing a traumatic event, a greater number of events, and more symptoms. They also found that the substance use preceded the traumatic events. Similarly, Breslau et al. (1991) found that early drug or alcohol use increased exposure to trauma, thereby leading indirectly to PTSD. In order to examine the reciprocal influences of substances and trauma, Kilpatrick et al. (1997) studied 3006 women over 2 years. At the first time point, if women were using drugs, but not alcohol, they had an increased risk of being physically or sexually assaulted over the next 2 years. After a new assault, there was an increased risk of both alcohol and drug abuse, even among women with no prior substance abuse or assault histories. Therefore, drug use puts women at risk for assault, which puts women at risk for both increased drug use and alcohol abuse. Further substance abuse not only increases the risk of further victimization, but it also complicates and interferes with recovery from the traumas already experienced.

Peritraumatic variables

Peri-trauma variables are all the factors the occur during a traumatic event which might affect reactions or recovery. The factors that will be examined in the rest of this chapter are the type of trauma, level of exposure, other relevant trauma variables such as acquaintanceship with the perpetrator in crime victims, cognitions and appraisals, behavior during the event, and peritraumatic dissociation.

Type of trauma

Resnick et al. (1993) conducted a national study of traumas among women. They found that the rate of PTSD was significantly higher among crime versus noncrime victims (26% vs. 9%). In the National Comorbidity Study (Kessler et al., 1995) participants were evaluated for PTSD for their one event if they had only one or for the most upsetting event if they had more than one. Among both men and women, rape was the trauma that was most likely to be the basis for the assessment of PTSD and the most likely associated with PTSD; 65% of men and 46% of women who were assessed for rape trauma had PTSD. In men, the events most likely to be associated with PTSD were rape, combat, childhood neglect, and childhood physical abuse. In women the traumas most likely to cause PTSD were rape, threat with a weapon, childhood physical abuse, and other qualifying traumas. The rates of PTSD for accidents, natural disasters, and witnessing traumas were very low compared to the interpersonal victimizations.

In interpreting these results, it must be kept in mind that, in rape, the violence exposure is uniformly high. The person was forced to submit to penetrative sex. Other traumatic events have greater variability in levels of exposure. In combat situations, there may be a great deal of variability in the level of threat, violence, or injury. Accidents and natural disasters also may also have varying levels of exposure from slight property loss to great injuries or death of loved ones. The next subsection will examine the effects of the level of exposure and its effects on trauma responses.

Level of exposure

Combat exposure. There have been a number of studies that have demonstrated the relationship between level of combat exposure and post-war symptoms. Foy, Sipprelle, Rueger, and Carroll (1984) found that both combat exposure and military adjustment predicted greater PTSD among Vietnam veterans. Buydens-Branchey, Noumair, and Branchey (1990) studied 84 Vietnam veterans and found that the duration of combat exposure was predictive of the prevalence and persistence of PTSD, with the intensity of combat or the fact of having been wounded predicting greater severity of PTSD. Breslau and Davis (1987) evaluated 69 Vietnam veterans who were inpatients in a Veterans Administration psychiatric unit. They found that cumulative exposure to combat stressors and participation in atrocities were independent risk factors for PTSD. Atrocities were torture, mutilation, or severe mistreatment of military personnel or civilians. These findings indicate that PTSD can result not only from victimization but also from committing acts.

Fontana and Rosenheck (1994) studied 5138 war-zone veterans from three wars who were seen in an outpatient clinical setting. The Vietnam veterans had more PTSD than the veterans of the other wars. The researchers found that the Vietnam veterans in their sample were exposed to more combat than the Korean veterans. They also found that the Vietnam veterans witnessed more abusive violence and were more frequently targets and observers of killing than World War II and Korean War veterans. In examining symptoms beyond PTSD, Boscarino (1995) examined 2490 Vietnam veterans and 1972 veterans who had served during the Vietnam era but not in Vietnam. Boscarino studied generalized anxiety, depression, alcohol abuse, and drug abuse as well as PTSD. He found that level of combat exposure was associated with PTSD, anxiety, and depression.

Disaster exposure. Carlier and Gersons (1997) studied the Bijlmermeer plane crash in the Netherlands in which an airplane crashed into an apartment building outside of Amsterdam. They studied a range of losses from the fewest material consequences to the highest level of injuries or losses. Losing a loved one, suffering material damage/losing home or being home at the time of the disaster were all significant predictors of PTSD 6 months later. Thompson et al. (1993) studied 1000 people from four southern US cities following Hurricane Hugo. They studied these disaster survivors at 12, 18, and 24 months post-hurricane with regard to a range of outcome symptoms: depression, anxiety, somatization, and general stress. Injury and life threat had the strongest effects but financial and personal losses were also distressing. Injury and life threat continued to influence the level of symptoms 2 years later. In a study of motor vehicle accidents, Blanchard et al. (1996) found that the extent of initial injury, but not ongoing injuries, predicted who had PTSD versus who had recovered 1 year later. In a statistical review of 52 studies of disasters, Rubonis and Bickman (1991) concluded that death rates have the strongest relationship to outcome regarding anxiety, depression, and distress.

Level of violence among crime victims. As mentioned earlier, when completed crimes (such as rape, robbery, or assault) are studied, all the victims are equally exposed in the sense that each of them experienced a sudden uncontrollable assault upon their person. So rather than studying exposure *per se*, researchers on crime tend to look at whether various assault variables (such as the severity of injuries, the length of the crime, presence of a weapon, threats, or number of assailants) affect subsequent victim reactions. The results of these research efforts have not been conclusive. For every study that has found that the brutality plays a role in later reactions, there is another study that did not find any effect.

Several studies have examined the effect that the brutality of the rape has upon the victim's reactions by developing brutality scores or indices based on several assault variables. Results of these efforts have been mixed. Atkeson et al. (1982) found the amount of rape "trauma" did not predict later reactions. Sales, Baum, and Shore (1984) observed that neither the presence nor extent of violence *per se* was strongly associated with victim reactions. However, Cluss, Boughton, Frank, Stewart, and West (1983), Ellis, Atkeson, and Calhoun (1981), and Norris and Feldman- Summers (1981) all found a combination of assault variables to be predictive of greater distress on some measures. Cluss et al. (1983) found that their "threat index" was significantly and positively correlated with self-esteem at an initial assessment but not at the 6- or 12-month follow-up. Norris and

Feldman-Summers (1981) found assault variables to be predictive of problems with psychosomatic symptoms but not with sexual satisfaction or frequency, or the level of reclusiveness.

Examination of individual assault variables has also yielded mixed results. Girelli, Resick, Marhoefer-Dvorak, and Hutter (1986) found that none of eight assault variables (e.g., threats, weapons, and injuries) predicted a range of assessed symptoms in rape victims seeking treatment. However, they found that subjective distress was predictive of later fear reactions. Resick (1988) examined a similar range of variables in a prospective study of male and female robbery victims and female rape victims. These crime victims were assessed five times between 1 month and 18 months post-crime. Assault variables played very little role in predicting reactions of rape victims or male robbery victims at any time point. The level of threats did predict PTSD symptoms among female robbery victims.

Sales et al. (1984) found that threats against the victim's life predicted symptomatology within the first 3 months after a rape but not at the follow-up assessment 6 months later. Four assault variables predicted follow-up symptomatology only: the number of assailants, physical threat, injury requiring medical care, and medical complications. Victims who developed PTSD in a study by Kilpatrick et al. (1987) were more likely to have been seriously injured than those who did not develop PTSD but did not differ as to whether a weapon was present. They also found cognitive appraisal of life threat to predict later PTSD.

In a later study Resnick et al. (1993) studied direct threat to life or receipt of injury in female victims. They found that the PTSD rate in the group that had both was twice that of the subgroup that had neither. Sales et al. (1984) have suggested that "it is possible that the actual violence of an attack is less crucial to victim reaction than the felt threat" (p. 125). It does appear that explicit threats or perceived life threat is more reliably predictive of trauma responses that other factual details of the violence. However, an indicator of severity of violence, the receipt of injury, does predict trauma reactions in a number of studies.

Acquaintanceship status

One within-trauma variable, which is unique to crime victimization, is the person's level of acquaintanceship with the perpetrator. The effect of this relationship on reactions and recovery has been studied almost exclusively in rape victims. Of course there are some crimes with very high rates of PTSD and other trauma reactions that are exclusively committed by intimates. Domestic violence, incest, and child abuse are committed by people the victim should be able to trust to keep them safe. All of these forms of intimate violence have strong trauma sequellae probably partially because of the person committing the acts, but also because, within the family, the violence is likely to recur.

There has been a common assumption in the public arena that some rapes are worse than others. Rapes by strangers are often assumed to be more traumatic for the victim. Although Ellis et al. (1981) and Thornhill and Thornhill (1990) found that women attacked by strangers had more problems with fear and depression afterward than women attacked by acquaintances, other researchers have not found this to be the case (Girelli et al., 1986; Kilpatrick et al., 1987; Koss, Dinero, Seibel, & Cox, 1988; Resick, 1988). Kilpatrick et al. (1987) compared the impact of stranger, marital, and date rapes and found no differences in mental health among the three groups. Koss et al. (1988) found no differences in depression, state anxiety, or sexual satisfaction between strangers, nonromantic acquaintances, casual dates, steady dates or spouses/family members. However, they did find lower ratings of relationship quality among women who were raped by spouses/family members than the other groups of acquaintance rape victims. They also found that acquaintance rape victims were less likely to tell anyone about the incident.

In the Resick (1988) study of rape and robbery victims, Resick found in her sample, that robbery victims were as likely to know their assailants as rape victims (72–79% of each sample, recruited through police reporting, were complete strangers with their assailant). Further, although not found with rape victims or male robbery victims, acquaintanceship status was associated with self-esteem problems with female robbery victims in the months following the crime. Greater acquaintance with the assailant was associated to lower self-esteem at 6, 12, and 18 months post-crime.

Acquaintanceship with the assailant may affect the victim in other ways. Stewart et al. (1987) compared rape victims who sought out immediate treatment with those who delayed receiving treatment. Women who delayed treatment were more likely to have known their assailants and less likely to have physically defended themselves. Perhaps these women experience more self-blame or perhaps they expect that others will blame them or not believe them. Given that these women are just as likely to experience trauma reactions as those who are raped by strangers, it is unfortunate that they are not seeking help sooner, or not at all.

Appraisals of safety

Several studies of rape victims have found that women who appraised the situation as "safe" prior to the assault had greater fear, PTSD, or depressive reactions than women who perceived themselves to be in a dangerous situation prior to the assault (Cascardi, Riggs, Hearst-Ikeda, & Foa, 1996; Frank & Stewart, 1984; Scheppele & Bart, 1983). For example, Cascardi et al. assessed 107 sexual assault victims and found that PTSD scores were significantly higher among those who perceived they were in a safe location at the time of the assault. Safe situations were their own homes, a friend's home, or other familiar locations. Alleys, parking lots, and streets were categorized as dangerous situations. When someone is attacked in what they perceived to be in a safe situation, it is even more shocking and inconceivable, both at the time and later, than situations in which violence appears to be more expected.

Mental defeat

Recently, Ehlers and her colleagues (Dunmore, Clark, & Ehlers, 1997; Ehlers, Clark et al., 1998; Ehlers, Maercker, & Boos, 1998) have introduced the concept of mental defeat and its relationship to PTSD. Mental defeat is more than just giving up, it is a perception that the victim has lost all autonomy; that is, a state of giving up efforts to retain one's identity as a human being with a will of one's own. Examples of mental defeat would be statements such as, "I became an object"; "The event destroyed who I was"; or "I just wanted him to kill me to get it over with". Mental defeat is different from a sense of uncontrollability. Even though an event may be totally outside of one's control, victims may still retain a clear sense of their own identity and can view the event as an isolated incident apart from the rest of their life and personality, rather than a self-shattering event.

Several studies have indicated that mental defeat during the trauma is related to PTSD and to treatment outcome. Dunmore et al. (1997) found that mental defeat discriminated assault victims with PTSD from those who did not have the disorder. Also in the same study, they found that mental defeat predicted PTSD at 6 and 9 months after the assault. In a study of political prisoners in socialist East Germany, Ehlers, Maercher, and Boos (1998) found that former prisoners with PTSD were more likely to have experienced mental defeat than those without PTSD. These results were found even when they statistically controlled for the severity of maltreatment during imprisonment, the unexpectedness of the imprisonment, perceived threats, and psychological maltreatment during imprisonment.

In a study of treatment outcome using prolonged exposure with sexual assault victims, Ehlers, Clark, Dunmore et al. (1998) found that mental defeat during the event effected treatment outcome. Prolonged exposure therapy (see Chapter 7) was implemented with sexual assault victims and the authors compared those who improved a great deal with those who improved only modestly. They found that those who did not improve as much with treatment were more likely to have experienced mental defeat. Because prolonged exposure does not include any type of cognitive therapy to help the client reinterpret the event, the authors concluded that additional cognitive therapy might be important for those who experienced mental defeat during the assault.

Peritraumatic dissociation

A number of studies have examined the relationship between peritraumatic dissociation and later problems with PTSD. Peritraumatic dissociation is the experience of unreality during a traumatic event. It can be experienced in a number of forms: losing track of time or blanking out; going on "automatic pilot"; a sense of unreality as if one were dreaming or watching a play; feeling as if one were floating above the scene; feeling disconnected from one's body or that one's body is distorted in some way; emotional numbing; or amnesia for parts of the event (see list of questions in Chapter 4, Box 4.2). Although relatively little is known about the mechanisms of peritraumatic dissociation at this time, it is thought by some to be a natural biological response to inescapable horror, for which some people are more prone than others. In fact, in the study of physiological responsivity among those with high peritraumatic dissociation discussed in the previous chapter (Griffin et al., 1997), peritraumatic dissociation was found to fall on a normal distribution much like other inherited traits. Others believe that dissociation is more likely in children and those who are abused in childhood may be more likely to dissociate during traumas in adulthood. In this view, dissociation is more of a learned response. There is some evidence that those who dissociate more were more likely to have been abused as children (Briere & Runtz, 1988; Irwin, 1996).

Whatever the mechanisms of peritraumatic dissociation turn out to be, there is good evidence that dissociating during the event is associated with greater levels of PTSD later. As a part of the Vietnam

Veterans Readjustment Study, male and female veterans were asked about peritraumatic dissociation even though the traumatic events had occurred two decades earlier (Marmar et al., 1994; Tichenor, Marmar, Weiss, Metzler, & Ronfeldt, 1996). They found that having dissociated during the traumatic events was strongly associated with having PTSD years later. Similarly, Bremner et al. (1992) compared Vietnam combat veterans, 53 with PTSD and 32 without PTSD. They found that those with PTSD reported more dissociation at the time of the combat trauma.

There were several studies that resulted from the San Francisco Bay Area earthquake in which Interstate freeway 880 collapsed and killed 44 people in 1989 (Marmar, Weiss, Metzler, & Delucchi, 1996; Marmar, Weiss, Metzler, Ronfeldt, & Foreman, 1996; Weiss, Marmar, Metzler, & Ronfeldt, 1995). This group of researchers studied three groups of emergency service personnel (firefighters, police, para-medics, and highway department workers): those who were at the site of the collapse, those who were working that day but were not at the disaster, and those who worked in San Diego, which was unaffected by the earthquake. Although overall, they found that those who worked in the disaster reported fairly low levels of distress at the time they were assessed (1.5 years later), they did find an association between dissociation and PTSD. After level of exposure, prior adjustment, social support, and years of experience on the job were all controlled, general dissociation and peritraumatic dissociation were predictive of level of PTSD. They also found that those with higher levels of peritraumatic dissociation were younger, experienced greater exposure to disaster, felt greater perceived threat and were more likely to cope by means of escape and avoidance.

Other researchers around the world have found similar relation-ships between peritraumatic dissociation and later PTSD. Holen (1993) found dissociation during disaster was associated with short-term symptoms. Carlson and Rosser-Hogan (1991) found the same relationship between severity of trauma, dissociative symptoms, and PTSD symptoms among Cambodian refugees. Shalev et al. (1996) studied hospital patients in Jerusalem who came into the emergency room and were hospitalized in surgery or orthopedic wards. The casualty victims were either military or civilian. These researchers examined whether a number of variables could predict PTSD status 6 months after the initial assessment. They studied age, gender, edu-cation, event severity, initial PTSD symptoms, peritraumatic dissociation, and level of anxiety. Only peritraumatic dissociation significantly predicted PTSD at the later time point.

Because peritraumatic dissociation appeared to have such a strong role in predicting later PTSD, David Spiegel and his associates (Spiegel et al., 1996), were particularly instrumental in introducing a new diagnosis to the *DSM-IV*: acute stress disorder. They studied both dissociative symptoms and anxiety symptoms immediately following firestorms in Berkeley/Oakland, California, and 7 months later. Through statistical comparisons, they determined that the early presence of three of a possible five dissociative symptoms and three of a possible five anxiety symptoms was the best combination in predicting later PTSD. However, as mentioned in Chapter 1, other researchers are now questioning these findings through further studies and some have found that knowing about peritraumatic dissociation may not improve prediction of PTSD beyond an assessment of initial severity of PTSD symptoms.

Other peritraumatic behaviors and emotions

The study of other peritraumatic emotions and behaviors of the victim and their influence on recovery from trauma has been studied less than peritraumatic dissociation. With regard to behavior, there is some evidence that active resistance to rape, even when the rape is completed, is predictive of fewer distress symptoms later (Bart & O'Brien, 1984; Janoff-Bulman, 1979; Selkin, 1978). However, in a study of female rape, robbery, and assault victims (Kaysen, Morris, & Resick, 2000), active behavioral resistance did not predict trauma responses at 1 month post-crime as well as fearful responses or shame/dissociation during the crime. Shame, numbing, dissociation, and anger were found to co-occur. At 3 months post-crime, the best predictor of distress was the level of 1-month distress, although the shame/dissociation factor was also a significant predictor. The assault victims reported the greatest level of active resistance strategies. Women who were raped reported more shame/dissociation and fearful responses during the crime than either assault or robbery victims.

Several studies have found that the perception of threat is a more influential predictor of distress than more objective indicators of the level of violence such as injuries or the use of weapons (Bernat, Ronfeldt, Calhoun, & Arias, 1998; Girelli et al., 1986). In a large study of university students, Bernat et al. found that emotional reactions during the trauma, panic symptoms, and peritraumatic dissociation were all associated with PTSD and all of these within-trauma reactions were interrelated.

A note of caution

Another factor that will have to be examined in the future is the reliability of reporting upon one's perceptions during a highly traumatic event, especially a long time after the event has passed. Southwick, Morgan, Nicolaou, and Charney (1997) conducted a prospective study of memory for serious combat-related traumas in veterans of Operation Desert Storm. They found that, of the veterans who were assessed about potentially traumatic experiences 1 month after the war and again 2 years later, only 12% of the research participants recalled the same events at both times. Seventy percent of the veterans recalled at least one event at 2 years that they had not reported at 1 month, and 46% did not report an event at 2 years that they had reported at 1 month. Those with PTSD were likely to report more traumatic events at 2 years than 1 month.

Although these findings point out that memories may not be fixed and unchanging, it is possible that the increase in reporting of traumatic events over time was due to earlier traumatic amnesia. Mechanic et al. (1998) studied the reported memory problems of 92 rape victims at 2 weeks and 3 months post-crime. At 2 weeks post-rape, 37% of the women reported having significant levels of amnesia for parts of the rape. By 3 months post-crime, only 16% reported significant amnesia. Mechanic et al. examined variables that were associated with the reports of failed memory. They found that those who reported greater peritraumatic dissociation during the rape were more likely to report greater amnesia later. They also found that rapes by known assailants resulted in more amnesia than rapes by strangers. They speculated that being raped by someone known to the victim is a greater betrayal and therefore more likely to result in avoidance of the memory.

These studies highlight the caution with which peritraumatic reactions must be viewed. While asking someone how she or he is feeling right now or what is happening now, one might assume that the responses are fairly valid. However, asking people to report on their psychological state or responses during moments of terror or horror might be less reliable. Although the memory of an extremely traumatic event might be indelibly etched in memory for some people, other people may have had difficulty encoding the memory at the time because of interfering emotions, head injuries, or substances imbibed. Others may have trouble retrieving the memories because of ongoing dissociation or other forms of avoidance. Only through repeated findings in research will we be able to determine if the reactions that are being reported represent typical patterns of response. With that caveat, it does appear that peritraumatic dissociation is a rather consistent predictor of later distress.

Summary

Pre-trauma and peri-trauma variables appear to have varying effects on recovery from traumatic events. Among the demographic variables, gender is the most consistent predictor although it tends to be confounded with type of trauma. Being older at the time of the trauma tends to be a predictor of better recovery, although middle-aged people with more responsibilities to children and parents may be a particularly stressed age group. Race/ethnicity does not appear to be a good predictor of reactions to trauma once rates of exposure have been controlled. Socioeconomic variables may be better predictors of exposure to violence than reactions to trauma.

Traumatic stress effects appear to be cumulative. Childhood sexual abuse history is a predictor of worse reactions to adult traumas and adult traumas impact reactions and recovery to subsequent events. Prior psychological problems in the trauma victim or the victim's family of origin may interfere with recovery from traumatic stressors. The type of trauma and level of exposure within the event is a consistent predictor of reactions and recovery. However, once among groups where exposure is uniformly high, such as rape victims, assault variables do not appear to have a major impact on reactions. Within-trauma cognitive reactions such as mental defeat and peritraumatic dissociation appear to be strong predictors of severity of reactions and may affect treatment as well.

Post-trauma risk factors and resources: Coping, cognitions, and social support

6

Aside from pre-trauma risk factors and within-trauma responses, the ways people interpret and cope with events and the ways others respond will affect the eventual outcome. Lazarus and Folkman (1984) have defined psychological stress as "a particular relationship between the person and the environment that is appraised by the person as taxing or exceeding his or her resources and endangering his or her well-being" (p. 19). They proposed that there are two critical processes that mediate the person–environment relationship: cognitive appraisal and coping.

Most events in life are open to interpretation. How one interprets, or appraises, the causes of the events, the meaning and consequences of the event, or even the event itself, will influence how the affected person will attempt to cope with the situation. Not only do the direct participants with the stressor play a role in interpreting and coping, but loved ones, friends and acquaintances, and even the community may play a role in cognitive appraisals that may not only affect the person's coping, but also the amount and quality of social support they receive.

Coping as defined by Folkman (1991), is "the changing thoughts and acts that the individual uses to manage the external and/or internal demands of a specific person environment transaction that is appraised as stressful" (p. 5). Folkman was describing a dynamic process in which appraisals, coping, and social support may be intertwined to affect the eventual outcomes of stressful situations. This chapter will focus on these post-trauma influences: cognitions, coping, and social support.

Post-trauma coping

Simply speaking, coping consists of the efforts someone makes to reduce their distress. Sometimes, as in the case of disaster, there is a great deal of clean-up activity and restoration of one's way of life that begins immediately and may take some time. Many traumatic events result in injury that must be treated. These pressing activities may usurp immediate energies so that the psychological reactions and recovery are delayed. When there are no restorative activities required, the person or people involved must still cope with the psychological aftermath.

Aside from being considered a post-trauma variable, coping could also be considered a pre-trauma risk factor. The style of coping a person has developed to deal with everyday stressors is likely to be the type of coping he/she will attempt to use to adjust to the more traumatic stressors as well. There is of course, no assurance that coping strategies for daily stress will be effective for catastrophic stressors. For example, if someone has been taught throughout his/her life to "sweep things under the rug", to avoid feelings and not deal with stressful events, this strategy may backfire with events that are too big, too important, and too emotionally laden to ignore.

Although the word "coping" has a connotation of a successful outcome, it should be remembered that coping strategies might be either effective or ineffective. When someone says, "I am coping the best that I can", that could mean that she or he is recovering from the event, or it could be said in exasperation because whatever is being attempted is not working to relieve his or her suffering. For example, the use of alcohol may be an attempt to shut down painful emotions or to obtain some needed but elusive sleep. Other people, in an attempt to be helpful, may even urge the traumatized person to have a drink. However, even if effective in the short run, the use of external substances even at its best does not lead one to a sense of mastery, and at its worst can lead to addiction and a complication of symptoms. On the other hand, having a good cry might look like the person is not coping to an outsider, but in fact may bring the traumatized person some relief. Ultimately, whether a coping strategy is effective or ineffective must be measured by the long-term outcome, how extreme the measure is, and whether there are any negative consequences from the use of the strategy.

At times it is difficult to distinguish between ineffective coping and psychological symptoms. One of the three symptom clusters of PTSD is concerned with avoidance of the traumatic memory and reminders.

Many people assume that they should be trying to push it away and even seek therapy with the expressed goal of avoiding the memory better. They do not realize that their attempts at coping are actually considered to be symptoms of a disorder. The combination of PTSD avoidance of reminders of a single event with a general tendency to avoid emotions or problems is a particularly toxic combination.

Attempting to avoid thinking about a traumatic event may not only be ineffective, it may actually backfire. Wegner, Schneider, Carter, and White (1987) conducted the first of a series of studies on thought suppression. During an initial period, they instructed one group of participants to think of anything, but to try not to think of a white bear (suppression condition). They instructed another group to think of a white bear (expression condition). During a second period, the instructions were reversed. The participants talked aloud during the periods and rang a bell whenever they thought of white bears. Although the group that was first asked to suppress their thoughts of white bears, did think about them less than the group that was asked to think of them, they had a rebound during the second period. In the second period, when asked to think of white bears, they thought about them more than the group that was originally asked to think of the bears.

This research paradigm has been applied to the problem of PTSD with similar findings. In samples of motor vehicle accident victims with or without acute stress disorder (Harvey & Bryant, 1998) and sexual assault survivors with and without PTSD (Shipherd & Beck, 1999), the rebound in thoughts was evident among those with ASD or PTSD following instructions to suppress thoughts about their traumas. In both cases, after a period of suppression (in which trauma thoughts were reduced but not actually completely suppressed), the groups with ASD or PTSD had a greater rebound of trauma thoughts than those without the disorders. It appears that attempts to avoid thinking about traumas may actually increase intrusive thoughts!

Coping can be classified along several dimensions. Behavioral coping is the action one takes in responding to the trauma. For a crime victim, it might be engaging in increased safety measures around one's home. It could also mean contacting the police or district attorney and following the progress of the criminal justice system. For disaster or accident victims it might be the reparative work to one's home or belongings. However, behavioral coping might also mean locking the doors of one's home and refusing to go out except to go to work, or avoiding people and withdrawing from social activities once viewed as pleasurable. Moving away from a place of residence may be viewed as adaptive behavioral coping if the place is objectively high risk (moving away from a high crime neighborhood or a flood plain), but could be maladaptive coping if one moves away from a city or region and away from family and friends to go to another city that has similar crime rates. The latter type of move might merely reflect over generalization of avoidance rather than any factual improvement in living conditions or risk reduction.

Emotional coping is concerned with affect regulation. It is possible that either too little or too much expression of emotion could be problematic. People with borderline personality disorder (BPD) are noted for their affect regulation problems (*DSM-IV*, APA, 1994). This includes wide mood swings over short periods of time, sometimes reminiscent of the mood swings of a very young child. For the person with BPD, even daily hassles may trigger a crisis response. Because their emotions feel so big and out of control, and the person has so few internal coping resources, people with BPD are at risk for doing impulsive and at times drastic things to attempt to shut down their feelings. Suicidal behavior, self-mutilation, or substance abuse are not uncommon methods of coping with overwhelming affect.

On the other hand, if someone has over-regulated affect or even a fear of emotion, the feelings that accompany a traumatic stressor may appear to be so overwhelming that the person will avoid them at all costs. The over-regulated person will attempt to avoid thinking about or talking about the trauma. He/she will attempt to minimize the importance or impact of the event. Although, while reducing symptoms in the short run, this avoidance strategy may prolong recovery by interfering with the emotional processing of the event. As will become evident in the next chapter on treatment, expression of affect (without become overwhelmed) is considered therapeutic while the avoidance of affect (and cognitive processing) is thought to be a maintaining factor in PTSD symptoms. The over-regulated person may also turn to external substances to reduce distress when sheer will power over thoughts and feelings fails. Even if the person is successful in avoiding the memory of the traumatic memory for a while, even years, eventually when reminded of the trauma or when vulnerable, the memory and affect will come back with full force because nothing has really changed or been resolved about the incident.

Research on coping

Early research on coping with stress began by trying to delimit the various ways in which people coped. However, it soon became evident that, rather than listing a variety of behaviors or cognitive coping strategies, these types of coping actually represented some fairly simple dimensions: problem-focused or emotion-focused coping as one dimension, approach or avoidance as another dimension (see Figure 6.1). Problem-focused coping is the effort someone makes to recognize, modify, or eliminate the impact of a stressor. Emotion-focused coping is the effort to regulate affect that results from traumatic exposure. Therefore, a person could engage in either approach or avoidance problem-focused coping, or approach or avoidance emotion-focused coping. Most of the coping scales that are used to assess coping with stress or traumatic stress contain some or all of these dimensions. However, the next section (Post-trauma attributions and cognitions) will give special attention to a number of cognitive strategies and appraisals separately because cognitive strategies have received the lion's share of research.

Coping styles have been studied across a number of trauma groups. In studies conducted with victims of motor vehicle accidents, rape, domestic violence, or combat, researchers have all found that symptoms and continued distress (PTSD, depression, and/or social adjustment) are associated with avoidance type coping (Bryant & Harvey, 1995; Cohen & Roth, 1987; Finn, 1985; Mitchell & Hodson, 1983; Nezu & Carnevale, 1987). Both problem-focused and emotion-focused coping have been found to be less among those with PTSD than those without the disorder. Although these studies find a consistent pattern of avoidance and reduced active coping, it is not clear whether the avoidance is limited to traumatic stress or whether this is a pattern that extends to everyday stress. Few studies have examined this question specifically.

In a study of repatriated prisoners of World War II, Fairbank, Hansen, and Fitterling (1991) compared ex-POWs with or without PTSD and a group of noncombat veterans. The coping scale that was used in this study examined eight types of coping: problem-focused coping, wishful thinking, detachment, seeking social support, focusing on the positive, self-blame, tension reduction, and keeping to self. The researchers compared coping with war memories and coping with recent life stressors. They found that the veterans with PTSD were more likely to use wishful thinking, self-blame, self-isolation, and seeking social support more than the other two groups. However, there were no significant differences in coping with current life stressors.

In contrast, Coffey, Leitenberg, Henning, Bennett, and Jankowski (1996) did find similarities in coping with general and traumatic

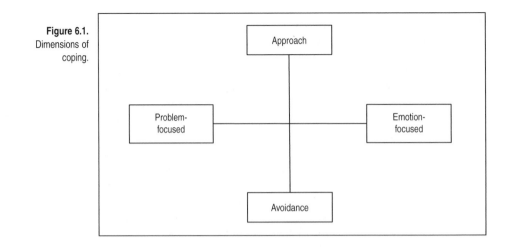

Figure 6.1.
Dimensions of
coping.

Approach

Problem-
focused

Emotion-
focused

Avoidance

stress. Coffey et al. studied a sample of 974 college students who were asked to report coping regarding dating violence and another stressful event. Of the total sample, 12.5% reported that they had been the victim of violence (slapped, kicked, bit, hit with fist, or hit with something) by a romantic partner. As might be predicted, the women who had been abused by a partner reported greater psychological distress than women who had never been abused by a partner. The women in the violence group were also more likely to have been the victims of sexual aggression, child physical and sexual abuse, and to have come from violent homes. However, when the other events were controlled for, the partner violence group still had more distress than the nonabused group. Furthermore, the abused group was more likely to use disengagement styles of coping not only for the abuse but also for other stressful events.

It is not clear why these two studies resulted in opposite results. Comparing aging combat veterans with young college-age women may be a bit like comparing apples with oranges. However, the World War II veterans have had many years to develop coping skills in their day to day lives and their traumas were long ago and far away. They may have been able to separate their combat memories more successfully than the young women who had been abused more extensively, at a younger age, and in their own environments. Repeated abuse, especially while young, may lead to more extensive patterns of avoidance and poor coping styles not just for the traumas, but for stressful events generally.

Very little is known about developmental level and coping styles. Vernberg et al. (1996) studied responses of 568 third- to fifth-grade children to Hurricane Andrew. They used a child version of a coping scale with four factors: positive, blame and anger, wishful thinking, and social withdrawal. All of the types of coping were associated with more PTSD symptoms, but blame and anger were more strongly associated than the other types of coping. The authors thought that even positive coping strategies were associated with more PTSD because it was so soon after the disaster and the children were still developing coping strategies.

In contrast to design of the previous studies that focused on groups with or without psychological disorders, Wolfe, Keane, Kaloupek, Mora, and Wine (1993) studied 152 nontreatment-seeking Vietnam veterans who thought they made a good adjustment. Those who recovered well from the war used nonavoidant coping styles. Coping style predicted current adjustment better than combat exposure. Another small study (10 participants) also examined Vietnam veterans who made a good adjustment, but the authors (Hendin & Haas, 1984) looked more at coping during the combat to identify what variables might affect adjustment later. They found that each of the veterans exhibited calmness under pressure, intellectual control, acceptance of fear, and a lack of excessively violent or guilt-arousing behavior. Perhaps these behaviors reflected prior adjustment as well as effective training.

There are a few studies that have examined gender and coping. Charlton and Thompson (1996) studied 108 treatment-seeking survivors of accidents, crime, and war (but not disasters). The research participants were assessed at the time they started treatment using a somewhat different measure of coping than some of the previous studies. Rather than more global concepts such as engagement and disengagement, they focused on more specific strategies: confrontational coping, distancing, self-controlling, seeking social support, accepting responsibility, escape-avoidance, planful (sic) problem solving, and positive reappraisal. The researchers found that men and women were similar on coping except on a subscale regarding accepting responsibility (men reported greater accepting responsibility). Most coping strategies, particularly escape/avoidance were consistently associated with high psychological distress. Positive reappraisal and distancing were associated with better outcome. These findings on sex differences contrast to Vingerhoets and Van Heck (1990), who found that women used more emotion-focused coping and men used more problem-focused coping.

Curle and Williams (1996) looked at gender differences in coping following a school bus accident in the Austrian Alps. They studied

25 adolescents 2 years after the nonfatal bus accident. Overall, psychological adjustment was good but there were gender differences, with girls showing poorer adjustment. Along with the differences in adjustment, there were gender differences in coping strategies. Girls used distraction and social withdrawal more than boys did. Sigmon, Greene, Rohan, and Nichols (1996) studied 19 male and 59 female adult survivors of childhood sexual abuse. The participants completed measures on abuse-specific coping and general coping. Four types of coping were examined: problem-focused, emotion-focused, avoidance, and acceptance. With regard to abuse-specific coping, there were no gender differences. Both genders used similar coping styles during childhood when the abuse was occurring: avoidance was most likely, emotion-focused coping was least frequent. As adults, however, men used greater acceptance strategies and women used more emotion-focused strategies. (However, men were older in this sample and women were more likely to have been sexually abused in adulthood.) They used similar levels of problem-focused and avoidant coping strategies and used the four kinds fairly evenly. Avoidance and emotion-focused coping in childhood predicted distress and other trauma symptoms in adulthood.

Post-trauma attributions and cognitions

One particular form of coping that has attracted a great deal of research is concerned with appraisals and attributions. This refers to how someone thinks about an event after it occurs. Most people appear to need to understand why events happen in order to attempt to predict and control future events. People also appear to need to make meaning of events in order to put them into a larger context of understanding themselves and the world. In social psychology, attribution theory has long been studied as the way in which people understand and attribute causes for events. In clinical psychology, the existential, cognitive, and constructivist orientations have all focused on how people construe meanings from events and the effects of those interpretations.

Attributions

Attribution theory, first applied to achievement settings, has been examined in clinical settings as well. Weiner (1985) proposed that when events are unexpected, people tend to look for explanations along several typical dimensions, internal–external, controllable–uncontrollable, and stable–unstable. Along the internal–external dimension are thoughts concerning whether the event was caused by oneself or factors outside of oneself. The controllable–uncontrollable dimension concerns the person's beliefs regarding how controllable they thought the event was. Stable–unstable refers to the persistence of these factors. Abramson, Seligman, and Teasdale (1978), in a revision of learned helpessness theory, added the dimension of global–specific, which refers to factors that are usually found or ones that were specific to this situation. Abramson et al. proposed that internal, stable, and global attributions of negative events are related to depression. Inasmuch as traumatic events represent events representing helplessness, researchers began to apply this model to traumatic stress (McCormick, Taber, & Kruedelbach, 1989). Some studies have focused on attributional style, which refers to one's propensity to respond in certain ways across situations. In these studies, research participants are given generic scenarios to respond rate. In other studies, participants are asked to rate their attributions about their own specific trauma. These studies are much more specific in determine someone's causal attributions about their trauma, but do not necessarily reflect a person's general style in viewing events.

Several studies have found a connection between attributional style and PTSD. McCormick et al. (1989) studied 99 patients admitted for treatment at an alcohol and gambling treatment program at a Veterans Administration Hospital. Twenty-six of the participants also met the criteria for PTSD. Those with PTSD had attributional styles consistent with the learned helplessness model: internal, global, and stable attributions. They advised therapists to help clients move their appraisals to more "universal helplessness" than personal helplessness and to view the event as time-limited and specific to the situation. Earlier, Perloff (1983) argued that prior to trauma, having a perception of unique invulnerability ("Bad things won't happen to me") as well as unique vulnerability ("Bad things always happen to me") may exacerbate reactions to traumatic events. Apparently, those people who believe they control their lives and environments (or have no control) make the poorest adjustments to events that are out of their control. She too recommended that the best stance was one of universal vulnerability ("Bad things can happen to anyone").

In two different studies, Joseph and his colleagues (Joseph, Brewin, Yule, & Williams, 1991, 1993) studied attributions following shipping disasters. They found that more internal (self-blame) and controllable attributions were associated with greater depression, intrusive recollections and anxiety 8 months to 1 year later. Wenninger and Ehlers (1998) compared the attributional styles of adult survivors of child sexual abuse (CSA) with a nontraumatized sample. They found that the CSA group had more internal, stable, and global attributions for negative events in their everyday life than the comparison sample. There were no differences on the controllability dimension. They then examined the relationship between attributional style and PTSD symptoms among the CSA survivors. They found that the global scale correlated significantly with PTSD and other trauma symptoms. Wenninger and Ehlers interpreted the findings to mean that there was a relationship between an inflexible and overgeneralized cognitive style and symptoms.

Falsetti and Resick (1995) examined causal attributions among college students who had been victims of crimes. They found that internal and stability attributions about their traumas predicted depression, internal and global attributions were associated with general distress, and internal, stability, and controllability attributions predicted PTSD.

Resick and Schnicke (1993) assessed causal attributions along the four dimensions controllable by others–uncontrollable by others, controllable by you–uncontrollable by you, internal–external, and stable–unstable. They found that after treating rape victims with a cognitive therapy (cognitive processing therapy, see Chapter 7), the women changed their attributions from believing that the cause of the rape was controllable by them, and internal to them. After treatment, their attributions changed to external and control by others. In other words, they blamed themselves less and the assailant more. However, there was no change on the stable–unstable dimension.

There have been a number of studies that have examined causal attributions among battered women (see Holtzworth-Munroe, Smutzler, & Sandin, 1997 for a review). Holtzworth-Monroe et al. drew several general conclusions regarding these studies. Women tend to blame their abusive spouses more than themselves, they are likely to attribute causality of his violence to relationship factors, and they believe that the violence is unstable (will not happen again). Holtzworth-Monroe et al. also concluded that severity of battering might change attributions. Women who were severely abused tended to blame their partners more, themselves less, and viewed the causes of abuse as more stable. Furthermore, Andrews and Brewin (1990) found that women who had been physically or sexually abused in childhood were more likely to make internal and stable attributions for the abuse than women who had not been abused in childhood.

Appraisals and coping

Lazarus and Folkman (1984) proposed that the way in which someone appraises an event will have a powerful influence in determining the level of stress reactions. From a social psychological framework, Janoff-Bulman (1992) has focused on fundamental assumptions that guide our interpretations of traumatic events. She proposes that there are three fundamental assumptions that people hold, and that help people feel that they personally are invulnerable to events such as crime: (1) Benevolence of the world, (2) Meaningfulness of the world, and (3) The self as worthy. The belief that the world is a benevolent place indicates that people believe that there are more positive outcomes than negative outcomes. The assumption of the meaningfulness of the world is an assumption that people directly control what happens to them through their own actions. The belief in the fairness of the world benevolence, that good things happen to good people and bad things happen to bad people, has been called the just world belief. Therefore, if you believe that you have worth, that good things are likely to happen to you, and that you control your own fate, then traumatic events such as crime should not happen to you. Hence, you feel a sense of invulnerability, what Perloff (1983) called "unique invulnerability".

With the backdrop of such assumptions intending to keep one feeling safe and in control, what happens then when a trauma occurs and these assumptions are challenged? According to some theorists (e.g., Frieze & Bookwala, 1996; Janoff-Bulman, 1992; McCann & Pearlman, 1992; Resick & Schnicke, 1992), messages that are strongly contradictory to one's beliefs about self and world must be reconstructed in some way to reconcile the discrepancy. Assimilation is the process of taking in new information. Accommodation is the process of changing one's beliefs, categories, and schemas to accept the new information (see Chapter 3).

Frieze and Bookwala (1996) suggested three cognitive coping strategies: denial of the traumatic event, redefinition of the event, and self-blame. All of these strategies might be viewed as assimilation. That is, if someone denies that the event happened or blames himself/herself for its occurrence, they are trying to regain their prior beliefs by refusing to take in this new, incompatible information. Redefinition of the event might be a form of assimilation if the reconstruction of the event serves to maintain old beliefs. However, there is another form of redefinition that might assist in coping. Some people engage in downward social comparison or event comparison in which they compare themselves to less fortunate others or compare their event to worse possible outcomes ("It could have been worse. I could have been badly injured or killed."). Some people are able to seek out positive benefits in the face of catastrophe ("I have a greater appreciation for life." "I am closer to my family now.").

Assimilation: Self-blame and guilt

Some researchers who have focused on self-blame (Bulman & Wortman, 1977; Lerner, 1980; Wortman, 1976) have proposed that victims are likely to accept responsibility for events in order to maintain a sense of control over their lives and to maintain the belief that the world is just and orderly. But at what cost are such attributions? Janoff-Bulman (1979) hypothesized that self-blame serves an adaptive function but that behavioral self-blame should be associated with more effective post-rape adjustment than characterological self-blame. Meyer and Taylor (1986) and Frazier (1990) did not find this to be the case. Although they too found high rates of self-blame in rape victims (50%), they found both characterological and behavioral self-blame were associated with poorer adjustment post-rape.

Wyatt, Notgrass, and Newcomb (1990) conducted a community study on rape and then analyzed the data of 55 women who had been raped. They found that 61% of the women attributed the rape to something about themselves. This self-blame was associated with both negative short-term and long-term effects. It should be pointed out here, however, that blaming oneself does not mean that rape victims do not blame the rapist. It is possible to blame oneself for a portion of the event and still blame someone else for other portions of the event.

In a review of attributional research with battered women, Holtzworth-Munroe et al. (1997) noted that, in a dozen studies on attributions, there was no study in which the majority of participants blamed themselves for their husband's violence. In most studies, the battered women tended to blame their husbands more than themselves.

Guilt is a combination of thoughts and feelings. The guilty person experiences an unpleasant feeling along with the belief that he/she should have thought, felt, or acted differently (Kubany, 1994). Guilt normally occurs when people feel they have violated their personal standards, are responsible for causing an event, or believe they were not justified in the actions they took (Kubany & Manke, 1995). However, it is quite possible that people are mistaken in their conclusions, due to faulty logic. Kubany and Manke (1995) have proposed four major sources of guilt among trauma survivors based on erroneous thinking.

(1) *Hindsight bias*. The belief that one "knew" what was going to happen before it was possible to "know" or that one dismissed or overlooked clues that "signaled" what was going to occur (p. 34).
(2) *Responsibility distortion*. The exaggerated perception of personal responsibility for causing the event or a related negative outcome (p. 35).
(3) *Justification distortion*. The belief that actions taken lacked sufficient justification (p. 38).
(4) *Wrongdoing distortion*. The exaggerated perception of personal wrongdoing (p. 41).

Hindsight bias, first studied and labeled as such by social psychologists (Fischoff, 1975), is the erroneous belief, after the fact and the outcomes are known, that one did or should have known the outcome at the time. Therefore, if someone knew ahead of time that something bad was going to happen, they could have and should have prevented it. And because they failed to prevent the event, they should be blamed and feel guilty. For example, young women who are raped by an acquaintance frequently state that they should have known that the man who attacked them would do such a thing. They blame themselves for having poor judgment even though there may have been no indicators that violence was imminent. It doesn't occur to them that if they had known the other person was a rapist, then they would have behaved very differently than they did. Sometimes people claim that they had a "feeling" that something was wrong and that they should have acted on the feeling. However, people often have "feelings" that are soon forgotten when the bad thing doesn't happen. Furthermore, there is no clear plan of action when one has a vague feeling that something is going to happen.

Responsibility distortion is the belief that one caused an event that is out of one's control. An example of responsibility distortion is the oldest child in a family who blames himself for the abuse of his mother by his father: "If only I had kept the younger kids quiet and out of the way, then Dad wouldn't have beaten up Mom." Combat veterans who blame themselves for the deaths of the men under their command who were ambushed is an another example. In both examples, the person blaming himself is ignoring the person who actually caused the violence and is, instead, assuming that he caused it. In fact, many events have multiple causes or reflect a chain of events.

Justification distortion refers to the erroneous belief that one has more good options available than there actually were and that one made poor choices at the time. People often fantasize about all of the things they could have done differently after an event. They assume that other choices were available to them at the time ("I should have fought him" says the incest survivor referring to herself at age 4) or that the outcome would have been better than the option they chose ("If I fought him, I would have succeeded in stopping him" or "If only I had stacked the sandbags higher the flood wouldn't have gotten in"—ignoring the fact that there was no more time and no more sandbags). People often forget, after the fact, that they may have only had a split second to make a decision under conditions of high stress or emotion and physical peril.

Wrongdoing distortion refers to a false conclusion that one has acted in a way that was inconsistent with personal beliefs and, hence, he/she has violated his or her moral code. The person with a perception of personal wrongdoing may then conclude that they are bad or weak. If a soldier is scared during battle, he may conclude that he has failed to be a good soldier and is weak. A sexual abuse survivor who has lost her virginity during an assault or experiences sexual arousal may conclude that she is bad if virginity were important to her or if she believed that sexual arousal implies complicity. Sometimes, in traumatic events, there is no good choice and no matter what one does, a negative outcome will occur. The expression "damned if you do and damned if you don't" is apt. If your moral values are that killing is always wrong, but also that one should defend one's country and be patriotic, then if you are drafted into the military and are placed into a situation where you must kill or your fellow soldiers will be killed, you are placed into a difficult dilemma. You may experience guilt afterwards no matter what you do, especially if you overlook the fact that both sides of the dilemma were there at the time. The idea that you killed someone may take such prominence that you forget that there was no other good option. The choice was killer or traitor. The book and movie *Sophie's Choice* dramatically depicts a woman who could not live with the guilt of the decision that was forced upon her by the

Nazis: to choose which of her children would die. In both of these examples, the people have not violated their moral code. They did not intend the outcome and had no options available that were consistent with their moral codes.

Aside from the research above linking self-blame and PTSD, Kubany et al. (1995) found a strong relationship between both PTSD and depression and trauma-related guilt severity with both Vietnam veterans and battered women. With a sample of 58 Vietnam combat veterans, they found that common sources of guilt were concerned with: not having done more and an inability to prevent death and suffering of civilians and other Americans; accidental killing or harm to others; or brutality and excessive use of force. Common sources of guilt among 50 battered women were associated with: talking back or not being quiet; not doing something well enough that the abuser wanted; not acting on warning signs of abuse; negative effects on the children; personal inadequacies; causing the partner distress by leaving; calling the police or pressing charges; and not leaving or getting help sooner.

Accommodation and over-accommodation

Accommodation should be the process of adapting beliefs just enough to take in new incompatible information without becoming extreme. A successful accommodation following crime by an acquaintance might be, "I can't trust all people but there are many people I can trust" or "I can't control all events, but I do have a lot of influence over events in my life". Successful accommodation allows the person to accept and adjust to the unexpected experience and to be able to adapt better to other stressors in the future. However, it is possible that one can change beliefs about oneself or the world too much following trauma or that one is raised with extreme beliefs that will affect functioning. Resick and Schnicke (1992) referred to this overgeneralization of beliefs as over-accommodation. Over-accom-modated beliefs are extreme and maladaptive and serve to limit a person's life choices and relationships. Examples of over-accommo-dated beliefs are "I can't trust anyone", "I can't make good decisions for myself", or "The world is so dangerous that I can't go out anywhere and be safe".

McCann, Sakheim, and Abrahamson (1988) proposed that the beliefs that are most likely to be disrupted following trauma are beliefs regarding safety, trust, power/control, esteem, and intimacy. They proposed that these beliefs can be referent to oneself, others, or both. Furthermore, although in many cases positive beliefs may be shattered by trauma, it is also possible that due to prior traumas or poor child rearing, negative beliefs may be seemingly confirmed by a traumatic event. For example, if someone had been victimized by family members in childhood and learned to distrust people, a later victimization would appear to be "proof" that no one is to be trusted.

Several studies have examined the relationship between disrupted cognitions and symptoms following traumatic events. Resick developed a self-report inventory for rape victims called the Personal Beliefs and Reactions Scale (PBRS) based on five schema areas that were identified by McCann et al. (1988) as likely to become disrupted following trauma: safety, trust, power/control, esteem, and intimacy (Resick, Schnicke, & Markway, 1991). Each of these scales had items reflecting disrupted beliefs regarding oneself or others. In addition to the five schema areas, the PBRS also included subscales on rape beliefs, self-blame, and undoing (assimilation). Mechanic and Resick (1998) found that rape victims with PTSD had significantly more disrupted beliefs on all of the subscales except negative rape beliefs and control than rape victims who did not have PTSD. As might be expected, women who were raped by acquaintances had more disrupted beliefs regarding self-blame, trust, control, and intimacy than those were raped by strangers. Furthermore, following successful treatment, disruptions in beliefs improved.

Wenninger and Ehlers (1998) conducted two studies, one in the United States and one in Germany, to examine the relationship between cognitions and symptoms among victims of child sexual abuse also using the PBRS. They found that safety, trust, esteem, intimacy, and the overall scales of self and other were associated with PTSD symptoms, depression, and anxiety. Both samples had very similar levels of psychological disruption and showed the same relationship between negative cognitions and psychological symptoms.

Using a different methodology, Roth and her colleagues (Lebowitz & Newman, 1996; Newman, Riggs, & Roth, 1997; Roth & Newman, 1991, 1992, 1993) assessed post-trauma schemas, which they refer to as themes, by examining and coding unstructured interviews. Their coding system attempts to assess both the affective and cognitive themes that are listed in Box 6.1. assess the following themes: helplessness, rage, fear, loss, shame, guilt, diffuse affect, benign world, meaningful world, trustworthiness of people, self-worth, self-blame, reciprocity, alienation, and legitimacy. The interview is conducted to determine how much the trauma victim has resolved the particular

BOX 6.1 Description of affective and cognitive themes (from Newman et al., 1997, *Journal of Traumatic Stress, 10*, published by Plenum Publishing Corporation)

Helplessness: Feelings of absolute powerlessness during exposure to a traumatic event that may generalize beyond the actual moments of the traumatic event(s).

Rage: Anger and hostility may be manifested directly (e.g., at perpetrators) or indirectly (e.g., guilt about one's anger, avoiding and distancing oneself from anger, fearing expression of anger would further endanger the self or others).

Fear: Fright and terror during exposure and after exposure to a traumatic event may continue as well as from fear of the event(s) being repeated.

Loss: Grief, regret, and mourning regarding the way portions of one's life have been altered by a traumatic event.

Shame: Deep feelings of embarrassment, humiliation, and mortification for being exposed to traumatic events.

Guilt: Feelings of culpability, the emotional self-reproach for having any role in the event, as well as reactions prior, during, and subsequent to the event(s).

Diffuse affect: Intense non-specific emotions, such as pain, misery, discomfort, and hurt.

Benign world: Ideas and expectations that the world is malevolent, dangerous, and/or unrewarding.

Meaningful world: Ideas and expectations that the world is unpredictable, unfair, and out of one's control.

People trustworthy: Ideas and expectations of others being dangerous, unhelpful, unfair, capable of deception, betrayal, and exploitation, and generally untrustworthy.

Self worthy: Expectation that one is an incompetent and incapable person who is not equipped to handle traumatic and nontraumatic situations.

Self-blame: The cognition of holding oneself responsible for being exposed to traumatic events, or for responding in a certain way to the experiences.

Reciprocity: Belief that as a result of the trauma a person is not worthy of equal relationships in which they can both give and receive support and nurturance and, in more intimate relationships, love.

Alienation: Feeling one is different, disconnected, detached, and set apart from other people or from their own self-definition.

Legitimacy: Feeling deviant about one's reactions, that one's feelings are somehow not valid, and/or that one is crazy, over-reacting, or deficient in response to the traumatic event(s).

themes that are relevant to his/her experience. Newman et al. (1997) studied a sample of 84 treatment seekers who had experienced at least one traumatic event. They fell into three groups: those without PTSD, those with PTSD, and those with complex PTSD. Following the coding of the interviews, the researchers found that those with and without PTSD did not differ from each other in the number of unresolved or irrelevant themes except for the complex PTSD group. Those with complex PTSD had both more unresolved themes and fewer nonrelevant themes. Furthermore, when they divided the group into those with interpersonal traumas (incest, crime), versus those with noninterpersonal traumas (disasters, accidents), they found that those with interpersonal traumas reported the most unresolved themes. The researchers concluded that only those people with the most severe levels of PTSD were showing thematic disruptions. They also pointed out that because the coding system was developed on incest survivors that the coding categories might have been particularly sensitive to interpersonal traumas.

Social influences on reactions and recovery

Social support

How people are treated after a traumatic event may well affect how they recover. Contrast the images of VE or VJ day from old newsreels, in which people were dancing in the streets and honoring the WWII veterans, with the television images of soldiers returning from Vietnam being reviled by rioting students at home. Surely such differences in their homecomings had an impact on how veterans viewed their experiences and how welcomed they felt upon their return home. Compare the likely reactions of two rape victims. In one case, her parents say, "I'm so sorry that it happened. What can we do to help?" versus another case, in which her parents say, "What were you doing there to begin with? What were you wearing? Didn't I warn you?" How others respond to one's traumas can greatly influence how victims interpret the events and whether they continue to share their experiences and reactions or withdraw and isolate themselves.

Like coping and cognitions, social support may reflect pre-existing influences as well as post-trauma responses. Knowing that one has supportive family and friends prior to an event can affect whether someone even discloses that something happened, much less discussing how the event is affecting him or her. Knowing that family or friends have been unsupportive or even dysfunctional may lead the trauma survivor to attempt to handle the situation alone. Perhaps less-than-optimal relationships are acceptable in everyday life when there is nothing particularly stressful to cope with. However, in times of great stress and trauma, need for supportive others increases while the inadequacies of relationships become all too obvious and a distressing factor to contend with.

Murphy (1988) has pointed out that there are two alternative schools of thought on social support. One is that social support is developed and maintained over time. Such social support is an antecedent to stress and is said to protect people from negative outcomes. This view emphasizes that low levels of social support are in and of themselves stressful and that high levels of social support prevent negative health effects. The other view, usually referred to as the buffering hypothesis, is that social support is only relevant under conditions of high stress. In other words, low levels of support are not inherently stressful but under conditions of high stress, those with high social support do better.

Murphy (1988) observed that the frequent complication in studying social support following trauma is that the trauma itself may include the loss of important social figures. For example, if someone's trauma is the unexpected death of one's spouse, there is not only traumatic bereavement but also a loss of a usual source of support— the spouse. In major disasters, not only families and neighbors, but entire communities, may be lost or displaced. For battered women, part of the *modus operandi* of batterers is the systematic isolation of their partners. Not only is the person who should be their key attachment figure subjecting them to violence, but they are separated from other possible sources of support and assistance. In these cases, it is very difficult to sort out the effects of social support in mediating the trauma versus the loss of social support figures as part of the trauma.

Social support is typically measured in one of two ways, quantity or quality. Quantity refers to network size, the number of people the respondent has regular contact with (friends, family, social groups, or professional helpers such as therapists or clergy), and how frequently the person has contact with these people. Quality of social support is typically measured as how well the person perceives they do or could receive support from others.

Social support comes in many forms. Flannery (1990), in a review of social support and psychological trauma, lists four types of helpful support: emotional support, information, social companionship, and instrumental support. Emotional support is the ability to confide and express feelings to others and their ability to listen empathetically. Information may be focused on the practical (e.g., information on available services, assisting with applications for aid, or giving normalizing facts, e.g., "Flashbacks and nightmares are typical post-trauma symptoms"). Information could also be that the problem is insoluble or that there is nothing to be done now about the event but cope—information presented in a supportive manner. Social companionship does not focus on the stressor *per se* but the mere presence of others may reduce one's sense of isolation and helplessness as well as to provide meaning to daily events. Instrumental support includes active behaviors to assist the person in need. Examples of this would be neighbors pitching in to help someone clean up after a tornado hits a person's house, bringing food over after the death of a loved one, running errands for someone who is overwhelmed. Financial assistance may come from family, friends, or the government and may come in the form of loans or gifts as part of instrumental support.

Stress, support, and psychological or physical outcomes

There is a large body of literature that has demonstrated a connection between social support and either mental or physical health, particularly in conjunction with general life stress. Although the effects are not typically strong, there have been research findings connecting good social support and healthy outcomes in a wide array of daily life stressors (Flannery, 1990). For example this relationship has been observed with college students, inner-city children, unemployed workers, blue-collar workers, business executives, new mothers, widows, and patients and parents of children with serious medical conditions. The relationship between social support and life-stress outcomes has been found with both psychological outcomes such as lower depression and anxiety but also with physical health outcomes and recovery from medical procedures.

Research on social support and trauma

Along with the research on general stress, the research on traumatic stress has demonstrated a relationship between social support and trauma outcomes across populations. For example, Davidson et al. (1991) conducted a population study of PTSD in North Carolina with 2985 participants. The social support measure included network size, amount of social interaction, and perceived adequacy of support. Although there was no difference in network size, those with PTSD had less social interaction and less adequate social support.

Barrett and Mizes (1988) studied 52 Vietnam veterans with regard to both social support and combat exposure. Veterans who received high social support reported fewer symptoms of PTSD and depression than those with lower social support. There was no interaction with combat exposure, meaning that social support had an independent influence on symptoms.

Using a large data set from a study of Vietnam veterans conducted by the Center for Disease Control in the US, Boscarino (1995) examined the effect of social support among 2490 Vietnam veterans and 1972 era veterans. Boscarino examined PTSD, depression, anxiety disorders, and substance abuse/dependence, as well as current social support. He measured social support as a single score that combined contact and quality of support. He found that current social support levels are important predictors of current mental health status. Vietnam veterans with lower quality social support are more likely to have a current diagnosis of PTSD, general anxiety, depression, or alcohol abuse (but not drug abuse), even after controlling for level of combat exposure. Boscarino divided the Vietnam veterans into three groups: low, average, and high social support. He found that those with low social support had nearly an 80% greater risk of PTSD than veterans with average support but nearly a 180% greater risk than veterans with high social support. These social support effects were even greater for generalized anxiety and depression. Although Boscarino hypothe- sized that low social support prevents the reduction of distress that might come from contact with similar victims or supportive others, he also pointed out that the relationship could be in the opposite direction, that great and chronic distress may deplete social support.

Keane, Scott, Chavoya, Lamparski, and Fairbank (1985) found some evidence of the depletion of social support among those with PTSD. These researchers compared Vietnam combat veterans with PTSD, Vietnam combat veterans who were well adjusted, and Vietnam era veterans who were not in combat but who were currently hospitalized in a veteran's hospital. They assessed social support for three time periods: preliminary, post-military, and at the present. Keane et al. studied network size as well as different types of support such as material, physical, sharing, or advice. They found that all three groups reported similar preliminary social support. However, whereas the two comparison groups either stayed stable or increased their social support after the military, those with PTSD reported a decrease in social support.

The previous studies were retrospective studies that could have been affected by the participants' current perceptions. However, a prospective study reported similar findings. In a study of British survivors of a cruise ship disaster in Greece, Joseph, Yule, Williams, and Andrews (1993), found that support received from family and friends decreased significantly over 18 months following the disaster. They also found that crisis support in the immediate aftermath of the disaster predicted better psychological outcome over time.

Green, Grace, and Gleser (1985) also examined the effects of social support years after an event. These researchers studied 117 people who had survived a fire a year earlier in a supper club in Kentucky in which 165 people died. For the follow-up assessment, 67 people participated 2 years after the fire. The researchers examined whether the amount of social support and the helpfulness of the support were related to psychological distress, substance abuse, and symptoms. At both time periods poor social support was related to more negative outcomes.

Conte and Schuerman (1987) compared 369 sexually abused children with 318 children recruited from the community. They found that the victim having a supportive relationship with an adult and the family having characteristics of poor family functioning were good predictors of the outcomes for the children. If the child had a supportive relationship with a nonoffending adult, he/she tended to do better. If the family showed more signs of dysfunction, he/she did worse.

Williams, Hodgkinson, Joseph, and Yule (1995) examined how negative attitudes toward emotional expression would be associated with higher levels of symptoms and lower level of received support. Williams et al. studied 73 survivors of a capsized ferry in Belgium in which, out of a total of 600 passengers and crew aboard, 193 died. The research participants were assessed 3 years later. Participants were given four questions that were summed: (1) I think you should always keep your feelings under control; (2) I think you should not burden other people with your problems; (3) I think getting emotional is a sign of weakness; and (4) I think other people don't understand your feelings. They found that the more that people endorsed those statements the more symptomatic they were and the lower the social support they received, reflecting the problem with keeping a "stiff upper lip".

Although there is clearly a relationship between social support and psychological symptoms following trauma, it has not been determined what the direction of the relationship might be. It is possible that poor social support affects how the victim of trauma processes and copes with the event. However, it is also possible that, because of the avoidance and withdrawal that accompany PTSD, victims isolate themselves from possible sources of support. It is also possible that having an ongoing problem such as PTSD or depression results in diminished support over time, that is, victims may wear out their supporters eventually. The problem with studying the effects of social support at any one given point in time is that support may wax or wane depending upon the apparent needs of the victims and their willingness to accept help and support. Social support is an ongoing process that reflects an interaction between people and is not easily captured in most cross-sectional research projects.

Summary

This chapter examined the effects of post-trauma coping, cognitions, and social support on reactions to and recovery from trauma. Attempts at coping reflect, in essence, the need to reduce distress, and are therefore only relevant to those who are distressed. Once a person has recovered from a traumatic event, there is no need to cope. However, it appears that active engagement with the problem at hand is a better method of coping than disengagement. Withdrawal and avoidance are consistently associated with greater post-trauma distress and failure to recover. An important aspect of coping is related to the meanings that are attached to the traumatic event. The more someone attributes blame to him/herself and feels guilt, the greater the distress and symptoms are likely to be. If someone attempts to keep his or her view of self or world intact by distorting the event (assimilation), there is also likely to be more distress if this is not successful. Furthermore, overgeneralizing beliefs ("No one can be trusted") in an attempt to feel safer is likely to result in greater anxiety and distress rather than recovery. Supportive people in the victim's life may help reduce cognitive distortions and assist with coping. However, victims sometimes, perhaps due to shame, guilt, or PTSD avoidance, isolate themselves from the very people who may be able to assist in recovery, resulting in a vicious cycle of distress and withdrawal, faulty attributions, and loss of support, resulting in chronic symptoms.

Treatment of traumatic stress reactions 7

Appropriate treatment for trauma depends upon a number of factors. Many people who have experienced a traumatic event recover naturally and do not need psychological or psychiatric treatment at all. Having supportive family and friends may be sufficient. For those with an adjustment disorder, stronger reactions but not a specific disorder such as PTSD or depression, general counseling or psychotherapy may be helpful. These types of therapy provide support, empathy, and an environment in which a person can explore the meaning of the event in the context of his or her life. As reactions become more severe and chronic, more specific interventions may be necessary. Comorbidity of two or more disorders also may complicate the treatment picture. The remainder of this chapter will describe approaches to treatment that are typically offered in response to trauma. Research evaluating these approaches will be provided where available. Somewhat more attention will be given to cognitive behavioral therapies because these therapy procedures are more specifically detailed and have been researched more thoroughly at this point. Nearly all of the available research and specific treatments have focused on PTSD rather than other trauma-related disorders, although many studies have examined the outcomes with other types of symptoms beyond those of PTSD.

Biological treatments

Medication is frequently offered by primary-care physicians and psychiatrists to deal with some of the symptoms that are problematic for trauma survivors. There are specific medications available for depression and anxiety. However, there is no medication that has been designed to treat the range of symptoms of PTSD. Researchers are now examining the effectiveness of medications that were developed to treat other disorders on the symptoms of PTSD. Because there appears to be dysregulation of a number of neurobiological systems among those with PTSD, pharmacotherapy (drug therapy) research has thus far only focused on one or another of the affected systems, but no one has yet studied how medications may best be combined for optimal effect. In fact, at this time there have only been fewer than a dozen controlled studies of pharmacotherapy for PTSD. Other reports of noncontrolled, nonblind studies (called open trials) have reported some promising findings, however. At this point in time, although PTSD treatment has not been well researched, research on medical intervention for acute stress disorder or the dissociative disorders is all but nonexistent.

In a review of psychopharmacological treatment of PTSD, Davidson and van der Kolk (1996) described principal goals of medications in PTSD. They are:

(1) Reduction of frequency and/or severity of intrusive symptoms.
(2) Reduction in the tendency to interpret incoming stimuli as recurrences of the trauma.
(3) Reduction in conditioned hyperarousal to stimuli reminiscent of the trauma, as well as in generalized hyperarousal.
(4) Reduction in avoidance behavior.
(5) Improvement in depressed mood and numbing.
(6) Reduction in psychotic or dissociative symptoms.
(7) Reduction of impulsive aggression against self and others.

Thus far, the systems that have received the most attention are the adrenergic, serotonergic, and benzodiazepine systems. The adrenergic system has been implicated with PTSD, and there is a great deal of research to indicate that those with PTSD have excessive adrenergic activity. Two drugs, clonidine and propranolol, have both been shown to reduce sympathetic arousal and adrenergic activity. Although there have only been a few open trials with these two medications (Kinzie & Leung, 1989; Kolb, Burris, & Griffiths, 1984; Perry, 1994), they appear promising in reducing traumatic nightmares, intrusive recollections, hypervigilence, insomnia, startle reactions, and angry outbursts; in other words, they appear to best affect the re-experiencing and arousal symptoms.

Several studies have indicated that serotonin abnormalities may be present in PTSD patients (Friedman & Southwick, 1995). In addition to the core symptoms of PTSD, serotonin has also been associated with symptoms that are frequently comorbid with PTSD, such as depression, suicidal ideation, impulsivity, substance abuse, and aggression. As a result, two controlled clinical trials (Brady et al., 2000; van der Kolk et al., 1994) and a number of open trials have examined selective serotonin reuptake inhibitors (SSRIs) such as fluoxetine (Prozac), sertraline (Zoloft) and fluvoxamine. Brady et al. (2000) conducted a well-designed, double-blind, controlled study in which sertraline was compared to a placebo control in 187 PTSD-positive civilian outpatients. Findings indicated that sertraline produced significantly greater improvements on PTSD avoidance/numbing and arousal scores than the placebo group.

Together, these studies have reported reductions in overall PTSD symptoms and in all three categories of symptoms: intrusion, arousal, and avoidance. The SSRIs have been the only medications that have found improvements in the numbing symptoms separate from depression.

There are two types of medications that affect both the adrenergic and serotonergic systems: tricyclic antidepressants (TCAs) and monoamine oxidase inhibitors (MAOIs). The majority of controlled psychopharmacology studies for PTSD in the literature have involved TCAs or MAOIs. The TCAs most frequently studied are imipramine, amitriptyline, and desipramine, while the MAOI usually studied has been phenelzine. These medications are effective for both depression and anxiety so their application to PTSD is a natural extension. Southwick et al. (1994) conducted a statistical analysis to examine the results of 15 studies on TCAs and MAOIs and found that these antidepressants were relatively effective for the re-experiencing symptoms but were not helpful for the avoidance and arousal symptoms.

Finally, although there is very little research, benzodiazepines such as alprazolam and clonazepam are frequently prescribed. These anti-anxiety agents, called anxiolytic drugs, are associated with reductions in anxiety and fear. There have been only a few studies of benzodiazepines in the treatment of PTSD and they have found improvements in anxiety, insomnia, irritability, and hyperarousal. Although critical of the lack of research and concerned about possible withdrawal and rebound effects when these anti-anxiety agents are removed, Davidson and van der Kolk (1996) and Friedman and Southwick (1995) have argued that there is a place for the benzo-diazipines when carefully regulated, particularly for the management of startle and hyperarousal symptoms in concert with other medications. However, they and others recommend the SSRI medications as the best option at this time.

Medication may help to relieve the severity of symptoms and may allow the affected person to sleep and to function. However, medication should not be considered a cure for these disorders. If the trauma survivor is using the reduction in anxiety or depression to further avoid dealing with the trauma memory, it is likely that these symptoms will re-emerge when the medication is discontinued. Medications also have a number of side-effects that may be troublesome. The greatest benefit of medication may be that it may assist a person to benefit from therapy (or from processing the trauma in other ways) without becoming overwhelmed.

Crisis intervention: A preventive approach

Crisis counseling was developed in the 1960s and 1970s along with crisis theory. Crisis theory presumed that the traumatic event upsets the person's homeostasis. Because usual coping mechanisms and strategies are overwhelmed due to the severity of the event, the person will either begin to develop new adaptive or maladaptive strategies. In either case, the distress will subside in about 6 to 8 weeks. Crisis intervention is a supportive therapy in which the client is helped to develop appropriate coping skills to deal with the event at hand. Although research on specific traumas such as rape dispelled the short time frame for recovery that was proposed by crisis theory, crisis intervention lives on. Most rape crisis centers and victim assistance agencies have a crisis orientation and emphasize brief counseling and supportive forms of therapy. Although crisis intervention may well be helpful in reducing or shortening trauma reactions, especially in those who do not develop diagnosable disorders, there is not much research demonstrating the efficacy of crisis intervention in trauma populations. Crisis counseling has been found to be helpful with the death of a partner (Parkes, 1980; Raphael, 1977) and accidents (Bordow & Porritt, 1979).

There is currently an intriguing study underway that may provide support for immediate intervention for rape victims. Based on prior research that high levels of distress immediately after the crime may be one of the best predictors of the development of PTSD, Resnick, Acierno, Holmes, Kilpatrick, and Jager (1999) have designed an intervention intended to reduce distress during the post-rape forensic medical examination at the hospital. Resnick et al. randomly assigned participants to treatment as usual (meeting with a rape crisis counselor and then the medical examination) or treatment as usual plus viewing a 17-minute videotape. The videotape has two components: one intended to provide information to reduce distress during the medical examination and the other to provide information intended to help prevent PTSD, depression, panic, and substance abuse.

In preliminary findings, Resnick et al. (1999) reported that those who viewed the videotape did report less distress during the medical examination and were able to retain the medical information they received during the examination better than those who had not viewed the videotape. Although the study is still ongoing, there is some preliminary evidence that this procedure may result in lower levels of distress at follow-up.

Critical incident stress debriefing (CISD) has been developed to deal with groups of people after a disaster subsequent to the crisis intervention movement of the 1970s. CISD focuses particularly on emergency workers, although it has been used with the victims of disaster as well. It evolved from military interventions to reduce impact of combat trauma with the purpose of returning the soldiers to the combat arena. CISD has been adapted to civilian disaster situations to assist workers in the aftermath (Mitchell, 1983). Usually CISD lasts several hours at one sitting and includes the following components:

(1) Introduction, with orientation to the process.
(2) Fact phase, in which group members describe their roles and tasks during the incident and provide facts for each other about what occurred.
(3) Thought phase, in which the group members are asked to remember their first thoughts during the incident.
(4) Reaction phase, during which members talk about the worst part of the experience and express their feelings.
(5) Symptom phase, in which members are asked to review their own physical, emotional, behavioral, and cognitive symptoms during the event and after.
(6) Teaching phase, where the debriefers provide information about the normalcy of these reactions and teach coping strategies and general health issues.
(7) Relating phase that closes the meeting and provides a summary and recommendations.

There are other models for stress debriefing (Armstrong, O'Callahan, & Marmar, 1991; Young, 1988). These vary with regard to the amount of teaching or client disclosure, but they all focus on providing information and assisting clients with coping in the immediate aftermath of trauma with the view toward prevention of longer-term problems. Some research projects have focused on individual rather than group intervention (Rose, Brewin, Andrews, & Kirk, 1999).

Although studies have varied somewhat with regard to the exact procedures implemented, there is growing outcome research at this point that single session interventions do not usually have the intended effect of preventing PTSD whether conducted in groups or individually. A few researchers have found CISD and other debriefing procedures to be helpful (Chemtob, Tomas, Law, & Cremniter, 1997; Ersland, Weisaeth, & Sund, 1989; Hytten & Hasle, 1989). However, at least 10 other studies have not found these interventions to be effective in preventing post-trauma symptomatology, or have found that those who received the interventions were doing worse than those who did not receive counseling (e.g., Bisson, Jenkins, Alexander, & Bannister, 1997; Kenardy et al., 1996; Rose et al., 1999).

Although one-session interventions may be too short to be effective, other early intervention techniques may hold more promise. Foa, Hearst-Ikeda, and Perry (1995) reported on the preliminary findings of a therapeutic intervention to prevent the development of PTSD in female rape and assault victims. This brief intervention was successful in reducing the symptoms of PTSD and depression beyond what would be expected during the natural recovery window. Although this study could be described in the later section on cognitive-behavioral interventions, because the focus was on prevention of chronic PTSD, in seems appropriate to describe it here. Rather than basing the therapy on crisis intervention or CISD, the intervention adapts a successful treatment for chronic PTSD to the immediate aftermath.

The intervention consists of four, 2-hour therapy sessions. During the first meeting, the therapist gathers information regarding symptoms and beliefs and presents an overview of the program. Normal reactions to trauma are described and the therapist makes note of any distorted beliefs the clients have regarding themselves or the world that are related to their experience. The therapist and clients also generate a list of situations and people who are objectively safe but the clients are avoiding.

In the second meeting, the list of avoided situations and people is organized into a hierarchy, based on the level of anxiety each item produces. The client is trained in relaxation and deep breathing. Next, a rationale for imaginal exposure is presented and then the client is asked to recall the experience aloud in present tense. While the client recounts the event, the therapist makes note of any distorted cognitions regarding self or world. Following the exposure component, the client and therapist engage in a Socratic dialogue (leading clients to understand their reasoning processes and beliefs through questions) to examine the accuracy of these beliefs. The client is sent home with an audiotape of the session with instructions to listen to it several times during the week and to confront daily some of the situations from the list.

During the third meeting, the client and therapist begin with a review of the homework followed by 45 minutes of imaginal exposure. The remainder of the session is devoted to cognitive restructuring. The client is given homework to listen to the audiotape everyday, to confront feared situations, and to use a daily diary to monitor negative thoughts, feelings, and cognitive distortions. At the fourth meeting, the client is again asked to engage in imaginal exposure (30 minutes), followed by cognitive restructuring for 45 minutes, using the homework records. The therapist reviews the skills the client has learned.

Results showed that at 2 months post-assault, victims who received the behavioral program (BP) had significantly less severe PTSD symptoms than victims in the control condition; 10% of the former group met criteria for PTSD as compared to 70% of the latter group; 5½ months post-assault, victims in the BP group were significantly less depressed than victims in the control group and had significantly less severe re-experiencing symptoms.

Bryant, Harvey, Dang, Sackville, and Basten (1998) conducted the first treatment study of acute stress disorder (ASD). Given that ASD predicts who will develop subsequent PTSD, the researchers were interested to see if early treatment of those with ASD would decrease the incidence of PTSD at post-treatment and at 6 months follow-up. Twenty-four victims of motor vehicle or industrial accidents in Australia were given five sessions of either cognitive behavior therapy (CBT) or supportive counseling within 2 weeks of their trauma. At post-treatment, only 8% of the CBT group met the criteria for PTSD compared to 83% of the supportive therapy group. At 6 months follow-up, 17% of the CBT group had PTSD, while 67% of the supportive therapy group had PTSD. The CBT treatment consisted of relaxation training, cognitive restructuring, and both imaginal and *in vivo* (live, in the environment) exposure. The supportive counseling condition included education about trauma, general problem-solving skills, and social support.

Psychodynamic therapies

Because Freud came to believe that the stories of abuse he heard from his patients were all fantasies and that neuroses were caused by intrapsychic conflicts rather than environmental sources, psycho-analytic and psychodynamic therapists paid little attention to treatment of trauma until the 1980s. However, modern psychodynamic thinking and therapy are much more attuned to the effects of environmental stressors on the clients' concept of themselves and others.

Beginning with Horowitz (1976) and his work on bereavement, psychodynamic therapy has taken a more cognitive approach to treatment, with the exploration of self and other schemas and the conflict produced by the trauma. In contrast to cognitive behavioral therapists, psychodynamic therapists place relatively more emphasis on the therapeutic relationship, transference and countertransference, and on developmental issues. However, both the psychodynamic and cognitive approaches have strong similarities with regard to the impact of the traumatic event on important beliefs and meanings for the client. The therapies that focus on helping the client derive more healthy meanings for the event, to help them reconstruct the event, are called constructivist theories and therapies (Herman, 1992b; McCann & Pearlman, 1990).

Lindy (1996) emphasized the importance of the re-experiencing symptoms and the client's tendency toward repetition of the trauma. Because the trauma memory intrudes into the present, it will intrude into the environment and relationship between the therapist and client. When the reenactment, or transference, of the traumatic material occurs within the safe environment of the therapy rela-tionship ("a secure holding environment"), the client and therapist can work through or come to understand how the trauma affected the client's inner sense of self. Lindy (1996) and van der Kolk, McFarlane, and van der Hart (1996) point out that the trauma memory must be transformed from a jumble of dissociated nonverbal images, sensations, and emotions to a narrative story. From there, the meanings of the event itself, the effects of prior traumas or early experiences and conflicts, and current relationships can be explored.

All psychodynamic therapists emphasize the importance of the therapeutic relationship (e.g., Lindy, 1996; Marmar et al., 1995; van der Kolk et al., 1996) as the crucial mechanism through which change is effected. Marmar et al. point out that when the clients retell their stories in the presence of a skilled therapist who remains calm, compassionate, and nonjudgmental, the situation begins to depressurize. Through this strong therapeutic alliance the client can continue to reduce the emotional toxicity of the event and put it into perspective with regard to prior experiences, current beliefs, and future expectations and goals.

Marmar et al. (1995), also have pointed out the distinction between simple or uncomplicated PTSD, PTSD with comorbid Axis I disorders, and complex PTSD, which they call a post-traumatic personality disorder. Uncomplicated PTSD can proceed as a brief therapy with the following steps: establishing a therapeutic alliance; focusing on self-concepts; working through conflicts; linkage of the presenting trauma with prior traumas; and attention to transference and countertransference. For those with comorbid Axis I disorders, treatment for PTSD proceeds the same way but the Axis I disorders are treated simultaneously with the PTSD. The one exception to this is substance abuse/dependence that must be treated prior to PTSD-focused therapy.

Treatment of complex PTSD, or PTSD personality disorder, is a much slower process that may be interspersed with hospitalizations for acute crisis, medication for affect regulation, and a multimodal approach including group therapy, family therapy, interpersonal skills training, and relapse prevention for substance abuse problems. Complex PTSD is more likely in people who were chronically or repeatedly abused in the context of childhood family abuse or war. PTSD effects generalize to all areas of functioning as a result of decades of untreated and unprocessed trauma that were inflicted during important developmental periods. As such, clients with complex PTSD exhibit severe problems with affect regulation, identity, interpersonal and vocational functioning, and dissociative reactions (Herman, 1992a; van der Kolk, 1996). The person with this array of symptoms may be diagnosed with borderline or narcissistic personality disorder. If the dissociative reactions are of sufficient magnitude that the person developed alternate identities, he/she may be diagnosed with dissociative identity disorder. A number of books have been written about treatment of dissociative identity disorder (multiple personality disorder) from a psychodynamic perspective (e.g., Putnam, 1989).

Both the treatment of personality disorders and dissociative disorders reflect a slow uncovering process of the traumatic material in the context of a strong therapeutic alliance. Trauma therapists are much more active and directive in intervening with maladaptive behavior than is typically seen in traditional psychoanalysis. However, the mechanism for change is still viewed within the transference of traumatic memories and relationships into the therapeutic environment where it is processed in the context of a safe, nonjudgmental relationship between client and therapist. It is believed that once the traumatic memories have been shared and digested, that dissociative boundaries will no longer be needed and the dissociative defense mechanisms will less frequently be activated.

Unfortunately, although there is anecdotal and case study information that psychodynamic therapy for trauma-related problems is effective, there is little controlled research to support this belief. However, in one study, Brom, Kleber, and Defares (1989) conducted a large-scale controlled study with 112 trauma survivors who were randomly assigned to systematic desensitization, psychodynamic treatment, hypnotherapy, and a waiting-list control group. Results showed that all three therapies proved more effective than the waiting-list control group in decreasing PTSD symptoms, and general psychopathology, but the three therapies were not significantly different from each other. The authors speculated that the similarity of results in the three treatment conditions may be due to the similarity in the behavior of the therapists, which they did not measure directly. Another interesting finding in this study was that the treatments also brought about changes in the more stable personality measures.

Cognitive-behavioral therapies

Descriptions of treatments

Coping skills: Stress inoculation training. Cognitive-behavioral therapies are rooted in learning theories, especially classical conditioning and operant avoidance. Early studies on sexual assault survivors, predating the concept of PTSD, focused exclusively on fear and anxiety reactions (Burgess & Holmstrom, 1974a, b; Calhoun et al., 1982; Kilpatrick, Resick, & Veronen, 1981; Kilpatrick & Veronen, 1984). The first treatment approach to be proposed for treating trauma-related symptoms was Stress Inoculation Training (SIT; Kilpatrick et al., 1982; Resick & Jordan, 1988; Veronen & Kilpatrick, 1983). SIT is a cognitive-behavioral treatment package originally developed by Meichenbaum (1974) for the management of anxiety. The goals of SIT are to help clients understand and manage their trauma-related fear reactions, resulting in decreased avoidance behavior. The reduction in avoidance of fear-producing stimuli was assumed to result in the extinction or habituation of these strong fear and anxiety reactions. The SIT protocol consists of three phases: education, skill-building, and application. SIT protocols range from 8 to 20 sessions depending on the needs of the client and the research study, but all versions use essentially the same component techniques. SIT can be conducted in either group or individual format.

The first session or two are the educational phase. Clients are given an explanation for their trauma symptoms based upon two-factor theory (classical conditioning of fears and escape or avoidance of fear cues). They are taught to identify their different modes (or channels) of response including emotions, behaviors, physical reactions, and thoughts. The therapist gives an overview of treatment to describe how the clients will be taught coping skills for each of the channels. During the application phase, clients are asked to practice and then engage these skills in their environment order to reduce their fear and anxiety in safe situations.

Usually, the first skill that is introduced during the skill-building phase is relaxation training. Clients are first taught progressive muscle relaxation and are asked to practice this during and between sessions. The use of relaxing imagery is also introduced. During the relaxation training sessions, the therapist also helps the clients identify where they tend to carry their stress (e.g., neck, jaw, etc.) and help them identify cues that trigger fear reactions. Finally, the clients are usually trained in some form of brief relaxation that they can use quickly and anywhere. The relaxation skills are introduced to assist in three channels of response: physical, emotional, and cognitive.

Coping skills designed to address the cognitive mode of response include thought stopping, covert rehearsal, problem solving, and guided self-dialogue (Kilpatrick et al., 1982; Resick & Jordan, 1988; Resnick & Newton, 1992). Thought stopping (Wolpe, 1958) is used to manage intrusive or obsessional thoughts that promote anxiety. Clients are taught that when they begin worrying, they are to say "stop" out loud at first, and eventually silently, to stop the circular thinking. Then they are instructed to redirect their thinking, perhaps to problem-solving steps or to factual danger assessment. Guided self-dialogue and cognitive restructuring both help the client identify irrational, faulty, or maladaptive thinking patterns and replace them with more positive and adaptive cognitions. Problem-solving skills help clients to generate and evaluate potential options.

Finally, role playing and covert modeling address behavioral avoidance. Both teach the client how to communicate effectively and resolve problems using appropriate social skills. During covert modeling, clients can imagine situations in which they are likely to experience fear reactions. They can imagine using the coping strategies they have been taught in these situations. Covert modeling is used as a practice step before clients engage in actual situations. Presumably, the cognitive rehearsal will decrease the likelihood of avoidance responses.

In the third phase of treatment, clients learn how to apply these coping skills step-by-step in daily situations that provoke anxiety. The steps of stress inoculation include: (1) assessing the probability of the feared event (including the discrimination of dangerous from safe situations; (2) managing avoidance behavior and fear reactions with cognitive restructuring, guided self-dialogue, and brief relaxation; (3) engaging in the feared behavior using problem-solving skills and skills learned via role-playing and covert modeling; (4) reinforcing oneself for using skills in the feared situation (Meichenbaum, 1974). Before ending treatment, the therapist helps the clients generate a fear hierarchy of events not addressed directly in therapy, which the clients are assigned to continue working on afterwards with these skills.

Exposure-based treatments. Just as SIT was developed originally for the treatment of general anxiety, the exposure therapies were developed to treat specific anxiety disorders, such as phobias or obsessive-compulsive disorder. Inasmuch as PTSD has been conceptualized as an anxiety disorder, then it is logical to adapt treatments for those disorders to trauma reactions.

Systematic desensitization (SD), developed by Wolpe (1958) for the treatment of phobias, has been attempted with trauma survivors, for the most part as single case studies or uncontrolled trials. In this treatment, the therapist and client generate a hierarchy of fear cues that resulted from the traumatic event or generalized from conditioned cues. Clients are exposed in imagination gradually, to increasingly fear-producing images. In SD, the client is trained in using relaxation skills, and is then confronted with fear cues in imagination, along a graded hierarchy, while in a relaxed state. Within each session, the exposures are brief, repetitive, and exclusively focused on one fear cue alone. Mastery of low-level fear cues are followed by exposure to the next cue higher up within the hierarchy.

Another exposure technique, called flooding or direct therapeutic exposure (DTE), was also introduced in the early 1980s in the treatment of PTSD. Flooding differs from SD in that the exposures are based on extended exposure to moderate or strong fear-producing cues. In addition to confronting fear cues in imagination, flooding also involves confrontation with the conditioned fear cues *in vivo*. A specific exposure protocol for PTSD, called prolonged exposure (PE) was the first flooding therapy that focused the imaginal exposures, not on current fear cues, but on remembering the traumatic event in detail (Foa, Rothbaum, Riggs, & Murdock, 1991). PE combines repeated detailed prolonged recall of the traumatic event with behavioral exposures outside of therapy.

The treatment protocol for PE usually consists of nine 90-minute sessions that include breathing retraining for relaxation, imaginal exposures to the entire trauma memory and *in vivo* exposures to trauma-related current cues. The first two sessions are devoted to information gathering, education about PTSD, explanations of treatment rationale, treatment planning, and breathing retraining. The remaining seven sessions focus on both imaginal and *in vivo* exposures. During the therapy sessions, the clients are asked to close their eyes, and to relive what happened to them aloud in the present tense with as much detail as possible, including sensory details (sights, smells, sounds, sensations), as well as emotions and thoughts. Usually, the exposure is repeated two or three times in each session depending on the length of the account. Sessions are audiotaped and clients listen to the tapes everyday between sessions, along with 45 minutes of *in vivo* exposure. During each exposure (every 10 minutes) and at home, clients are asked to keep a record of their anxiety levels using Subjective Units of Distress (SUDS) ratings ("On a scale from 0 to 100, how distressed are you?"). During initial exposures, anxiety is expected to be high. With repeated exposures in the safe therapy setting, anxiety diminishes.

In vivo exposures consist of instructions to gradually confront safe situations that evoke moderate levels of anxiety and then follow up with confrontations of more fearful situations. Subjective Units of Distress are assessed within the exposures to monitor emotional processing, and subsequent habituation (decrease) of anxiety. Although the *in vivo* exposures may be conducted alone, the client is encouraged to begin with a coach, a trusted person who can accompany the client through exposures.

> Marilyn sought treatment 1 year after an automobile accident that left her with chronic back and neck pain as well as PTSD. During a rainstorm, Marilyn was struck

from the rear just after she came to a stop at a stoplight. Her car was forced into the car in front of her. Because of her injuries, Marilyn did not attempt to drive for several months following the accident. When she did begin driving again, she was quite anxious and spent more time looking in her rearview mirror than the road ahead. Whenever she had to come to a stop, her heart began racing and she braced herself for a crash. Occasionally she had flashbacks of her accident, particularly on rainy days. She had occasional nightmares and expressed feelings of helplessness. Marilyn refused to drive after dark or during rainy weather, which nearly resulted in her losing her job due to absenteeism. It was her need for employment and the eroding of support from family and friends that brought her into treatment.

Treatment consisted of imaginal and behavioral exposure. Although her re-experiencing symptoms and emotions regarding the accident diminished during the imaginal exposure, and she made some progress driving in the evening, Marilyn continued to look into the rearview mirror so much that the therapist feared she would have another accident. In order to help her with this, the therapist had the client drive around quiet university campus parking lots with the rearview mirrors covered. Although she was initially quite anxious, Marilyn's fear diminished and she grew more comfortable. In the process of doing these exposures, Marilyn realized that during the accident she had looked back but there wasn't anything she could have done to prevent the accident. She also realized that looking back excessively would not prevent an accident, but might actually precipitate one. She and the therapist discussed how frequently Marilyn might safely glance into her mirrors and she practiced more moderate behavior. By the end of treatment, Marilyn was no longer reporting PTSD symptoms although she did report having some lingering tension on rainy days. She was not avoiding driving, however, and had not missed any work due to avoidance.

Marks, Lovell, Noshirvani, Livanou, and Thrasher (1998) have conducted exposure therapy somewhat differently than Foa, Rothbaum et al. (1991). Their version of the therapy includes five sessions of imaginal exposure and then five sessions of live exposure. During the imaginal exposure, clients are asked to relive the experience aloud in first person present tense about the details of their experience and then to imagine and describe critical aspects of the event (rewind and hold). Clients listen to their therapy tapes daily between sessions. During the live exposure portion of therapy, clients (most often therapist-accompanied) progress through a hierarchy of trauma-related stimuli that are feared, avoided, and disabling. They are asked to practice the live exposure for an hour a day between sessions.

Cognitive-behavioral therapy techniques. Cognitive processing therapy (CPT) was developed in order to facilitate the expression of affect and the appropriate accommodation of the traumatic event with more general schemas regarding oneself and the world (Resick & Schnicke, 1992, 1993). Resick and Schnicke (1992) argued that PTSD is not just focused on one emotion, fear. Other strong emotions such as anger, humiliation, shame, and sadness may well result from the trauma. Furthermore, they also emphasized the content of the meaning elements as an important focus. Drawing upon the work of cognitive and constructivist theorists, Resick and Schnicke proposed that beliefs about the traumatic event might become distorted (assimilation) in the victim's attempt to maintain old beliefs and schemas about themselves and the world. However, although accommodation of the new event into the person's memory and beliefs is desirable, over-accommodation (overgeneralization) may lead to extreme distortions about the safety or trustability of others or overly harsh judgments about oneself. Resick (1995) has proposed that the normal and expected emotions that would likely result from danger, loss, and inflicted harm as those that will abate through exposure. However, emotions that are the product of distorted thinking (e.g., "I should have prevented the event", leading to guilt and shame) may continue to be manufactured and will not necessarily habituate. Resick proposed direct intervention into the meaning elements as an important component of therapy.

Developed originally for use with rape and crime victims, CPT was adapted from basic cognitive techniques explicated by Beck and Emery (1985). However, whereas Beckian cognitive therapy usually focuses on challenging current maladaptive beliefs, CPT begins with the trauma memory and focuses on feelings, beliefs, and thoughts that directly emanated from the traumatic event. The therapist then helps the clients examine whether the trauma appeared to disrupt or confirm beliefs prior to this experience, and how much the clients have overgeneralized (over-accommodated) from the event to their beliefs about themselves and the world. Clients are then taught to challenge their own self-statements and to modify their extreme beliefs to bring them into balance.

After an educational session in which the symptoms of PTSD are described and explained with information processing theory, clients are asked to consider and write about what it means to them that the event happened. After reading and discussing the impact statement in session two with an eye toward identifying problematic beliefs and cognitions (stuck points), clients are then taught to identify the connection between events, thoughts, and feelings and to practice at home with worksheets. The next two sessions of therapy are for the client to recall the trauma in detail and to access their affect as well as their beliefs. Clients are asked to write an account of the event including thoughts, feelings, and sensory details. Clients read the account to the therapist and reread it daily. After rewriting the account, the therapy moves into the cognitive challenging phase. Using a Socratic style of therapy, the therapist teaches clients to ask questions regarding their assumptions and self-statements in order to begin challenging them. Clients are then taught how to use work-sheets to challenge and replace maladaptive thoughts and beliefs. In the early stages of the cognitive therapy, the focus is typically on the client's self-blame and attempts to undo the event after the fact (assimilation). In the final five sessions, the therapy progresses systematically through common areas of cognitive disruption: safety, trust, control, esteem, and intimacy. Over-accommodated beliefs on these themes are challenged with regard to both self and others.

> After going to a movie one night, David was accosted by two young men in a dark parking lot. They asked him for money. When he refused, one of the young men pulled out a knife. David swore at them and turned to run. The young man with the knife suddenly lunged at him and stabbed him in the shoulder. The two men ran away after grabbing his wallet. Two years after the incident, David was referred to therapy by his sister who was concerned because he seemed depressed.
>
> The therapist diagnosed both PTSD and depression. In addition to the assault, David reported that as a child he had been physically and emotionally abused by his father, who was an alcoholic. Although David had never used

alcohol before, he found himself drinking in the evening, particularly before going to bed. He expressed fear of becoming like his father. Cognitive processing therapy was implemented. When David wrote his statement about the meaning of the event, it became clear that David was harboring a great deal of self-blame for the incident. He kept playing over in his mind ways he could have handled the situation differently or more heroically. It was also evident that he was fearful of going out, was ashamed that he was fearful, and had begun judging himself harshly in many ways. David was afraid that if others knew how he felt, they would ridicule or reject him. As a result, he withdrew socially and became more and more depressed.

Aside from exposure through writing about and reading over his account of the incident, David learned to challenge his self-blame about the crime through a series of assignments with worksheets. He came to realize that blame belonged to the assailants, not to him, and that their behavior was not predictable or controllable by his actions or inactions. He also realized that he had been assuming other people were all sharing his harsh self-judgments; that he had been "mindreading" rather than finding out what the people in his life actually thought. Through the cognitive therapy, David began to identify negative patterns of thinking that predated the assault and prob-ably resulted from the childhood abuse. He was able to challenge these beliefs, not only with regard to the assault, but the child abuse as well. As he began to reassess his thoughts and assumptions and replace them with more balanced beliefs, his PTSD symptoms and depression began to lift and he had less desire to drink. David began to reconnect with friends and family and was able to resume going out without difficulty.

Research has also focused on adapting the current therapeutic techniques in the development of cognitive-behavioral packages for the treatment of PTSD in sexually abused children. Deblinger, McLeer, and Henry (1990) have developed a 12-session cognitive behavioral intervention program that includes modeling/coping skills training, gradual exposure, followed by education/prevention training. In the modeling/coping skills part, the therapist models calm behavior to abuse-related disclosures. Coping skills training helps the children to express their emotions effectively and cope with anxiety. Also, relaxation skills and mediated self-talk help children cope with abuse-related anxiety. In the second part, consisting of graded exposure, the children are encouraged to use coping strategies while confronting abuse-related memories. The therapist also offers alternative exposure methods, such as imagery, doll play, drawing, reading, letter writing, poetry, and singing. The children are allowed to pick the exposure technique of their choice so as to help them regain a sense of control. The third part involves education/ prevention training which is provided to help the children make sense of their abusive experiences and to identify and respond more effectively to inappropriate advances or interactions in the future. The treatment program also included a non-offending parent intervention consisting of several cognitive-behavioral strategies as well. The aim of this component is to help the parents behaviorally analyze their interactions with their children, and identify and alter maladaptive parent–child interactions that may inadvertently foster the maintenance of PTSD symptoms and behavior problems.

Marks et al. (1998) have examined a form of cognitive therapy that does not include any type of exposure component. In this form of cognitive restructuring, clients are taught how thoughts, feelings, and behavior are linked in order to identify dysfunctional thoughts and common thinking errors; to generate more rational responses; and to reappraise beliefs and attributions about themselves, the trauma, and the world. After being helped to identify negative automatic thoughts, clients are asked to monitor their thoughts with daily diaries and to challenge them with Socratic questioning and probabilistic reasoning. From specific thoughts, the clients then move to appraising and modifying distorted beliefs about the traumatic event, themselves, the world, and the future. Clients are assigned homework in which they identify, monitor, challenge, and modify negative thoughts and beliefs.

Results of treatment outcome studies

Stress inoculation training. Resick, Jordan, Girelli, Hutter, and Marhoefer-Dvorak (1988) looked at the effectiveness of SIT, assertion training, and supportive psychotherapy for rape victims. Each therapy was conducted in a group format for 2-hour sessions for 6 weeks. SIT resulted in significant improvements from pre- to post-treatment on a range of self-report measures. These changes were maintained at 6 months follow-up. However, there were no differences between the three therapies; they were found to be equally effective.

Foa, Rothbaum et al. (1991) compared 45 rape victims who were randomly assigned to SIT, prolonged exposure (PE), supportive counseling, and no treatment controls, and found SIT and PE clients significantly improved on measures of PTSD, depression, and anxiety. Of the stress inoculation training group, 50% no longer met criteria for PTSD; 40% of those treated with prolonged exposure also no longer met criteria for PTSD. In contrast, 90% of the supportive counseling group, and all the victims on the waiting-list, still had PTSD. However, while scores for SIT clients were the most improved at post treatment, there was a trend for PTSD scores to be the most improved at 3 months follow-up for PE clients. Foa, Rothbaum et al. (1991) argued that this is because SIT provides short-term relief from anxiety via anxiety management, whereas PE may provide more long-term relief because the emotional and cognitive processing that occurs during exposures may result in permanent changes in the traumatic memory. It should be noted, however, that clients in the SIT condition did not confront feared situations with *in vivo* exposure as described earlier because the researchers did not want any procedures to overlap in the two comparison conditions in this study.

Exposure techniques. Frank et al. (1988) compared the effectiveness of SD with cognitive therapy on a sample of sexual assault victims. They also compared the effectiveness of the two treatments on two victim groups, recent victims (<4 weeks) and delayed victims (>4 weeks). The results showed that both the victim groups showed significant pre- to post-treatment gains with both treatments on several self-report measures and there were no differences between the treatment modalities.

Brom, Kleber, and Defares (1989) conducted a large scale controlled study with 112 trauma survivors who were randomly assigned to SD, psychodynamic treatment, hypnotherapy, and a waiting-list control group. Results showed that although SD proved more effective than the waiting-list control group in decreasing PTSD symptoms, and general psychopathology, it was not significantly different from either psychodynamic therapy, or hypnotherapy. The authors speculated that the similarity of results in the three treatment conditions may be due to the similarity in the behavior of the therapists, which they did not measure directly. Another interesting finding in this study was that the treatments also brought about changes in the more stable personality measures, a finding not seen in a study conducted by Hyer, Woods, Bruno, and Boudewyns (1989). One explanation for this may be that the sample in the Brom et al. (1989) study was less chronic (<5 years), and more heterogeneous (bereavement, acts of violence, traffic accidents) than the sample in the Hyer et al. study (Vietnam veterans with chronic PTSD).

Haynes and Mooney (1975) were the first to use flooding successfully with four physical and sexual assault victims. Flooding was also used successfully by Rychtarik, Silverman, Van Landingham, and Prue (1984) to treat an incest case. Black and Keane (1982) in a single case study of a 55-year-old World War II veteran, with a 36-year history of psychological problems, demonstrated the effectiveness of flooding treatment over a 2-year follow-up period. A series of other case studies and noncontrolled trials demonstrating the effectiveness of flooding therapy in the treatment of PTSD in war victims (Fairbank, Gross, & Keane, 1983; Fairbank & Keane, 1982; Johnson, Gilmore, & Shenoy, 1982; Keane & Kaloupek, 1982; Schindler, 1980) and in accident victims (McCaffrey & Fairbank, 1985) followed.

Keane, Fairbank, Caddell, and Zimering (1989), in a clinical trial, randomly assigned 24 Vietnam veterans with PTSD either to a group receiving 14–16 sessions of flooding therapy or to a waiting-list control. Therapy sessions were approximately 90 minutes in length and typically included 15 minutes of reviewing intersession activities, 10 minutes of relaxation therapy, 45 minutes of flooding, 10 minutes of relaxation, and 10 minutes of integrating any new information or emotions that were evoked as a function of imagery just presented. The subjects were assessed on standard psychometric instruments at pre- and post-treatment and at 6-month follow-up. Results were that the clients receiving flooding therapy reported significantly more improvement than the waiting-list controls on the re-experiencing dimension of PTSD, anxiety, and depression. Therapist ratings on startle reactions, memory and concentration problems, impulsivity, irritability, and legal problems were all significantly lower in the flooding group compared to the control group.

Cooper and Clum (1989) compared the effectiveness of flooding to current combat cues with a "standard" treatment in a group of Vietnam veterans suffering from PTSD. Specifically, flooding was utilized to supplement the traditional individual and group treatment given for Vietnam veterans suffering from PTSD. This standard treatment plus flooding was then compared to a control group that received standard treatment only. Results showed that the addition of flooding was effective with regard to self-report symptoms directly related to the traumatic event(s), anxiety, and sleep disturbance.

Boudewyns and Hyer (1990) conducted a controlled study to compare direct therapeutic exposure to current combat cues with a traditional therapy for PTSD in 51 Vietnam veterans. They improved on Cooper and Clum's (1989) design by adding physiological measures of heart rate, EMG, and skin conductance in their outcome measures. At follow-up, patients who displayed decreased physiological responding also demonstrated improvement on a community adjustment measure tapping anxiety/depression, alienation, vigor, and confidence in skills at follow-up.

As described earlier, in their first comparison study of PE with SIT, Foa, Rothbaum et al. (1991) found a trend at 3 months post-treatment for those who received PE to be reporting fewer symptoms. In a larger, controlled study using a combination treatment, Foa et al. (1999) examined the differential effects of SIT and PE on trauma symptoms by conducting a study on sexual assault victims that compared the efficacy of PE alone, SIT alone, and a treatment program that combined SIT and PE. Results showed that at post-treatment the combination of treatments did not improve upon the effectiveness of either treatment alone. Both treatments, singly or in combination, were very effective in treating PTSD and the results were maintained over months of follow-up.

Cognitive processing therapy/cognitive therapy. Resick and Schnicke (1992) compared rape victims who received cognitive processing therapy with a waiting-list comparison sample and found CPT to be highly effective. There was a significant reduction in symptoms of PTSD and depression and significant improvement in social adjustment. At 6 months post-treatment, none of the women treated were diagnosed with PTSD. In a controlled trial with 171 rape victims comparing CPT and PE, Resick, Nishith, Weaver, Astin, and Feuer (2000) have found that CPT and PE are equally and highly effective in treating PTSD and depression but CPT appears superior in reducing guilt. In neither study did the nontreatment comparison samples report any improvement. At post-treatment, only 17% of the participants still met the criteria for PTSD and on average the participants showed a 70% decrease in symptoms. These findings were maintained through a 9-month follow-up.

Chard (2000) had adapted CPT for treating symptoms (PTSD, depression, and disrupted self-esteem and cognitions) among adult survivors of child sexual abuse. In this modification, CPT has been expanded to 17 weeks with both group and individual treatment in the first 9 weeks and group treatment thereafter. Additional modules have been added to the original protocol to address developmental impact, communication training, and social support. In a controlled study comparing CPT with a waiting list control, Chard found that those receiving active treatment showed significant and large improvements in symptoms compared to the no treatment group, which did not change.

Implementing a cognitive-behavioral program with 19 sexually abused girls acting as their own controls, Deblinger et al. (1990) found significant improvements from pre- to post-treatment on measures of PTSD, internalizing behaviors, externalizing behaviors, state/trait anxiety, and depression. In another study examining the differential effects of child or nonoffending mother participation in a cognitive-behavioral intervention designed to treat PTSD, Deblinger, Lipp-mann, and Steer (1996) found that mothers assigned to the experimental treatment condition described significant decreases in their children's externalizing behaviors and increases in effective parenting skills; the children of these mothers reported significant reductions in depression. Also, the children who were assigned to the experimental intervention exhibited greater reductions in PTSD symptoms as compared to the children in the control group.

Marks et al. (1998) compared four groups: exposure therapy, cognitive restructuring, exposure combined with cognitive restructuring, and relaxation training. The participants were 87 men and women who had PTSD from a range of traumatic stressors; 77 participants completed treatment and 52 completed the 36-week follow-up. The authors found that, overall, the cognitive, exposure, and combined treatments were more effective than relaxation, but there were no major differences between any of the three treatments. The treatment gains were maintained through the 6-month follow-up.

Another study, also conducted in Great Britain, compared cognitive therapy with exposure (Tarrier et al., 1999). After 4 weeks of self-monitoring of symptoms to insure that their PTSD was persistent, 72 men and women were assigned to either cognitive therapy or imaginal exposure. A range of traumas resulting in PTSD was treated: 52% were crime victims, 34% had experienced accidents (particularly motor vehicle accidents), and the remaining 15% had experienced other traumas. The researchers found similar results to the Marks et al. study; both groups improved significantly but neither form of therapy was superior to the other.

Eye movement desensitization and reprocessing therapy

EMDR technique

Eye movement desensitization and reprocessing therapy (EMDR) is a controversial therapy that evolved, not from theory or application of effective techniques for other disorders, but from a personal observation. As originally developed by Shapiro (1989, 1995), EMDR was based on a chance observation that troubling thoughts were resolved when her eyes followed the waving of leaves during a walk in the park. Shapiro developed EMDR on the basis of this observation and argued that lateral eye movements facilitate cognitive processing of the trauma. In the early presentations of EMDR, it was touted as a one-session cure for a range of disorders. However, more recent studies are typically of trauma-related symptoms with a course more similar to the other trauma therapies. EMDR is now described as an eight-phase treatment that includes: history taking, client preparation, target assessment, desensitization, installation, body scan, closure, and re-evaluation of treatment effects. EMDR includes both exposure and cognitive components as well as the lateral eye movements.

In the EMDR protocol, a client is asked to identify and focus on a traumatic image or memory (target assessment phase). Next, the therapist elicits negative belief statements about the memory. The client is asked to assign a rating to the memory and negative beliefs on an 11-point scale of distress and to identify the physical location of the anxiety. The therapist helps the client generate positive thoughts that would be preferable to associate with the memory. These are rated on a 7-point scale of how much the client believes the statement. Once the therapist has instructed the client in the basic EMDR procedure, the client is asked to do four things simultaneously (desensitization phase): (1) visualize the memory; (2) rehearse the negative thoughts; (3) concentrate on the physical sensations of the anxiety; and (4) visually track the therapist's index finger. While the client does this, the therapist rapidly moves his/her index finger rapidly back and forth 30–35 cm from the client's face, with two back and forth movements per second. These are repeated 24 times. Then the client is asked to blank out the memory and take a deep breath. Subsequently, the client brings back the memory and thoughts and rates the level of distress. Sets of eye movements are repeated until the distress rating equals 0 or 1. At this point, the client describes how he/she feels about the positive cognition and gives a rating for it (installation phase).

Research on eye movement desensitization and reprocessing

EMDR has been controversial for a number of reasons including lack of theoretical foundation for the eye movements and lack of empirical data with sound methodology. In her own controlled study of EMDR, Shapiro (1989) reported that 22 combat veterans with PTSD were successfully treated with one 90-minute session of EMDR. Unfortunately, she based this on subjective distress ratings, which are measures of the process within sessions rather than objective, standardized measures of treatment outcome.

Several studies have found significant reductions in symptoms of PTSD and related symptomotology such as depression or anxiety in subjects who received EMDR when compared to nontreatment controls (Rothbaum, 1995; Wilson, Becker, & Tinker, 1995). Others have found significant improvements in subjects who received EMDR and no outcome differences when compared to other treatments for PTSD (Boudewyns, Hyer, Peralme, Touze, & Kiel, 1995; Carlson, Chemtob, Rusnak, Hedlund, & Muraoka, 1995; Vaughan et al., 1994). Unfortunately, the majority of these studies have serious methodological shortcomings such as inclusion of stressors that do not meet the Criterion A definition of a traumatic stressor (Wilson et al., 1995) or inclusion of substantial numbers of subjects who did not meet diagnostic criteria for PTSD (Vaughan et al., 1994; Wilson et al., 1995).

However, in a sample of 61 combat veterans, all of whom met diagnostic criteria for PTSD, Boudewyns et al. (1995) found EMDR to be equally effective as direct therapeutic exposure in reducing symptoms of PTSD, depression, anxiety, and heart rate. In this study, subjects were randomly assigned to one of three groups. All three groups received the standard treatment at their facility, which consisted of eight group therapy sessions and a few spontaneous individual sessions. One group received only this form of treatment; the second and third groups also received five to eight sessions of either EMDR or prolonged exposure. All three groups improved significantly on symptoms of PTSD. The group therapy only group did not improve on depression and showed increases in anxiety and heart rate, whereas the two other groups improved on all measures.

Although Shapiro maintains that lateral eye movements are an essential therapeutic component of EMDR, studies that have examined this have found mixed results. Renfrey and Spates (1994) treated a sample of 23 trauma victims with standard EMDR, or another variation in which no lateral eye movements were induced and subjects were instructed to fix their visual attention. All three groups improved significantly on measures of PTSD, depression, anxiety, heart rate, and subjective distress scores at post-treatment and at 1–3 month follow-up. No differences were found among treatments. Devilly, Spence, and Rapee (1998) compared EMDR to two control conditions with Vietnam veterans in Australia. One of the control conditions was identical to EMDR except for the eye movements. Instead of lateral eye movements, clients were asked to fix their gaze on a black box that emitted a flashing light while imagining the trauma. The other control condition was treatment as usual from their therapists. Devilly et al. found that both of the treatment groups improved somewhat compared to the treatment as usual group but the two experimental groups did not differ statistically. At a 6-month follow-up, the treatment gains were not maintained for either experimental group.

Devilly and Spence (1999) compared EMDR with cognitive-behavior therapy (a combination of exposure, SIT, and cognitive therapy) in a mixed sample of trauma survivors with PTSD in Australia. They found that while EMDR was somewhat effective, the cognitive-behavior therapy package was superior. The results were maintained over a 3-month follow-up.

It does not appear that lateral eye movements are an essential component of EMDR. EMDR forces the client to think about the trauma, to identify the negative cognitions associated with the trauma, and to work toward positive cognitions as they process the traumatic memory. Without the lateral eye movements, EMDR is quite similar to other forms of cognitive/exposure therapy that facilitate the processing of the traumatic memory. Therefore, any efficacy demonstrated by EMDR may be more attributable to engagement of the traumatic memory and the facilitation of information processing than to eye movements. However, treatments that have more extensive behavioral and imaginal exposure as well as cognitive therapy are likely to be more effective.

Summary

This chapter reviewed the therapies that have evolved from both biological information regarding PTSD, and also from psychological theories of PTSD. Although there is no one medication that can be viewed as sufficient to treat the full range of PTSD symptoms, there are medications, such as the SSRIs, which may provide some relief.

However, it should be remembered that medication is only effective as long as the client continues to take the medication, and that relapse is likely upon discontinuation. Also, many PTSD patients find the side-effects of some medications to be sufficiently bothersome that they discontinue the medication.

Therapy, particularly cognitive-behavior therapy, holds greater promise for the successful treatment of PTSD. There have been a number of research projects that have demonstrated therapy to be effective in reducing the symptoms of PTSD and depression resulting from traumatic events. To date, no one treatment has been shown to be more effective overall than the others. This may be an artefact of relatively small sample sizes in complex comparison studies or may simply reflect the fact these treatments are equally effective. Alternatively, this may reflect the overlap in treatment applications. Each of the treatments examined in this chapter is really a treatment package consisting of various components, some of which are similar across treatments. In other words, because all of the treatments may involve these elements to some degree, it is not clear what are the crucial elements for resolution of PTSD symptoms. Resick and Schnicke (1993) have noted that one reason that so many treatment comparison studies for PTSD have not found differences among treatments may be due to the fact that almost all of the treatments include, either formally or informally, corrective information that may facilitate information processing. Understanding this will be important for the refinement of these existing techniques as well as the development of new treatments.

As more progress is made in evaluating different types of treatment, it will become increasingly possible to identify the different markers for recovery that will enable better patient–treatment matching. The treatments themselves need to be dismantled systematically so it becomes possible to determine the active components and the minimum number of sessions that are required to bring about therapeutic success. Adaptations of treatments for people with complex symptom pictures with comorbid disorders will likely receive greater research attention in the future. Also, long-term follow-up of therapy studies will be needed to determine whether gains made during treatment are permanent. Most studies, due to expense, are only able to track participants for a few months after completion of therapy.

References

Abrahams, M.J., Price, J., Whitlock, F.A., & Williams, G. (1976). The Brisbane floods, January 1974: Their impact on health. *Medical Journal of Australia, 2,* 936–939.

Abramson, L., Seligman, M., & Teasdale, J. (1978). Learned helplessness in humans: Critique and reformulation. *Journal of Abnormal Psychology, 57,* 49–74.

Alvazzi del Frate, A., & Patrignani, A. (1995). *Women's victimization in developing countries.* Rome: United Nations Publication (United Nations Interregional Crime and Justice Research Institute).

Alvazzi del Frate, A., Zvekic, U., & van Dijk, J.J. (1993). *Understanding crime: Experiences of crime and crime control.* Rome: United Nations Publication (United Nations Interregional Crime and Justice Research Institute).

American Psychiatric Association. (1980). *Diagnostic and statistical manual of mental disorders* (3rd ed.). Washington, DC: Author.

American Psychiatric Association. (1987). *Diagnostic and statistical manual of mental disorders* (3rd rev. ed.). Washington, DC: Author.

American Psychiatric Association. (1994). *Diagnostic and statistical manual of mental disorders* (4th ed.). Washington, DC: Author.

Amick-McMullan, A., Kilpatrick, D.G., & Resnick, H.S. (1991). Homicide as a risk factor for PTSD among surviving family members. *Behavior Modification, 15,* 545–559.

Andrews, B., & Brewin, C. (1990). Attributions of blame for marital violence: A study of antecedents and consequences. *Journal of Marriage and Family, 52,* 757–767.

Armstrong, K., O'Callahan, W., & Marmar, C. (1991). Debriefing Red Cross disaster personnel: The Multiple Stressor Debriefing Model. *Journal of Traumatic Stress, 4,* 581–593.

Atkeson, B.M., Calhoun, K.S., Resick, P.A., & Ellis, E.M. (1982). Victims of rape: Repeated assessment of depressive symptoms. *Journal of Consulting and Clinical Psychology, 50,* 96–102.

Barrett, D.H., Resnick, H.S., Foy, D.W., Dansky, B.S., Flanders, W.D., & Stroup, N.E. (1996). Combat exposure and adult psychosocial adjustment among US Army veterans serving in Vietnam, 1965–1971. *Journal of Abnormal Psychology, 105,* 575–581.

Barrett, T.W., & Mizes, J.S. (1988). Combat level and social support in the development of posttraumatic stress disorder in Vietnam veterans. *Behavior Modification, 12,* 100–115.

Bart, P.B., & O'Brien, P.H. (1984). Stopping rape: Effective avoidance strategies. *Signs, 10,* 83–101.

Basoglu, M., Paker, M., Paker, O., Oezmen, E., Marks, I., Incesu, C., Sahin, D., & Sarimurat, N. (1994). Psychological effects of torture: A comparison of tortured with nontortured political activists in Turkey. *American Journal of Psychiatry, 151*, 76–81.

Beck, A.T., & Emery, G. (1985). *Anxiety disorders and phobias: A cognitive perspective.* New York: Basic Books.

Becker, J.V., Skinner, L.J., Abel, G.G., Axelrod, R., & Cichon, J. (1984). Sexual problems of sexual assault survivors. *Women and Health, 9*, 5–20.

Beckham, J.C., Feldman, M.E., Kirby, A.C., Hertzberg, M.A., & Moore, S.D. (1997). Interpersonal violence and its correlates in Vietnam veterans with chronic posttraumatic stress disorder. *Journal of Clinical Psychology, 53*, 859–869.

Beebe, G.W. (1975). Follow-up stories of World War II and Korean war prisoners: II. Morbidity, disability, and maladjustments. *Journal of Epidemiology, 101*, 400–442.

Bennet, G. (1968). Bristol floods 1968: Controlled survey of effects on health of local community disaster. *British Medical Journal, 3*, 454–458.

Bernat, J.A., Ronfeldt, H.M., Calhoun, K.S., & Arias, I. (1998). Prevalence of traumatic events and peritraumatic predictors of posttraumatic stress symptoms in a nonclinical sample of college students. *Journal of Traumatic Stress, 11*, 645–664.

Bisson, J., Jenkins, P., Alexander, J., & Bannister, C., (1997). A randomised controlled trial of psychological debriefing for victims of acute burn trauma. *British Journal of Psychiatry, 171*, 78–81.

Black, J.L., & Keane, T.M. (1982). Implosive therapy in the treatment of combat related fears in a World War II veteran. *Journal of Behavior Therapy and Experimental Psychiatry, 13*, 163–165.

Blanchard, E.B., Hickling, E.J., Buckley, T.C., Taylor, A.E., Vollmer, A., & Loos, W.R. (1996). Psychophysiology of posttraumatic stress disorder related to motor vehicle accidents: Replication and extension. *Journal of Consulting and Clinical Psychology, 64*, 742–751.

Bolin, R., & Klenow, D. (1982–1983). Response of elderly to disaster: An age stratified analysis. *International Journal of Aging and Human Development, 16*, 283–296.

Bordow, S., & Porritt, D. (1979). An experimental evaluation of crisis intervention. *Social Science and Medicine, 13a*, 251–256.

Boscarino, J.A. (1995). Post-traumatic stress and associated disorders among Vietnam veterans: The significance of combat exposure and social support. *Journal of Traumatic Stress, 8*, 317–336.

Boudewyns, P.A., & Hyer, L. (1990). Physiological response to combat memories and preliminary treatment outcome in Vietnam veteran PTSD patients treated with direct therapeutic exposure. *Behavior Therapy, 21*, 63–87.

Boudewyns, P.A., Hyer, L.A., Peralme, L., Touze, J., & Kiel, A. (1995, August). *Eye movement desensitization and reprocessing (EMDR) and exposure therapy in the treatment of combat-related PTSD: An early look.* Paper presented at the annual meeting of the American Psychological Association, New York.

Brady, K., Pearlstein, T., Asnis, G.M., Baker, D., Rothbaum, B., Sikes, C.R., & Farfel, G.M. (2000). Efficacy and safety of sertraline treatment of posttraumatic stress disorder: A randomized controlled trial. *Journal of the American Medical Association, 283*, 1837–1844.

Bremner, J., Southwick, S., Brett, E., Fontana, A., Rosenheck, R., & Charney, D.S. (1992). Dissociation and posttraumatic stress disorder in Vietnam combat veterans. *American Journal of Psychiatry, 149*, 328–332.

Bremner, J.D., Randall, P., Scott, T.M., Bronen, R.A., Seibyl, J.P., Southwick, S.M., Delaney, R.C., McCarthy, G., Charney, D.S., & Innis, R.B. (1995).

MRI-based measurement of hippocampal volume in combat-related PTSD. *American Journal of Psychiatry, 152,* 973–981.

Bremner, J.D., Randall, P., Vermetten E., Staib, L., Bronen, R.A., Mazure, C., Capelli, S., McCarthy, G., Innis, R.B., & Charney, D.S (1997). MRI-based measurement of hippocampal volume in PTSD related to childhood physical and sexual abuse: A preliminary report. *Biological Psychiatry, 41,* 23–32.

Bremner, J.D., Scott, T.M., Delaney, R.C., Southwick, S.M., Mason, J.W., Johnson, D.R., Innis, R.B., McCarthy, G., & Charney, D.S. (1993). Deficits in short-term memory in posttraumatic stress disorder. *American Journal of Psychiatry, 150,* 1015–1019.

Bremner, J.D., Southwick, S.M., Johnson, D.R., Yehuda, R., & Charney, D.S. (1993). Childhood physical abuse and combat-related posttraumatic stress disorder in Vietnam veterans. *American Journal of Psychiatry, 150,* 235–239.

Breslau, N., Davis, G., Andreski, P., Peterson, E., & Schultz, L. (1997). Sex differences in posttraumatic stress disorder. *Archives of General Psychiatry, 54,* 1044–1048.

Breslau, N., & Davis, G.C. (1987). Posttraumatic stress disorder: The stressor criterion. *Journal of Nervous and Mental Disease, 175,* 255–264.

Breslau, N., Davis, G.C., Andreski, P., & Peterson, E. (1991). Traumatic events and posttraumatic stress disorder in an urban population of young adults. *Archives of General Psychiatry, 48,* 216–222.

Brewin, C.R., Andrews, B., Rose, S., & Kirk, M. (1999). Acute stress disorder and posttraumatic stress disorder in victims of violent crimes. *American Journal of Psychiatry, 156,* 360–366.

Brewin, C.R., Dalgleish, T., & Joseph, S. (1996). A dual representation theory of posttraumatic stress disorder. *Psychological Review, 103,* 670–686.

Briere, J., & Runtz, M. (1988). Symptomatology associated with childhood sexual victimization in a nonclinical adult sample. *Child Abuse and Neglect, 12,* 51–59.

Brom, D., Kleber, R.J., & Defares, P.B. (1989). Brief psychotherapy for posttraumatic stress disorders. *Journal of Consulting and Clinical Psychology, 57,* 607–612.

Bryant, R.A., & Harvey, A.G. (1995). Avoidant coping style and post-traumatic stress following motor vehicle accidents. *Behaviour, Research, and Therapy, 33,* 631–635.

Bryant, R.A., Harvey, A.G., Dang, S.T., Sackville, T., & Basten, C. (1998). Treatment of acute stress disorder: A comparison of cognitive-behavioral therapy and supportive counseling. *Journal of Consulting and Clinical Psychology, 66,* 862–866.

Bulman, R., & Wortman, C. (1977). Attributions of blame and coping with the "real world": Severe accident victims react to their lot. *Journal of Personality and Social Psychology, 35,* 351–363.

Burgess, A., & Holmstrom, L. (1974a). The rape trauma syndrome. *American Journal of Psychiatry, 131,* 981–986.

Burgess, A., & Holmstrom, L. (1974b). *Rape: Victims of crisis.* Bowie, MD: R.J. Brady.

Burgess, A., & Holmstrom, L. (1979). *Rape: Crisis and recovery.* Bowie, MD: R.J. Brady.

Burgess, A.W., & Holmstrom, L.L. (1978). Recovery from rape and prior life stress. *Research in Nursing and Health, 1,* 165–174.

Burnam, M.A., Stein, J.A., Golding, J.M., Siegel, J.M., Sorenson, S.B., Forsythe, A.B., & Telles, C.A. (1988). Sexual assault and mental disorders in a community population. *Journal of*

Consulting and Clinical Psychology, 56, 843–850.

Butler, R.W., Braff, D.L., Rausch, J.L., Jenkins, M.A., Sprock, J., & Geyer, M.A. (1990). Physiological evidence of exaggerated startle response in a subgroup of Vietnam veterans with combat-related PTSD. American Journal of Psychiatry, 147, 1308–1312.

Buydens-Branchey, L., Noumair, D., & Branchey, M. (1990). Duration and intensity of combat exposure and posttraumatic stress disorder in Vietnam veterans. Journal of Nervous and Mental Disease, 178, 582–587.

Byrne, C.A., Resnick, H.S., Kilpatrick, D.G., Best, C.L., & Saunders, B.E. (1999). The socioeconomic impact of interpersonal violence on women. Journal of Consulting and Clinical Psychology, 67, 362–366.

Byrne, C.A., & Riggs, D.S. (1996). The cycle of trauma: Relationship aggression in male Vietnam veterans with symptoms of posttraumatic stress disorder. Journal of Research in Childhood Education, 11, 213–225.

Calhoun, K.S., Atkeson, B.M., & Resick, P.A. (1982). A longitudinal examination of fear reaction in victims of rape. Journal of Counseling Psychology, 29, 655–661.

Cannon, W.B. (1914). The emergency function of the adrenal medulla in pain and the major stress emotions. American Journal of Physiology, 3, 356–372.

Carlier, I., & Gersons, B. (1997). Stress reactions in disaster victims following the Bijlmermeer plane crash. Journal of Traumatic Stress, 10, 329–335.

Carlson, E.B., & Rosser-Hogan, R. (1991). Trauma experiences, posttraumatic stress, dissociation, and depression in Cambodian refugees. American Journal of Psychiatry, 148, 1548–1551.

Carlson, J.G., Chemtob, C.M., Rusnak, K., Hedlund, N.L., & Muraoka, M.Y. (1995, June). Eye movement desensitization and reprocessing for combat-related posttraumatic stress disorder: A controlled study. Paper presented at the fourth annual meeting of the European Conference on Traumatic Stress, Paris, France.

Cascardi, M., Riggs, D.S., Hearst-Ikeda, D., & Foa, E.B. (1996). Objective rating of assault safety as predictors of PTSD. Journal of Interpersonal Violence, 11, 65–78.

Cashman, L., Molnar, C., & Foa, E. (1995, November). Comorbidity of DSM-III-R axis I and II disorders with acute and chronic post-traumatic stress disorder. A paper presented at the 29th annual convention of the Association for the Advancement of Behavior Therapy, Washington, DC.

Cassiday, K.L., McNally, R.J., & Zeitlin, S.B. (1992). Cognitive processing of trauma cues in rape victims with post-traumatic stress disorder. Cognitive Therapy and Research, 16, 283–295.

Chard, K.M. (2000). Cognitive processing therapy for sexual abuse: An outcome study. Unpublished manuscript, University of Kentucky.

Charlton, P.F., & Thompson, J.A. (1996). Ways of coping with psychological distress after trauma. British Journal of Clinical Psychology, 35, 517–530.

Charney, D.S., Woods, S.W., Goodman, W.K., & Heninger, G.R., (1987). Neurobiological mechanisms of panic anxiety: Biomechanical and behavioral correlates of yohimbine induced panic attacks. American Journal of Psychiatry, 144, 1030–1036.

Charney, D.S., Woods, S.W., & Price, L.H. (1990). Noradrenergic dysregulation in panic disorder. In J.C. Ballinger (Ed.), Neurobiology of panic disorder (pp. 91–105). New York: Wiley Liss.

Chemtob, C., Hamada, R., Roitblat, H., & Muraoka, M. (1994). Anger, impulsivity, and anger control in combat-related posttraumatic stress disorder. *Journal of Consulting and Clinical Psychology, 62*(4), 827–832.

Chemtob, C., Roitblat, H.L., Hamada, R.S., Carlson, J.G., & Twentyman, C.T. (1988). A cognitive action theory of post-traumatic stress disorder. *Journal of Anxiety Disorders, 2,* 253–275.

Chemtob, C., Tomas, S., Law, W., & Cremniter, D. (1997). Postdisaster psychological interventions: A field study of the impact of debriefing on psychological distress. *American Journal of Psychiatry, 154,* 415–417.

Cimino, J., & Dutton, M. (1991, August). *Factors influencing the development of PTSD in battered women.* A paper presented at the 99th Convention of the American Psychological Association, San Francisco.

Cluss, P.A., Boughton, J., Frank, L.E., Stewart, B.D., & West, D.G. (1983). The rape victims: Psychological correlates of participation in the legal process. *Criminal Justice and Behavior, 10,* 342–357.

Coffey, P., Leitenberg, H., Henning, K., Bennett, R.T., & Jankowski, M.K. (1996). Dating violence: The association between methods of coping and women's psychological adjustment. *Violence and Victims, 11,* 227–238.

Cohen, L.J., & Roth, S. (1987). The psychological aftermath of rape: Long-term effects and individual differences in recovery. *Journal of Social and Clinical Psychology, 5,* 525–534.

Conte, J.R., & Schuerman, J.R. (1987). Factors associated with an increased impact of child sexual abuse. *Child Abuse and Neglect, 11,* 201–211.

Cooper, N.A., & Clum, G.A. (1989). Imaginal flooding as a supplementary treatment for PTSD in combat veterans: A controlled study. *Behavior Therapy, 20,* 381–391.

Cottler, L., Compton, W., Mager, D., Spitznagel, E., & Janca, A. (1992). Posttraumatic stress disorder among substance users from the general population. *American Journal of Psychiatry, 149,* 664–670.

Curle, C.E., & Williams, C. (1996). Post-traumatic stress reactions in children: Gender differences in the incidence of trauma reactions at two years and examination of factors influencing adjustment. *British Journal of Clinical Psychology, 35,* 297–309.

Davidson, J., & van der Kolk, B. (1996). The psychopharmacological treatment of posttraumatic stress disorder. In B.A. van der Kolk, A.C. McFarlane, & L. Weisaeth (Eds.), *Traumatic stress: The effects of overwhelming experience on mind, body, and society* (pp. 510–524). New York: Guilford Press.

Davidson, J.R.T., Hughes, D., Blazer, D.G., & George, L.K. (1991). Post-traumatic stress disorder in the community: An epidemiological study. *Psychological Medicine, 21,* 713–721.

Davis, L.L., Suris, A., Lambert, M.T., Heimberg, C., & Petty, F. (1997). Posttraumatic stress disorder and serotonin: New direction for research and treatment. *Journal of Psychiatry and Neuroscience, 22,* 318–326.

Deblinger, E., Lippmann, J., & Steer, R., (1996). Sexually abused children suffering posttraumatic stress symptoms: Initial treatment outcome findings. *Child Maltreatment, 1,* 310–321.

Deblinger, E., McLeer, S.V., & Henry, D. (1990). Cognitive behavioral treatment for sexually abused children suffering post-traumatic stress: Preliminary findings. *Journal of American Academy of Child and Adolescent Psychology, 29,* 747–752.

DeKeseredy, W.S., Schwartz, M.D., & Tait, K. (1993). Sexual assault and stranger aggression on a Canadian university campus. *Sex Roles, 28,* 263–277.

Deutsch, H. (1945). *The psychology of women: A psychoanalytic interpretation:*

Vol. 2. Motherhood. New York: Grune & Stratton.

Devilly, G.J., & Spence, S.H. (1999). The relative efficacy and treatment distress of EMDR and a cognitive-behavior trauma treatment protocol in the amelioration of posttraumatic stress disorder. *Journal of Anxiety Disorders, 13,* 131–157.

Devilly, G.J., Spence, S.H., & Rapee, R.M. (1998). Statistical and reliable change with eye movement desensitization and reprocessing: Treating trauma within a veteran population. *Behavior Therapy, 29,* 435–455.

Drossman, D.A., Leserman, J., Nachman, G., Zhiming, L., Gluck, H., Toomey, T., & Mitchell, M. (1990). Sexual and physical abuse in women with functional or organic gastrointestinal disorders. *Annals of Internal Medicine, 113,* 828–833.

Dunmore, E., Clark, D.M., & Ehlers, A. (1997). *Cognitive predictors of chronic PTSD after assault.* Unpublished manuscript, University of Oxford, UK.

Ehlers, A., Clark, D.M., Dunmore, E., Jaycox, L., Meadows, E., & Foa, E.B. (1998). Predicting response to exposure treatment in PTSD: The role of mental defeat and alienation. *Journal of Traumatic Stress, 11,* 457–471.

Ehlers, A., Maercker, A., & Boos, A. (1998). *PTSD following political imprisonment: The role of mental defeat, alienation, and perceived permanent change.* Unpublished manuscript, University of Oxford, UK.

Ellis, E.M., Atkeson, B.M., & Calhoun, K.S. (1981). An assessment of long-term reaction to rape. *Journal of Abnormal Psychology, 90,* 263–266.

Ersland, S., Weisaeth, L., & Sund, A. (1989). The stress of rescuers involved in an oil rig disaster: "Alexander L. Kielland": 1980. *Acta Psychiatrica Scandinavica, 80,* 38–49.

Fairbank, J.A., Gross, R.T., & Keane, T.M. (1983). Treatment of post-traumatic stress disorder: Evaluation of outcome with a behavioral code. *Behavior Modification, 7,* 557–568.

Fairbank, J.A., Hansen, D.J., & Fitterling, J.M. (1991). Patterns of appraisal and coping across different stressor conditions among former prisoners of war with and without posttraumatic stress disorder. *Journal of Consulting and Clinical Psychology, 59,* 274–281.

Fairbank, J.A., & Keane, T.M. (1982). Flooding for combat-related stress disorders: Assessment of anxiety reduction across traumatic memories. *Behavior Therapy, 13,* 499–510.

Falsetti, S.A., & Resick, P.A. (1995). Causal attributions, depression, and posttraumatic stress disorder in victims of crime. *Journal of Applied Social Psychology, 25,* 1027–1042.

Felitti, V.S. (1991). Long-term medical consequences of incest, rape, and molestation. *South Medical Journal, 84,* 328–331.

Finn, J. (1985). The stresses and coping behavior of battered women. *Social Casework, 66,* 341–349.

Fischoff, B. (1975). Hindsight does not equal foresight: The effect of outcome knowledge on judgement under uncertainty. *Journal of Experimental Psychology: Human Perception and Performance, 1,* 288–299.

Flannery, R. (1990). Social support and psychological trauma: A methodological review. *Journal of Traumatic Stress, 3,* 593–611.

Foa, E.B. (1996, November). Conceptualization of post-trauma psychopathology as failure in emotional processing. In P.A. Resick (Chair), *Information processing theories: Variations on a theme.* Symposium conducted at the 12th annual meeting of the International Society for Traumatic Stress Studies, San Francisco.

Foa, E.B., Dancu, C.V., Hembree, E.A., Jaycox, L.H., Meadows, E.A., & Street,

G.P. (1999). A comparison of exposure therapy, stress inoculation training, and their combination for reducing posttraumatic stress disorder in female assault victims. *Journal of Consulting and Clinical Psychology, 67*, 194–200.

Foa, E.B., Feske, U., Murdock, T.B., Kozak, M.J., & McCarthy, P.R. (1991). Processing of threat-related material in rape victims. *Journal of Abnormal Psychology, 100*, 156–162.

Foa, E.B., Hearst-Ikeda, D., & Perry, K.J. (1995). Evaluation of a brief cognitive behavioral program for the prevention of chronic PTSD in recent assault victims. *Journal of Consulting and Clinical Psychology, 63*, 948–955.

Foa, E.B., Riggs, D.S., & Gershuny, B.S. (1995). Arousal, numbing, and intrusion: Symptom structure of PTSD following assault. *American Journal of Psychiatry, 152*, 116–120.

Foa, E.B., Rothbaum, B.O., Riggs, D.S., & Murdock, T.B. (1991). Treatment of post-traumatic stress disorder in rape victims: A comparison between cognitive behavioral procedures and counseling. *Journal of Consulting and Clinical Psychology, 59*, 715–723.

Foa, E.B., Steketee, G., & Rothbaum, B.O. (1989). Behavioral/cognitive conceptualization of post-traumatic stress disorder. *Behavior Therapy, 20*, 155–176.

Folkman, S. (1991). Coping across the life span: Theoretical issues. In M. Cummings, A. Greene, & K.N. Karrakar (Eds.), *Life span developmental psychology: Perspectives on stress and coping* (pp. 3–19). Hillsdale, NJ: Lawrence Erlbaum Associates Inc.

Fontana, A., & Rosenheck, R. (1994). Traumatic war stressors and psychiatric symptoms among World War II, Korean, and Vietnam war veterans. *Psychology and Aging, 9*, 27–33.

Foy, D., Sipprelle, C., Rueger, D., & Carroll, E. (1984). Etiology of posttraumatic stress disorder in Vietnam veterans: Analysis of premilitary, military and combat exposure influences. *Journal of Consulting and Clinical Psychology, 52*, 79–87.

Frank, E., Anderson, B., Stewart, B.D., Dancu, C., Hughes, C., & West, D. (1988). Efficacy of cognitive behavior therapy and systematic desensitization in the treatment of rape trauma. *Behavior Therapy, 19*, 403–420.

Frank, E., & Anderson, B.P. (1987). Psychiatric disorders in rape victims: Past history and current symptomatology. *Comprehensive Psychiatry, 28*, 77–82.

Frank, E., & Stewart, B.D. (1984). Physical aggression: Treating the victims. In E.A. Bleckman (Ed.), *Behavior modification with women* (pp. 245–272). New York: Guilford.

Frank, E., Turner, S., & Stewart, B. (1980). Initial response to rape: The impact of factors within the rape situation. *Journal of Behavioral Assessment, 62*, 39–53.

Frank, E., Turner, S., Stewart, B., Jacob, M., & West, D. (1981). Past psychiatric symptoms and the response to sexual assault. *Comprehensive Psychiatry, 22*, 479–487.

Fraser, F., & Wilson, E.M. (1918). The sympathetic nervous system and the "irritable heart of soldiers". *British Medical Journal, 2*, 27–29.

Frasier, P. (1990). Victims attributions and postrape trauma. *Journal of Personality and Social Psychology, 59*, 298–304.

Freedy, J.R., Shaw, D., Jarrell, M.P., & Masters, C.R. (1992). Towards an understanding of the psychological impact of natural disasters: An application of the conservation resources stress model. *Journal of Traumatic Stress, 5*, 441–454.

Freud, S. (1896). The aetiology of hysteria. Paper presented at The Society for Psychiatry and Neurology, Vienna,

Austria. Reprinted in J.M. Masson, *The assault on truth* (pp. 252–282). New York: HarperCollins.

Freud, S. (1917). *Introductory lectures on psychoanalysis.* New York: Liveright.

Friedman, M.J., & Schnurr, P.P. (1995). The relationship between trauma, posttraumatic stress disorder, and physical health. In M.J. Friedman, D.S. Charney, & A.Y. Deutch (Eds.), *Neurobiological and clinical consequences of stress: From normal adaptations to posttraumatic stress disorder* (pp. 507–524). Philadelphia: Lippincott-Raven.

Friedman, M.J., & Southwick, S.M. (1995). Towards pharmacotherapy for post traumatic stress disorder. In M.J. Friedman, D.S. Charney, & A.Y. Deutch (Eds.), *Neurobiological and clinical consequences of stress: From normal adaptation to post traumatic stress disorder* (pp. 465–482). Philadelphia: Lippincott-Raven.

Frieze, I.H., & Bookwala, J. (1996). Coping with unusual stressors: Criminal victimization. In M. Zeidner & N.S. Endler (Eds.), *Handbook of coping: Theory, research, applications* (pp. 303–321). New York: John Wiley & Sons.

Frueh, B., Brady, K., & de Arellano, M. (1998). Racial differences in combat-related PTSD: Empirical findings and conceptual issues. *Clinical Psychology Review, 18,* 287–305.

Garner, J., & Fagan, J. (1997). Victims of domestic violence. In R.C. Davis, A.J. Lurigio, & W.G. Skogan (Eds.), *Victims of crime* (2nd ed.; pp. 53–85). Thousand Oaks, CA: Sage Publications.

Gavey, N. (1991). Sexual victimization prevalence among New Zealand University students. *Journal of Consulting and Clinical Psychology, 59,* 464–466.

Gelles, R., & Straus, M. (1988). *Intimate violence.* New York: Simon & Schuster Inc.

Gidycz, C.A., Coble, C.N., Latham, L., & Layman, M.J. (1993). A sexual assault experience in adulthood and prior victimization experiences: A prospective analysis. *Psychology of Women Quarterly, 17,* 151–168.

Gidycz, C.A., Layman, M.J., Dowdall, C., Gylys, J., Crothers, M., & Matorin, A. (1997, November). The prediction of victimization and revictimization in women: The role of attitudinal variables. In M. Cloire (Chair), *Sexual revictimization of women: Risk factors and prevention strategies,* Symposium conducted at the 31st annual AABT convention, Miami Beach, FL.

Girelli, S.A., Resick, P.A., Marhoefer-Dvorak, S., & Hutter, C.K. (1986). Subjective distress and violence during rape: Their effects on long-term fear. *Victims and Violence, 1,* 35–46.

Gleason, W.J. (1993). Mental disorders in battered women: An empirical study. *Violence and Victims, 8,* 53–68.

Goldstein, G., van Kammen, W., Shelly, C., Miller, D.J., & van Kammen, D.P. (1987). Survivors of imprisonment in the Pacific theater during World War II. *American Journal of Psychiatry, 144,* 1210–1213.

Green, B., Grace, M., Lindy, J., Glesser, G., & Leonard, A. (1990). Risk factors for PTSD and other diagnoses in a general sample of Vietnam veterans. *American Journal of Psychiatry, 147,* 729–733.

Green, B., Lindy, J., Grace, M., & Leonard, B. (1992). Chronic posttraumatic stress disorder and diagnostic comorbidity in a disaster sample. *Journal of Nervous and Mental Disease, 180,* 760–766.

Green, B.L., Grace, M.C., & Gleser, G.C. (1985). Identifying survivors at risk: Long-term impairment following the Beverly Hills Supper Club fire. *Journal of Consulting and Clinical Psychology, 53,* 672–678.

Griffin, M.G., Resick, P.A., & Mechanic, M.B. (1997, August). Objective assessment of peritraumatic dissociation: Psychophysiological indicators. *American Journal of Psychiatry, 154*(8), 1081–1088.

Gurvits, T.G., Shenton, M.R., Hokama, H., Ohta, H., Lasko, N.B., Bilbertson, M.W., Orr, S.P., Kikinis, R., Jolesz, F.A., McCarley, R.W., & Pitman, R.K. (1996). Magnetic resonance imaging study of hippocampal volume in chronic, combat-related PTSD. *Biological Psychiatry, 40*, 1091–1099.

Harvey, A.G., & Bryant, R.A. (1998). The effect of attempted thought suppression in acute stress disorder. *Behaviour Research and Therapy, 36*, 583–590.

Haynes, S.N., & Mooney, D.K. (1975). Nightmares: Etiological, theoretical, and behavioral treatment considerations. *Psychological Record, 25*, 225–236.

Helzer, J.E., Robins, L.N., & McEvoy, L. (1987). Post-traumatic stress disorder in the general popuation: Findings of the epidemiologic catchment area survey. *New England Journal of Medicine, 317*, 1630–1634.

Hendin, H., & Haas, A. (1984). Combat adaptations of Vietnam veterans without posttraumatic stress disorders. *American Journal of Psychiatry, 141*, 956–960.

Herman, J.L. (1992a). Complex PTSD: A syndrome in survivors of prolonged and repeated trauma. *Journal of Traumatic Stress, 5*, 377–391.

Herman, J.L. (1992b). *Trauma and recovery*. New York: Basic Books.

Hobfoll, S. (1989). Conservation of resources: A new attempt at conceptualizing stress. *American Psychologist, 44*, 513–524.

Hobfoll, S. (1991). Trauma stress: A theory based on rapid loss of resources. *Anxiety Research, 4*, 187–197.

Hobfoll, S., & Lilly, R. (1993). Resource conservation as a strategy for community psychology. *Journal of Community Psychology, 21*, 128–148.

Hobfoll, S.E., Lomranz, J., Eyal, N., Bridges, A., & Tzemach, M. (1989). Pulse of a nation: Depressive mood reactions of Israelis to the Israel–Lebanon war. *Journal of Personality and Social Psychology, 56*, 1002–1012.

Holen, A. (1989). A longitudinal study of the occurrence and persistence of posttraumatic health problems in disaster survivors. *Stress Medicine, 7*, 11–17.

Holen, A. (1993). The North Sea oil rig disaster. In J.P. Wilson & B. Raphael (Eds.), *International handbook of traumatic stress syndromes* (pp. 471–478). New York: Plenum.

Holmes, M.R., & St. Lawrence, J.S. (1983). Treatment of rape-induced trauma: Proposed behavioral conceptualization and review of the literature. *Clinical Psychology Review, 3*, 417–433.

Holmes, T.H., & Rahe, R.H. (1967). The Social Readjustment Rating Scale. *Journal of Psychosomatic Research, 11*, 213–218.

Holtzworth-Monroe, A., Smutzler, N., & Sandin, B. (1997). A brief review of the research on husband violence: Part II. The psychological effects of husband violence on battered women and their children. *Aggression and Violent Behavior, 2*, 179–213.

Horowitz, M.J. (1976). *Stress response syndromes*. New York: Jason Aronson.

Horowitz, M.J. (1986). *Stress response syndromes* (2nd ed.). New York: Jason Aronson.

Hubbard, J., Realmuto, G.M., Northwood, A.K., & Masten, A.S. (1995). Comorbidity of psychiatric diagnoses with posttraumatic stress disorder in survivors of childhood trauma. *Journal of the American Academy of Child and Adolescent Psychiatry, 34*, 1167–1173.

Huerta, F., & Horton, R. (1978). Coping behavior of elderly flood victim. *Gerontologists, 18*, 541–546.

Hyer, L., Summers, M.N., Boyd, S., Litaker, M., & Boudewyns, P. (1996). Assessment of older combat veterans with the clinician-administered PTSD scale. *Journal of Traumatic Stress, 9*, 587–594.

Hyer, L., Woods, M.G., Bruno, R., & Boudewyns, P. (1989). Treatment outcomes of Vietnam veterans with PTSD and the consistency of the MCMI. *Journal of Clinical Psychology, 45*, 547–552.

Hytten, K., & Hasle, A. (1989). Fire fighters: A study of stress and coping. *Acta Psychiatrica Scandinavica, 80*, 50–55.

International Federation of Red Cross and Red Crescent Societies. (1993). *World Disasters Report: 1993*. Dordrecht, The Netherlands: Martinus Nijhoff Publishers.

International Federation of Red Cross and Red Crescent Societies. (1996). *World Disasters Report: 1996*. Oxford, UK: Oxford University Press.

Irwin, H.J. (1996). Traumatic childhood events, perceived availability of emotional support, and the development of dissociative tendencies. *Child Abuse and Neglect, 20*, 701–707.

Jaffe, P., Wolfe, D.A., Wilson, S., & Zak, L. (1986). Emotional and physical health problems of battered women. *Canadian Journal of Psychiatry, 31*, 625–629.

Janet, P. (1911). *L'état mental des hysteriques* (2nd ed.). Paris: Alcan.

Janet, P. (1919). *Les médications psychologiques*. Paris: Felix Alcan.

Janoff-Bulman, R. (1979). Characterological versus behavioral self-blame: Inquiries into depression and rape. *Journal of Personality and Social Psychology, 37*, 1798–1809.

Janoff-Bulman, R. (1985). The aftermath of victimization: Rebuilding shattered assumptions. In C.R. Figley (Ed.), *Trauma and its wake: The study and treatment of post-traumatic stress disorder* (pp. 15–35). New York: Brunner/Mazel.

Janoff-Bulman, R. (1992). *Shattered assumptions: Towards a new psychology of trauma*. New York: The Free Press.

Janoff-Bulman, R., & Wortman, C.B. (1977). Attributions of blame and coping in the "real world": Severe accident victims react to their lot. *Journal of Personality and Social Psychology, 35*, 351–363.

Johnson, G.H., Gilmore, J.D., & Shenoy, R.Z. (1982). Use of a flooding procedure in the treatment of a stress-related anxiety disorder. *Journal of Behavior Therapy and Experimental Psychiatry, 13*, 235–237.

Jongedijk, R.A., Carlier, I.V., Schreuder, B.J., & Gersons, B.P. (1996). Complex posttraumatic stress disorder: An exploratory investigation of PTSD and DESNOS among Dutch war veterans. *Journal of Traumatic Stress, 9*, 577–586.

Joseph, S.A., Brewin, C.R., Yule, W., & Williams, R. (1991). Causal attributions and psychiatric symptoms in survivors of the Herald of Free Enterprise disaster. *British Journal of Psychiatry, 159*, 542–546.

Joseph, S.A., Brewin, C.R., Yule, W., & Williams, R. (1993). Causal attributions and post-traumatic stress in adolescents. *Journal of Clinical Psychology and Psychiatry, 34*, 247–253.

Joseph, S.A., Yule, W., Williams, R., & Andrews, B. (1993). Crisis support in the aftermath of disaster: A longitudinal perspective. *British Journal of Clinical Psychology, 32*(2), 177–185.

Kardiner, A. (1941). The traumatic neuroses of war. *Psychosomatic Medicine Monographs, 1* (Nos. 2 & 3).

Kaysen, D., Morris, M., & Resick, P.A. (2000). Factor analysis of peritraumatic responses and distress in female crime victims. *Manuscript submitted for publication*.

Keane, T., Scott, W., Chavoya, G., Lamparski, D., & Fairbank, J. (1985). Social support in Vietnam veterans with post-traumatic stress disorder: A comparative analysis. *Journal of Consulting and Clinical Psychology, 53,* 95–102.

Keane, T., & Wolfe, J. (1990). Comorbidity in post-traumatic stress disorder: An analysis of community and clinical studies. *Journal of Applied Social Psychology, 20,* 1776–1788.

Keane, T.M., Fairbank, J.A., Caddell, J.M., & Zimering, R.T. (1989). Implosive (flooding) therapy reduces symptoms of PTSD in Vietnam combat veterans. *Behavior Therapy, 20,* 245–260.

Keane, T.M., & Kaloupek, D.G. (1982). Imaginal flooding in the treatment of post-traumatic stress disorder. *Journal of Consulting and Clinical Psychology, 50,* 138–140.

Keane, T.M., Kolb, L.C., Kaloupek, D.G., Orr, S.P., Blanchard, E.B., Thomas, R.G., Hsieh, F.Y., & Lavori, P.W. (1998). Utility of psychophysiological measurement in the diagnosis of posttraumatic stress disorder: Results from a department of veterans affairs cooperative study. *Journal of Consulting and Clinical Psychology, 66,* 914–923.

Keane, T.M., Zimering, R.T., & Caddell, R.T. (1985). A behavioral formulation of PTSD in Vietnam veterans. *The Behavior Therapist, 8,* 9–12.

Kemp, A., Rawlings, E., & Green, B. (1991). Post-traumatic stress disorder (PTSD) in battered women: A shelter sample. *Journal of Traumatic Stress, 4,* 137–148.

Kenardy, J., Webster, R., Lewin, T., Carr, V., Hazell, P., & Carter, G. (1996). Stress debriefing and patterns of recovery following a natural disaster. *Journal of Traumatic Stress, 9,* 37–49.

Kessler, R., Sonnega, A., Bromet, E., Hughes, M., & Nelson, C. (1995). Post-traumatic stress disorder in the National Comorbidity Survey. *Archives of General Psychiatry, 52,* 1048–1060.

Kilpatrick, D.G., Acierno, R., Resnick, H.S., Saunders, B.E., & Best, C.L. (1997). A 2-year longitudinal analysis of the relationships between violent assault and substance use in women. *Journal of Consulting and Clinical Psychology, 65,* 834–847.

Kilpatrick, D.G., Edmunds, C.N., & Seymour, A.K. (1992). *Rape in America: A report to the nation.* Arlington, VA: National Victim Center.

Kilpatrick, D.G., Resick, P., & Veronen, L. (1981). Effects of a rape experience: A longitudinal study. *Journal of Social Issues, 37,* 105–122.

Kilpatrick, D.G., Saunders, B.E., Amick-McMullan, A., & Best, C.L. (1989). Victim and crime factors associated with the development of crime-related post-traumatic stress disorder. *Behavior Therapy, 20,* 199–214.

Kilpatrick, D.G., & Veronen, L.J. (1984). *The psychological impact of crime.* Washington, DC: National Institute of Justice.

Kilpatrick, D.G., Veronen, L.J., & Best, C.L. (1985). Factors predicting psychological distress among rape victims. In C.R. Figley (Ed.), *Trauma and its wake* (pp. 113–141). New York: Brunner/Mazel.

Kilpatrick, D.G., Veronen, L.J., & Resick, P.A. (1979a). The aftermath of rape: Recent empirical findings. *American Journal of Orthopsychiatry, 49,* 658–669.

Kilpatrick, D.G., Veronen, L.J., & Resick, P.A. (1979b). Assessment of the aftermath of rape: Changing patterns of fear. *Journal of Behavioral Assessment, 1,* 113–148.

Kilpatrick, D.G., Veronen, L.J., & Resick, P.A. (1982). Psychological sequelae to rape: Assesssment and treatment strategies. In D.M. Dolays, R.L. Meredith, & A.R. Ciminero (Eds.), *Behavioral medicine: Assessment and* treatment strategies (pp. 473–497). New York: Plenum Press.

Kilpatrick, D.G., Veronen, L.J., Saunders, B.E., Best, C.L., Amick-McMullan, A., & Paduhovich, J. (1987). The psychological impact of crime: A study of randomly surveyed crime victims (Final report, Grant No. 84–IJ-CX-0039). National Institute of Justice, Washington, DC.

Kimerling, R., & Calhoun, K.S. (1994). Somatic symptoms, social support and treatment seeking among sexual assault victims. Journal of Clinical Psychology, 62, 333–340.

Kinzie, J.D., Boehnlein, J.K., Leung, P.K., Moore, L.J., Riley, C., & Smith, D. (1990). The prevalence of posttraumatic stress disorder and its clinical significance among Southeast Asian refugees. American Journal of Psychiatry, 147, 913–917.

Kinzie, J.D., & Leung, P. (1989). Clonidine in Cambodian patients with posttraumatic stress disorder. Journal of Nervous and Mental Disease, 177, 546–550.

Kluznik, J.C., Speed, N., VanValkenberg, C., & Magraw, R. (1986). Forty-year follow-up of United States prisoners of war. American Journal of Psychiatry, 143, 1443–1446.

Kolb, L.C., Burris, B.C., & Griffiths, S. (1984). Propranolol and clonidine in the treatment of the chronic post-traumatic stress disorders of war. In B.A. van der Kolk (Ed.), Post-traumatic stress disorder: Psychological and biological sequelae (pp. 97–107). Washington, DC: American Psychiatric Press.

Koss, M., Gidycz, C., & Wisniewski, N. (1987). The scope of rape: Incidence and prevalence of sexual aggression and victimization in a national sample of higher education students. Journal of Consulting and Clinical Psychology, 55, 162–170.

Koss, M.P., Dinero, T.E., Seibel, C.A., & Cox, S.L. (1988). Stranger and acquaintance rape: Are there differences in the victim's experience? Psychology of Women Quarterly, 12, 1–24.

Koss, M.P., Koss, P., & Woodruff, W. (1991). Deleterious effects of criminal victimization on women's health and medical utilization. Archives of Internal Medicine, 151, 342–357.

Kosten, T.R., Mason, J.W., Giller, E.L., Ostroff, R.B., & Harkness, L. (1987). Sustained urinary norepinephrine and epinephrine elevation in PTSD. Psychoneuroendocrinology, 12, 13–20.

Kubany, E.S. (1994). A cognitive model of guilt typology in combat-related PTSD. Journal of Traumatic Stress, 7, 3–19.

Kubany, E.S., Abueg, F.R., Owens, J.A., Brennan, J.M., Kaplan, A.S., & Watson, S.B. (1995). Initial examination of a multidimensional model of trauma-related guild: Applications to combat veterans and battered women. Journal of Psychopathology and Behavioral Assessment, 17, 353–376.

Kubany, E.S., & Manke, F.P. (1995). Cognitive therapy for trauma-related guilt: Conceptual bases and treatment outlines. Cognitive and Behavioral Practice, 2, 27–61.

Kuch, K., & Cox, B.J. (1992). Symptoms of PTSD in 124 survivors of the Holocaust. American Journal of Psychiatry, 149, 337–340.

Kulka, R.A., Schlenger, W.E., Fairbank, J.A., Hough, R.L., Jordan, B.K., Marmar, C.R., & Weiss, D.S. (1990). Trauma and the Vietnam war generation. New York: Brunner/Mazel.

Lang, P.J. (1977). Imagery in therapy: An information processing analysis of fear. Behavior Therapy, 8, 862–886.

Lazarus, R.S., & Folkman, S. (1984). Stress, appraisal, and coping. New York: Springer Publishing Company.

Lebowitz, L., & Newman, E. (1996). The role of cognitive-affective themes in the assessment and treatment of trauma reactions. *Clinical Psychology and Psychotherapy, 3,* 196–207.

LeDoux, J.E. (1987). Emotion. In F. Plum (Ed.), *Handbook of physiology: Nervous system V.* Washington, DC: American Physiological Society.

Lerner, M.J. (1980). *The belief in a just world.* New York: Plenum.

Lindy, J.D. (1996). Psychoanalytic psychotherapy of post-traumatic stress disorder: The nature of the relationship. In B.A. van der Kolk, A.C. McFarlane, & L. Weisaeth (Eds.), *Traumatic stress: The effects of overwhelming experience on mind, body, and society* (pp. 525–536). New York: Guilford Press.

Linehan, M.M. (1993). *Cognitive-behavioral treatment of borderline personality disorder.* New York: Guilford Press.

MacDonald, C., Chamberlain, K., & Long, N. (1997). Race, combat, and PTSD in a community sample of New Zealand Vietnam war veterans. *Journal of Traumatic Stress, 10,* 117–124.

Mahoney, M., & Lyddon, W. (1988). Recent developments in cognitive approaches to counseling and psychotherapy. *Counseling Psychologist, 16,* 190–234.

Marhoefer-Dvorak, S., Resick, P.A., Hutter, C.K., & Girelli, S.A. (1988). Single versus multiple incident rape victims: A comparison of psychological reactions to rape. *Journal of Interpersonal Violence, 3,* 145–160.

Marks, I., Lovell, K., Noshirvani, H., Livanou, M., & Thrasher, S. (1998). Treatment of post-traumatic stress disorder by exposure and/or cognitive restructuring: A controlled study. *Archives of General Psychiatry, 55,* 317–325.

Marmar, C., Weiss, D., Metzler, T., & Delucchi, K. (1996). Characteristics of emergency services personnel related to peritraumatic dissociation during critical incident exposure. *American Journal of Psychiatry, 153,* 94–102.

Marmar, C., Weiss, D., Metzler, T.,

Ronfeldt, H., & Foreman, C. (1996). Stress responses of emergency services personnel to the Loma Prieta earthquake interstate 880 freeway collapse and control traumatic incidents. *Journal of Traumatic Stress, 9,* 63–85.

Marmar, C.R., Weiss, D.S., & Pynoos, R.S. (1995). Dynamic psychotherapy of post-traumatic stress disorder. In M.J. Friedman, D.S. Charney, & A.Y. Deutch (Eds.), *Neurobiological and clinical consequences of stress: From normal adaptation to post traumatic stress disorder* (pp. 495–506). Philadelphia: Lippincott-Raven.

Marmar, C.R., Weiss, D.S., Schlenger, W.E., Fairbank, J.A., Jordan, B.K., Kulka, R.A., & Hough, R.L. (1994). Peritraumatic dissociation and posttraumatic stress in male Vietnam theater veterans. *American Journal of Psychiatry, 151,* 902–907.

Mason, J.W., Giller, E.L., Kosten, T.R., Ostroff, R.B., & Podd, L. (1986). Urinary-free cortisol levels in post-traumatic stress disorder patients. *Journal of Nervous and Mental Disease, 174,* 145–159.

Masson, J.M. (1985). *The assault on truth: Freud's suppression of the seduction theory.* New York: Harper Collins Publishers.

Mayou, R., Bryant, B., & Duthie, R. (1993). Psychiatric consequences of road traffic accidents. *British Medical Journal, 307,* 647–651.

McCaffrey, R.J., & Fairbank, J.A. (1985). Post-traumatic stress disorder associated with transportation accidents: Two case studies. *Behavior Therapy, 16,* 406–416.

McCahill, T., Meyer, L., & Fischman, A. (1979). *The aftermath of rape.* Lexington, MA: Heath.

McCann, I., & Pearlman, L. (1992). Constructivist self-development theory: A theoretical framework for assessing and treating traumatized college students. *Journal of American College Health, 40,* 189–196.

McCann, I.L., & Pearlman, L.A. (1990). *Psychological trauma and the adult survivor: Theory, therapy, and transformation.* New York: Brunner/Mazel.

McCann, I.L., Sakheim, D.K., & Abrahamson, D.J. (1988) Trauma and victimization: A model of psychological adaptation. *Counseling Psychologist, 16,* 531–594.

McCormick, R.A., Taber, J.I., & Kruedelbach, N. (1989). The relationship between attributional style and post-traumatic stress disorder in addicted patients. *Journal of Traumatic Stress, 2,* 477–487.

McFarlane, A., & Papay, P. (1992). Multiple diagnoses in posttraumatic stress disorder in the victims of a natural disaster. *Journal of Nervous and Mental Disease, 180,* 498–504.

McFarlane, A.C. (1988). The longitudinal course of posttraumatic morbidity: The range of outcomes and their predictors. *Journal of Nervous and Mental Disease, 176,* 30–39.

McFarlane, A.C. (1989). The aetiology of post-traumatic morbidity: Predisposing, precipitating and perpetuating factors. *British Journal of Psychiatry, 154,* 221–228.

McNally, R.J., Kaspi, S.P., Riemann, B.C., & Zeitlin, S.B. (1990). Selective processing of threat cues in post-traumatic stress disorder. *Journal of Abnormal Psychology, 99,* 398–402.

Meakins, J.C., & Wilson, R.M. (1918). The effect of certain sensory stimulation on the respiratory rate in case of so-called "irritable heart". *Heart, 7,* 17–22.

Mechanic, M.B., & Resick, P.A. (1998). The personal beliefs and reactions scale: Assessing rape-related cognitions. *Manuscript submitted for publication.*

Mechanic, M.B., Resick, P.A., & Griffin, M.G. (1994, November). The role of cognitive schemata in persistent PTSD following sexual assault. In M.B. Mechanic & D.S. Riggs (Co-Chairs), *Cognitive schemata in female victims of sexual assault.* Symposium conducted at the 28th annual convention of the Association for Advancement of Behavior Therapy, San Diego, CA.

Mechanic, M.B., Resick, P.A., & Griffin, M.G. (1998). A comparison of normal forgetting, psychopathology, and information-processing models of reported amnesia for recent sexual trauma. *Journal of Consulting and Clinical Psychology, 66,* 948–957.

Meichenbaum, D. (1974). *Cognitive behavior modification.* Morristown, NJ: General Learning Press.

Melick, M., & Logue, J. (1985/1986). The effect of disaster on the health and well-being of older women. *International Journal of Aging and Human Development, 21,* 27–38.

Meyer, C.B., & Taylor, S.E. (1986). Adjustment to rape. *Journal of Personality and Social Psychology, 50,* 1226–1234.

Mitchell, J. (1983). When disaster stikes . . .: The critical incident stress debriefing process. *Journal of Emergency Medical Services, 8,* 36–39.

Mitchell, R., & Hodson, C. (1983). Coping with domestic violence: Social support and psychological health among battered women. *American Journal of Community Psychology, 11,* 629–654.

Morgan, C., Grillon, C., Southwick, S., Davis, M., & Charney, D. (1996). Exaggerated acoustic startle reflex in Gulf War veterans with posttraumatic stress disorder. *American Journal of Psychiatry, 153,* 64–68.

Mowrer, O.H. (1947). On the dual nature of learning: A reinterpretation of "conditioning" and "problem solving". *Harvard Educational Review, 17,* 102–148.

Murphy, S. (1988). Mediating effects of interpersonal and social suppport on mental health 1 and 3 years after a natural disaster. *Journal of Traumatic Stress, 1,* 155–172.

Newman, E., Riggs, D., & Roth, S. (1997). Thematic resolution and PTSD: An empirical investigation of the relationship between meaning and trauma-related diagnosis. *Journal of Traumatic Stress, 10,* 197–214.

Nezu, A.M., & Carnevale, G.J. (1987). Interpersonal problem solving and coping reactions of Vietnam veterans with posttraumatic stress disorder. *Journal of Abnormal Psychology, 96,* 155–157.

Nishith, P., Mechanic, M.B., & Resick, P.A. (2000). Prior interpersonal trauma: The contribution to current PTSD symptoms in female rape victims. *Journal of Abnormal Psychology, 109,* 20–25.

Nishith, P., Weaver, T.L., Resick, P.A., & Uhlmansiek, M.H. (1999). General memory functioning at pre- and post-treatment in female rape victims with PTSD. In L.M. Williams & V.L. Banyard (Eds.), *Trauma and memory* (pp. 47–55). Thousand Oaks, CA: Sage Publications.

Norris, F., & Kaniasty, K. (1994). Psychological distress following criminal victimization: Cross-sectional, longitudinal, and prospective analyses. *Journal of Consulting and Clinical Psychology, 10,* 239–261.

Norris, F.H. (1992). Epidemiology of trauma: Frequency and impact of different potentially traumatic events on different demographic groups. *Journal of Consulting and Clinical Psychology, 60,* 409–418.

Norris, J., & Feldman-Summers, S. (1981). Factors related to the psychological impacts of rape on the victim. *Journal of Abnormal Psychology, 90,* 562–567.

Orr, S.P., Lasko, N.B., Metzger, L.J., Berry, N.J., Ahern, C.E., & Pitman, R.K. (1998). Psychophysiologic assessment of women with posttraumatic stress disorder resulting from childhood sexual abuse. *Journal of Consulting and Clinical Psychology, 66,* 906–913.

Parkes, C.M. (1980). Bereavement counselling: Does it work? *British Medical Journal, 281,* 3–6.

Pelcovitz, D., van der Kolk, B.A., Roth, S., Mandel, F.S., Kaplan, S., & Resick, P. (1997). Development of a criteria set and a structured interview for disorders of extreme stress (SIDES). *Journal of Traumatic Stress, 10,* 3–16.

Perloff, L.S. (1983). Perceptions of vulnerability to victimization. *Journal of Social Issues, 39,* 41–61.

Perry, B.D. (1994). Neurobiological sequellae of childhood trauma: Post traumatic stress disorders in children. In M. Murburg (Ed.), *Catecholamines in posttraumatic stress disorder: Emerging concepts* (pp. 233–276). Washington, DC: American Psychiatric Press.

Perry, B.D., Giller, E.L., & Southwick, S.M. (1987). Altered platelet alpha2 adrenergic binding sites in post-traumatic stress disorder. *American Journal of Psychiatry, 144,* 1511–1512.

Perry, B.D., Pollard, R.A., Blakley, T.L., Baker, W.L., & Vigilante, D. (1995). Childhood trauma, the neurobiology of adaptation, and "use-dependent" development of the brain: How "states" become "traits". *Infant Mental Health Journal, 16,* 271–291.

Phifer, J. (1990). Psychological distress and somatic symptoms after natural disaster: Differential vulnerability among older adults. *Psychology and Aging, 5,* 412–420.

Pitman, R., Orr, S., Forgue, D., Altman, B., & deJong, J. (1990). Psychophysiologic responses to combat imagery of Vietnam veterans with posttraumatic stress disorder versus other anxiety disorders. *Journal of Abnormal Psychology, 99,* 49–54.

Pitman, R., Orr, S., Forgue, D., deJong, J., & Claiborn, J.M. (1987). Psychophysiologic assessment of posttraumatic stress disorder imagery in Vietnam combat veterans. *Archives of General Psychiatry, 44,* 970–975.

Price, J. (1978). Some age-related effects of the 1974 Brisbane floods. *Australian and New Zealand Journal of Psychiatry, 12,* 55–58.

Prins, A., Kaloupek, D.G., & Keane, T.M. (1995). Psychophysiological evidence for autonomic arousal and startle in traumatized adult populations. In M.J. Friedman, D.S. Charney, & A.Y. Deutch (Eds.), *Neurobiological and clinical consequences of stress: From normal adaptation to post-traumatic stress disorder.* Philadelphia: Lippincott-Raven.

Putnam, F.W. (1989). *Diagnosis and treatment of multiple personality disorder.* New York: Guilford Press.

Ramsay, R., Gorst-Unsworth, C., & Turner, S.W. (1993). Psychiatric morbidity in survivors of state organized violence including torture: A retrospective series. *British Journal of Psychiatry, 162,* 55–59.

Raphael, B. (1977). Preventive intervention with the recently bereaved. *Archives of General Psychiatry, 34,* 1450–1454.

Rauch, S.L., van der Kolk, B.A., Fisler, R.E., Alpert, N.M., Orr, S.P., Savage, C.R., Fischman, A.J., Jenike, M.A., & Pitman, R.K. (1996). A symptom provocation study of posttraumatic stress disorder using positron emission tomography and script-driven imagery. *Archives of General Psychiatry, 53,* 380–387.

Renfrey, G., & Spates, C.R. (1994). Eye movement desensitization: A partial dismantling study. *Journal of Behavior Therapy and Experimental Psychiatry, 25,* 231–239.

Resick, P., Nishith, P., Weaver, T.L., Astin, M., & Feuer, C.A. (2000). *A comparison of cognitive processing therapy, prolonged exposure, and a waiting condition for the treatment of posttraumatic stress disorder in female rape victims.* Unpublished manuscript, University of Missouri-St. Louis.

Resick, P.A. (1988). *Reactions of female and male victims of rape and robbery* (a final report, Grant No. 85–IJ-CX-0042). Washington, DC: National Institute of Justice.

Resick, P.A. (1995, May). *Cognitive processing therapy for rape victims.* Workshop conducted at conference on PTSD, sponsored by Manchester University in conjunction with the British Association for Behavioural and Cognitive Psychotherapies, Manchester, UK.

Resick, P.A., Calhoun, K.S., Atkeson, B.M., & Ellis, E.M. (1981). Social adjustment in victims of sexual assault. *Journal of Consulting and Clinical Psychology, 49,* 705–712.

Resick, P.A., & Jordan, C.G. (1988). Group stress inoculation training for victims of sexual assault: A therapist's manual. In P.A. Keller & S.R. Heyman (Eds.), *Innovations in clinical practice: A source book* (pp. 99–111). Sarasota, FL: Professional Resource Exchange.

Resick, P.A., Jordan, C.G., Girelli, S.A., Hutter, C.K., & Marhoefer-Dvorak, S. (1988). A comparative outcome study of behavioral group therapy for sexual assault victims. *Behavior Therapy, 19,* 385–401.

Resick, P.A., & Schnicke, M.K. (1992). Cognitive processing therapy for sexual assault victims. *Journal of Consulting and Clinical Psychology, 60,* 748–756.

Resick, P.A., & Schnicke, M.K. (1993). *Cognitive processing therapy for rape victims: A treatment manual.* Newbury Park, CA: Sage Publications.

Resick, P.A., Schnicke, M.K., & Markway, B.G. (1991, November). *The relation between cognitive content and PTSD.* Paper presented at the 25th annual convention of the Association for the Advancement of Behavior Therapy, New York.

Resnick, H., Acierno, R., Holmes, M., Kilpatrick, D.G., & Jager, N. (1999). Prevention of post-rape psychopathology: Preliminary findings of a controlled acute rape treatment study. *Journal of Anxiety Disorders, 13,* 359–370.

Resnick, H., Yehuda, R., Pitman, R., & Foy, D. (1995). Effect of previous trauma on acute plasma cortisol level following rape. *American Journal of Psychiatry, 152,* 1675–1677.

Resnick, H.S., Kilpatrick, D.G., Dansky, B.S., Saunders, B.E., & Best, C.L. (1993). Prevalence of civilian trauma and posttraumatic stress disorder in a representative national sample of women. *Journal of Consulting and Clinical Psychology, 61,* 984–991.

Resnick, H.S., & Newton, T. (1992). Assessment and treatment of post-traumatic stress disorder in adult survivors of sexual assault. In D.W. Foy (Ed.), *Treating PTSD: Cognitive-behavioral strategies.* New York: Guilford Press.

Riggs, D.S., Rothbaum, B.O., & Foa, E.B. (1995). A prospective examination of symptoms of posttraumatic stress disorder in victims of nonsexual assault. *Journal of Interpersonal Violence, 10,* 201–214.

Rimsza, M.E., & Berg, R.A. (1988). Sexual abuse: Somatic and emotional reactions. *Child Abuse and Neglect, 12,* 201–208.

Rose, S., Brewin, C.R., Andrews, B., & Kirk, M. (1999). A randomised trial of psychological debriefing for victims of violent crime. *Psychological Medicine, 29,* 793–799.

Roth, S., & Newman, E. (1991). The process of coping with sexual trauma. *Journal of Traumatic Stress, 4,* 279–297.

Roth, S., & Newman, E. (1992). The role of helplessness in the recovery process for sexual trauma survivors. *Canadian Journal of Behavioural Science, 24,* 220–232.

Roth, S., & Newman, E. (1993). The process of coping with incest for adult survivors: Measurement and implications. *Journal of Interpersonal Violence, 8,* 363–377.

Roth, S., Newman, E., Pelcovitz, D., van der Kolk, B., & Mandel, F.S. (1997). Complex PTSD in victims exposed to sexual and physical abuse: Results from the DSM-IV field trial for posttraumatic stress disorder. *Journal of Traumatic Stress, 10,* 539–555.

Rothbaum, B.O. (1995, November). *A controlled study of EMDR for PTSD.* Poster presented at the 29th meeting of the Association for Advancement of Behavior Therapy, Washington DC.

Rothbaum, B.O., Foa, E.B., Riggs, D.S., Murdock, T., & Walsh, W. (1992). A prospective examination of post-traumatic stress disorder in rape victims. *Journal of Traumatic Stress, 5,* 455–475.

Rotter, J.B. (1954). *Social learning and clinical psychology.* Englewood Cliffs, NJ: Prentice Hall.

Rubonis, A., & Bickman, L. (1991). Psychological impairment in the wake of disaster: The disaster–psychopathology relationship. *Psychological Bulletin, 109,* 384–399.

Ruch, L., & Chandler, S. (1980). An evaluation of a center for sexual assault. *Women and Health, 5,* 45–63.

Ruch, L.O., Chandler, S.M., & Harter, R.A. (1980). Life change and rape impact. *Journal of Health and Social Behavior, 21,* 248–260.

Ruch, L.O., & Leon, J.J. (1983). Sexual assault trauma and trauma change. *Women and Health, 8,* 5–21.

Russell, D.E. (1984). *Sexual exploitation: Rape, child sexual abuse and workplace harassment.* Newbury Park, CA: Sage.

Rychtarik, R.G., Silverman, W.K., Van Landingham, W.P., & Prue, D.M. (1984). Treatment of an incest victim with implosive therapy: A case study. *Behavior Therapy, 15,* 410–420.

Sales, E., Baum, M., & Shore, B. (1984). Victim readjustment following assault. *Journal of Social Issues, 40,* 117–136.

Sapolsky, R.M., Uno, H., Rebert, C.S., & Finch, C.E. (1990). Hippocampal damage associated with prolonged stress exposure in primates. *Journal of Neuroscience, 10,* 2897–2902.

Scheppele, K.L., & Bart, P.B. (1983). Through women's eyes: Defining danger in the wake of sexual assault. *Journal of Social Issues, 39,* 63–80.

Schetky, D.H. (1990). A review of the literature on the long-term effects of childhood sexual abuse. In R.P. Kluft (Ed.), *Incest-related syndromes of adult psychopathology* (pp. 35–54). Washington, DC: American Psychiatric Press.

Schindler, F.E. (1980). Treatment of systematic desensitization of a recurring nightmare of a real life trauma. *Journal of Behavior Therapy and Experimental Psychiatry, 11,* 53–54.

Selkin, J. (1978). Protecting personal space: Victim and resister reactions to assaultive rape. *Journal of Community Psychology, 6*(3), 263–268.

Selye, H. (1976). *The stress of life.* New York: McGraw-Hill. (Original work published 1956.)

Shalev, A.Y., Peri, T., Canetti, L., & Schreiber, S. (1996). Predictors of PTSD in injured trauma survivors. *American Journal of Psychiatry, 53,* 219–224.

Shalev, A.Y., Sahar, T., Freedman, S., Peri, T., Glick, N., Brandes, D., Orr, S.P., & Pitman, R.K. (1998). A prospective study of heart rate response following trauma and the subsequent development of posttraumatic stress disorder. *Archives of General Psychiatry, 55,* 553–559.

Shapiro, F. (1989). Eye movement desensitization: A new treatment for post traumatic stress disorder. *Journal of Behavior Therapy and Experimental Psychiatry, 20,* 211–217.

Shapiro, F. (1995). *Eye movement desensitization and reprocessing: Basic principles, protocols, and procedures.* New York: Guilford.

Shipherd, J.C., & Beck, J.G. (1999). The effects of suppressing trauma-related thoughts on women with rape-related posttraumatic stress disorder. *Behaviour Research and Therapy, 37,* 99–112.

Shore, J., Tatum, E., & Vollmer, W. (1986). Psychiatric reactions to disaster: The Mount St. Helen's experience. *American Journal of Psychiatry, 143,* 590–595.

Sierles, F., Chen, J., McFarland, R., & Taylor, M. (1983). Posttraumatic stress disorder and concurrent psychiatric illness: A preliminary report. *American Journal of Psychiatry, 140,* 1177–1179.

Sigmon, S.T., Greene, M.P., Rohan, K.J., & Nichols, J.D. (1996). Coping and adjustment in male and female survivors of childhood sexual abuse. *Journal of Child Sexual Abuse, 5,* 57–75.

Smith, E., Robins, L., Przybeck, T., Goldring, E., & Solomon, S. (1986). Psychosocial consequences of disaster. In J.H. Shore (Ed.), *Disaster stress studies: New methods and findings* (pp. 49–76). Washington, DC: American Psychiatric Press.

Southwick, S., Yehuda, R., & Giller, E. (1993). Personality disorders in treatment seeking combat veterans with posttraumatic stress disorder. *American Journal of Psychiatry, 150,* 1020–1023.

Southwick, S.M., Krystal, J.H., Morgan, A.C., Johnson, D., Nagy, L., Nicolaou, A., Henninger, G.R., & Charney, D.S. (1993). Abnormal noradrenergic function in posttraumatic stress disorder. *Archives of General Psychiatry, 50,* 266–274.

Southwick, S.M., Morgan, A.C., Bremner, J.D., Nagy, L., Krystal, J.H., & Charney, D.S. (1990, December). *Yohimbine and M-CPP effects in PTSD patients.* Poster presented at the annual meeting of the American College of Neuropharmacology, Puerto Rico.

Southwick, S.M., Morgan, A.C., Nicolaou, A.L., & Charney, D.S. (1997). Consistency of memory for combat-related traumatic events in veterans of Operation Desert Storm. *American Journal of Psychiatry, 154*, 173–177.

Southwick, S.M., Yehuda, R., Giller, E.L., & Charney, D.S. (1994). Use of tricyclics and monoamine oxidase inhibitors in the treatment of PTSD: A quantitative review. In M.M. Murburg (Ed.), *Catecholamine function in post-traumatic stress disorder: Emerging concepts* (pp. 293–305). Washington, DC: American Psychiatry Press.

Spiegel, D. (1991). Dissociation and trauma. In A. Tasman & S. Goldfinger (Eds.), *American psychiatric press review of psychiatry, Vol. 10* (pp. 261–275). Washington, DC: American Psychiatric Press.

Spiegel, D., Koopman, C., Cardeña, E., & Classen, C. (1996). Dissociative symptoms in the diagnosis of acute stress disorder. In W.J. Ray (Ed.), *Handbook of dissociation*. New York: Plenum Press.

Spielberger, C.D. (1966). *Anxiety and behavior*. New York: Academic Press.

Spiro, A., Schnurr, P., & Aldwin, C. (1994). Combat-related posttraumatic stress disorder symptoms in older men. *Psychology and Aging, 9*, 17–26.

Starkman, M.N., Gebarski, S.S., Berent, S., & Schteingart, D.E. (1992). Hippocampal formation volume, memory of dysfunction, and cortisol levels in patients with Cushing's syndrome. *Biological Psychiatry, 32*, 756–765.

Stein, M., Walker, J., Hazen, A., & Forde, D. (1997). Full and partial posttraumatic stress disorder: Findings from a community survey. *American Journal of Psychiatry, 154*, 1114–1119.

Stewart, B.D., Hughes, C., Frank, E., Anderson, B., Kendall, K., & West, D. (1987). The aftermath of rape: Profiles of immediate and delayed treatment seekers. *Journal of Nervous and Mental Disease, 175*, 90–94.

Straus, M., Gelles, R., & Steinmetz, S. (1980). *Behind closed doors: A survey of family violence in America*. New York: Doubleday.

Stretch, R.H. (1991). Psychosocial readjustment of Canadian Vietnam veterans. *Journal of Consulting and Clinical Psychology, 59*, 188–189.

Stretch, R.H., Vail, J.D., & Maloney, J.P. (1985). Posttraumatic stress disorder among army nurse corps Vietnam veterans. *Journal of Consulting and Clinical Psychology, 53*, 704–708.

Stroop, J.R. (1935). Studies of interference in serial verbal reaction. *Journal of Experimental Psychology, 18*, 643–662.

Sutker, P., Davis, J., Uddo, M., & Ditta, S. (1995). War zone stress, personal resources, and PTSD in Persian Gulf war returnees. *Journal of Abnormal Psychology, 104*, 444–452.

Sutker, P.B., Winstead, D.K., Galina, Z.H., & Allain, A.N. (1991). Cognitive deficits and psychopathology among former prisoners of war and combat veterans of the Korean conflict. *American Journal of Psychiatry, 148*, 67–72.

Tarrier, N., Pilgrim, H., Sommerfield, C., Faragher, B., Reynolds, M., Graham, E., & Barrowclough, C. (1999). A randomized trial of cognitive therapy and imaginal exposure in the treatment of chronic posttraumatic stress disorder. *Journal of Consulting and Clinical Psychology, 67*, 13–18.

Taylor, S., Kuch, K., Koch, W.J., Crockett, D.J., & Passey, G. (1998). The structure of posttraumatic stress symptoms. *Journal of Abnormal Psychology, 107*, 154–160.

Thompson, M.P., Norris, F.H., & Hanacek, B. (1993). Age differences in the psychological consequences of Hurricane Hugo. *Psychology and Aging, 8*, 606–616.

Thornhill, N.W., & Thornhill, R. (1990). An evolutionary analysis of psychological pain following rape: II. The effects of stranger, friend, and family-member offenders. *Ethology and Sociobiology, 11*, 177–193.

Thrasher, S.M., Dalgleish, T., & Yule, W. (1994). Information processing in post-traumatic stress disorder. *Behavior Research and Therapy, 32*, 247–254.

Tichenor, V., Marmar, C.R., Weiss, D.S., Metzler, T.J., & Ronfeldt, H.M. (1996). The relationship of peritraumatic dissociation and posttraumatic stress: Findings in female Vietnam theater veterans. *Journal of Consulting and Clinical Psychology, 64*, 1054–1059.

van der Kolk, B.A. (1994). The body keeps the score: Memory and the evolving psychobiology of posttraumatic stress. *Harvard Review of Psychiatry, 1*(5), 253–265.

van der Kolk, B.A. (1996). The complexity of adaptation to trauma: Self-regulation, stimulus discrimination, and characterological development. In B.A. van der Kolk, A.C. McFarlane, & L. Weisaeth (Eds.), *Traumatic stress: The effects of overwhelming experience on mind, body, and society* (pp. 182–213). New York: Guilford Press.

van der Kolk, B.A., Dryfuss, D., Michaels, M., Berkowitz, R., Saxe, G., & Goldenberg, I. (1994). Fluoxetine in post-traumatic stress disorder. *Journal of Clinical Psychiatry, 55*, 517–522.

van der Kolk, B., McFarlane, A., & van der Hart, O. (1996). A general approach to treatment of posttraumatic stress disorder. In B.A. van der Kolk, A.C. McFarlane, & L. Weisaeth (Eds.), *Traumatic stress: The effects of overwhelming experience on mind, body, and society* (pp. 417–440). New York: Guilford Press.

van der Kolk, B., & van der Hart, O. (1989). Pierre Janet and the breakdown of adaptation in psychological trauma. *American Journal of Psychiatry, 146*(12), 1530–1540.

van Dijk, J.J. (1997, August). *Criminal victimization and victim empowerment in an international perspective: Key results on fifty nations of the international crime victims surveys: 1989–1996*. Keynote address at the ninth international symposium on Victimology, Amsterdam.

van Velsen, C., Gorst-Unsworth, C., & Turner, S. (1996). Survivors of torture and organized violence: Demography and diagnosis. *Journal of Traumatic Stress, 9*, 181–193.

Vaughan, K., Armstrong, M.S., Gold, R., O'Connor, N., Jenneke, W., & Tarrier, N. (1994). A trial of eye movement desensitization compared to image habituation training, and applied muscle relaxation in posttraumatic stress disorder. *Journal of Behavior Therapy and Experimental Psychiatry, 25*, 283–291.

Vernberg, E.M., La Greca, A.M., Silverman, W.K., & Prinstein, M.J. (1996). Prediction of posttraumatic stress symptoms in children after Hurricane Andrew. *Journal of Abnormal Psychology, 105*, 237–248.

Veronen, L.J., & Kilpatrick, D.G. (1983). Stress management for rape victims. In D. Meichenbaum & M.E. Jaremko (Eds.), *Stress reduction and prevention* (pp. 341–374). New York: Plenum.

Veronen, L.G., Kilpatrick, D.G., & Resick, P.A. (1979). Treating fear and anxiety in rape victims: Implications for the criminal justice system. In W.H. Parsonage (Ed.), *Perspectives on victimology* (pp. 148–159). Beverly Hills, CA: Sage Publications.

Vingerhoets, A., & Van Heck, G. (1990). Gender, coping and psychosomatic symptoms. *Psychological Medicine, 20,* 125–135.

Vrana, S.R., Roodman, A., & Beckham, J.C. (1995). Selective processing of trauma-relevant words in posttraumatic stress disorder. *Journal of Anxiety Disorders, 9,* 515–530.

Wagner, A.W., & Linehan, M.M. (1998). Dissociative behavior. In V.M. Follette, J.I. Ruzek, & F.R. Abueg (Eds.), *Cognitive-behavioral therapies for trauma* (pp. 191–225). New York: Guilford Press.

Waigandt, A., Wallace, D.L., Phelps, L., & Miller, D. (1990). The impact of sexual assault on physical health status. *Journal of Traumatic Stress, 3,* 93–102.

Weaver, T., & Clum, G. (1995). Psychological distress associated with interpersonal violence: A meta analysis. *Clinical Psychology Review, 15,* 115–140.

Weaver, T.L., & Chard, K.M. (1997). *Physical impact and posttraumatic stress disorder associated with partner violence: A meta-analysis.* Unpublished manuscript, University of Missouri-St. Louis.

Wegner, D.M., Schneider D.J., Carter, S.R., & White, T.L. (1987). Paradoxical effects of thought suppression. *Journal of Personality and Social Psychology, 53,* 5–13.

Weiner, B. (1985). An attributional theory of achievement motivation and emotion. *Psychological Review, 92,* 548–573.

Weiss, D., Marmar, C., Metzler, T., & Ronfeldt, H. (1995). Predicting symptomatic distress in emergency services personnel. *Journal of Consulting and Clinical Psychology, 63,* 361–368.

Wells, J., Hobfoll, S., & Lavin, J. (1997). Resource loss, resource gain, and communal coping during pregnancy among women with multiple roles. *Psychology of Women Quarterly, 21,* 645–662.

Wenninger, K., & Ehlers, A. (1998). Dysfunctional cognitions and adult psychological functioning in child sexual abuse survivors. *Journal of Traumatic Stress, 11,* 281–300.

Williams, R.M., Hodgkinson, P., Joseph, S., & Yule, W. (1995). Attitudes to emotion, crisis support, and distress 30 months after the capsize of a passenger ferry disaster. *Crisis Intervention, 1,* 209–214.

Wilson, S.A., Becker, L.A., & Tinker, R. (1995). Eye movement desensitization and reprocessing (EMDR) treatment for psychologically traumatized individuals. *Journal of Consulting and Clinical Psychology, 63,* 928–937.

Wirtz, P.W., & Harrell, A.V. (1987). Assaultive versus nonassaultive victimization: A profile analysis of psychological response. *Journal of Interpersonal Violence, 2,* 264–277.

Wolfe, J., Keane,, T.M., Kaloupek, D.G., Mora, C.A., & Wine, P. (1993). Patterns of positive readjustment in Vietnam combat veterans. *Journal of Traumatic Stress, 6,* 179–193.

Wolpe, J. (1958). *Psychotherapy by reciprocal inhibition.* Stanford, CA: Stanford University Press.

Wortman, C.B. (1976). Casual atttributions and personal control. In J.H. Harvey, W.J. Ickes, & R.F. Kidd (Eds.), *New directions in attribution research, Vol. 1.* Hillsdale, NJ: Lawrence Erlbaum Associates Inc.

Wyatt, G.E., Notgrass, C.M., & Newcomb, M. (1990). Internal and external mediators of women's rape experiences. *Psychology of Women Quarterly, 14,* 153–176.

Yehuda, R. (1997). Sensitization of the hypotahlamic-pituitary-adrenal axis in posttraumatic stress disorder. In R. Yehuda & A. McFarlane (Eds.), *Psychobiology of posttraumatic stress disorder: Annals of the New York Academy of Sciences, Vol. 821* (pp. 57–75). New York: Academy of Sciences.

Yehuda, R. (1998). Resilience and vulnerability factors in the course of adaptation to trauma. *National Center for Post-Traumatic Stress Disorder Clinical Quarterly, 8,* 3–5.

Yehuda, R., Boisoneau, D., Lowy, M.T., & Giller, E.L. (1995). Dose-response changes in plasma cortisol and lymphocyte glucocorticoid receptors following dexamethasone administration in combat veterans with and without post-traumatic stress disorder. *Archives of General Psychiatry, 52,* 583–593.

Yehuda, R., Boisoneau, D., Mason, J.W., & Giller, E.L. (1993). Glucocorticoid receptor number and cortisol excretion in mood, anxiety, and psychotic disorders. *Biological Psychiatry, 34,* 18–25.

Yehuda, R., Giller, E.L., Levengood, R.A., Southwick, S.M., & Siever, L.J. (1995). Hypothalamic-pituitary-adrenal functioning in post-traumatic stress disorder: Expanding the concept of the stress response spectrum. In M.J. Friedman, E.S. Charney, & A.Y. Deutch (Eds.), *Neurobiological and clinical consequences of stress: From normal adaptation to PTSD* (pp. 351–365). Philadelphia: Lippincott-Raven.

Yehuda, R., Perry, B.D., Southwick, S.M., & Giller, E.L. (1990). Platelet alpha2 adrenergic binding in PTSD, generalized anxiety disorder and major depressive disorder. In *New Research Abstracts, 143.* New York: American Psychiatric Association.

Yehuda, R., Southwick, S., Giller, E., Ma, X., & Mason, J.W. (1992). Urinary catecholamine excretion and severity of PTSD symptoms in Vietnam combat veterans. *Journal of Nervous and Mental Disease, 180,* 321–325.

Yehuda, R., Southwick, S.M., Mason, J.W., & Giller, E.L. (1990). Interactions of the hypothalamic-pituitary-adrenal axis and the catecholaminergic system of the stress disorder. In E.L Giller (Ed.), *Biological assessment and treatment of PTSD.* Washington, DC: American Psychiatric Press.

Young, M. (1988). The crime victims movement. In F. Ochberg (Ed.), *Post-traumatic therapy and victims of violence* (pp. 13–57). New York: Brunner/Mazel.

Zatzick, D., Marmar, C., Weiss, D., & Metzler, T. (1994). Does trauma-linked dissociation vary across ethnic groups? *Journal of Nervous and Mental Disease, 182,* 576–582.

Zigmond, M., Finlay, J., & Sved, A. (1995). Neurochemical studies of central noradrenergic responses to acute and chronic stress: Implications for normal and abnormal behavior. In M.J. Friedman, E.S. Charney, & A.Y. Deutch (Eds.), *Neurobiological and clinical consequences of stress: From normal adaptation to PTSD.* Philadelphia: Lippincott-Raven.

Author index

Note: References to *boxes*, *figures* and *tables* are indicated in *italics*.

Thornhill, N.W. 109
Thornhill, R. 109
Thrasher, S. 154–5, 158, 162
Thrasher, S.M. 68
Tichenor, V. 112
Tinker, R. 164
Tomas, S. 146
Toomey, T. 27
Touze, J. 164
Turner, S. 42, 103, 104
Turner, S.W. 42
Twentyman, C.T 67
Tzemach, M. 59

Uddo, M. 98
Uhlmansiek, M.H. 92
Uno, H. 83, 92

Vail, J.D. 41
van der Hart, O. 63, 148
van der Kolk, B. 53, 63, 142, 143, 148
van der Kolk, B.A. 53, 82, 92, 93, 143, 149
van Dijk, J.J. 35, 36*t*
van Heck, G. 123
van Kammen, D.P. 41
van Kammen, W. 41
van Landingham, W.P. 160
van Valkenberg, C. 41
van Velsen, C. 42
Vaughan, K. 164
Vermetten, E. 92

Vernberg, E.M. 98, 122–3
Veronen, L. 150
Veronen, L.G. 4, 5*t*
Veronen, L.J. 5, 65, 70, 102, 108, 109, 150, 151
Vigilante, D. 4, 82, 93, 101
Vingerhoets, A. 123
Vollmer, A. 7, 87, 107
Vollmer, W. 97
Vrana, S.R. 68

Wagner, A.W. 66
Waigandt, A. 27
Walker, J. 31, 37, 38
Wallace, D.L. 27
Walsh, W. 6*f*, 44
Watson, S.B. 131
Weaver, T. 69, 96, 97, 98, 100
Weaver, T.L. 27, 92, 161
Webster, R. 146
Wegner, D.M. 119
Weiner, B. 124–5
Weisaeth, L. 146
Weiss, D. 98, 112
Weiss, D.S. 19, 25, 26, 27, 40–1, 49–50, 51, 63, 64, 97, 98, 99, 104, 112, 148–9
Wells, J. 59
Wenninger, K. 126, 132
West, D. 104, 109, 159
West, D.G. 107
White, T.L. 119
Whitlock, F.A. 27
Williams, C. 123–4

Williams, G. 27
Williams, R. 125–6, 138
Williams, R.M. 138
Wilson, E.M. 85
Wilson, R.M. 85
Wilson, S. 27
Wilson, S.A. 164
Wine, P. 123
Winstead, D.K. 92
Wirtz, P.W. 102
Wisniewski, N. 30, 33
Wolfe, D.A. 27
Wolfe, J. 52, 123
Wolpe, J. 151, 152
Woodruff, W. 27
Woods, M.G. 160
Woods, S.W. 90
Wortman, C. 128
Wortman, C.B. 69, 128
Wyatt, G.E. 128

Yehuda, R. 52, 52*t*, 81, 84, 90, 91–2, 101, 143
Young, M. 145
Yule, W. 68, 125–6, 138

Zak, L. 27
Zatzick, D. 98
Zeitlin, S.B. 68
Zhiming, L. 27
Zigmond, M. 83
Zimering, R.T. 65, 160
Zvekic, U. 35

Subject index

Note: References to *boxes, figures* and *tables* are indicated in *italics*.

and social support 135, 138

Disorders see Clinical disorders; Prevalence of disorders

Disorders of extreme stress, not otherwise specified (DESNOS) 13, 53

Dissociation 20, 25
in acute stress disorder 18, 19
in complex PTSD 54
Janet's theories 62–3
learned behavior 66
neurobiology 93
peritraumatic 87, 88b, 88f, 98, 111–13, 114
in PTSD 14b, 15–16
race and risk of trauma 98

Dissociative amnesia 18, 20–1, 22, 66 see also Peritraumatic dissociation

Dissociative fugue 21–2

Dissociative identity disorder (DID) (formerly Multiple personality disorder) 22–4, 149–50

Distress 10, 15b, 16, 18

Divorce 25, 100

Domestic violence see also Battered women
coping styles 121, 122
effects on reactions to rape 103–4
prevalence 32, 33, 34, 37
PTSD 42

Dopamines 93

Drug abuse/dependence
after sexual assault 46–7, 46t
comorbidity 22, 25, 26, 47, 50–1
and coping 120
and PTSD 48, 49t, 50
and reactions to trauma 104–5

and self-reported health problems 27
and victimization 104–5

Dual representation theory 73–6

Education and risk of trauma 99–100

Emotional abuse 103–4

Emotions see also Affect
and coping 120, 121
processing trauma 74–6, 75t, 120
responses 83–4
and social support 135, 138

Employment 26

Endogenous morphines see Endorphines

Endorphines 82

Environment, invalidating 66

Epidemiological studies 47, 48–9, 49t

Epinephrine (adrenaline) 79, 81, 85, 90

Eye movement desensitization and reprocessing therapy (EMDR) 163–5

Fear 66–7, 74, 143, 150–1 see also Phobias

Fight–flight response 80–1, 82–3, 93

Fire
disorders following 50
prevalence 37–8
prior psychological functioning and response to 104
PTSD 45, 50, 113
and social support 138

Flashbacks 14b, 15, 18, 61–2, 72, 74
in PTSD 90, 91, 92

Flooding
direct therapeutic exposure 152–3, 160–1
prolonged exposure 153–4, 159, 161

Fluoxetine (Prozac) 143

Fluvoxamine 143

Freezing 4, 93

Functional impairment 10, 15b, 16, 18, 20, 24–6

Gender
accidents 38, 99
coping strategies 123–4
physical assault variables 34, 35–7, 36t, 99, 108
PTSD 39, 54, 105–6, 108
risk of trauma 98–9
type of trauma 105–6

Glucocorticoids 80, 81–2, 83, 92

Guilt 129–31, 161 see also Self-blame

Helplessness 125

Hippocampus 83, 84, 92

Holocaust survivors 42

Homicide, family survivors 11–12, 34–5, 35t, 44–5, 96

Hormones 79

Hypothalamus 79

Hysteria 60–2, 61b

Imipramine 143

Immune system 81–2

Impulse control 54

Impulsivity 22

Incest 12, 27, 62, 103–4, 160

Information processing theory 66–8

Learning difficulties 25

Learning theory 64–6

Physical disorders 26–8, 82

Physiological arousal 14*b*, 16, 18, 84, 142, 143

"Physioneurosis" 85

Pituitary gland 79

Post-trauma risk factors and resources 40–5, 48, 49–51 *see also* Cognitions (post-trauma); Coping; Social support

Post-traumatic stress disorder (PTSD) 12–17, 22 *see also* Post-trauma risk factors and resources; Psychological risk factors; Psychophysiological reactivity
after bereavement 11–12
anger 71
at-risk populations 40–5
and attribution 125
battered women 42–3
central nervous system abnormalities 92–3
child abuse 42
combat veterans 40–1, 106
comorbidity 47–55, 49*t*, 50, 75, 141, 149
complex/associated features 53–4, 149
crime victims 7, 42–5, 107–8
date rape 17
delayed onset 7
diagnostic criteria 13, 14–15*b*, 15–16
disasters 40, 45, 50, 106–7, 112
disorders of extreme stress, not otherwise specified (DESNOS) 13, 53
domestic violence 42

emotional processing 74–6, 75*t*
fear 66–7
and fight–flight reaction 83
fire trauma 45, 50, 113
Holocaust survivors 42
homicide, family survivors 44–5
and information processing theory 66–8
and learning theory 64–6
motor vehicle accident victims 7, 40, 45
neglect 42
neuroendocrine abnormalities 89–92, 142–3
and personality disorders 51–4, 149
physical assault victims 40, 42, 44, 52–3, 52*t*
predicting 19
prevalence 39–45, 54
prospective studies 5–8, 43–4
rape victims 6, 6*f*, 17, 40, 42, 43, 44, 52–3, 52*t*, 105
refugees 41, 42, 50, 112
retrospective studies 8, 43
sadness 71
and self-reported health problems 27
sex differences 39, 54, 105–6, 108
sexual assault victims 40, 42
shame 71
and social-cognitive theories 68
startle response 16, 89, 143
and stress response 83, 84

torture victims 42
treatment *see* Treatment of traumatic stress reactions
type of trauma 105–6
Vietnam veterans 12, 25–6, 40–1, 49–50, 104, 106
war 40, 41

Prevalence of disorders 30, 38, 45, 54–5
anti-social personality disorder (ASPD) 52
at-risk populations 40–5, 49–51
battered women 42–3
child abuse victims 42
combat veterans 40–1
crime victims 42–5
depression 43, 46–7, 46*t*
disaster victims 40, 45, 46
domestic violence victims 42
fire trauma 45
Holocaust survivors 42
homicide, family survivors 44–5
motor accident vehicle victims 40, 45
neglect 42
physical assault victims 40, 42
psychological disorders 46–7, 46*t*
PTSD 39–45, 54
rape victims 40, 42, 43, 44
refugees 41, 42
sexual assault victims 40, 42, 46–7, 46*t*
studies, prospective/retrospective 43–4
torture victims 42
Vietnam veterans 40–1
war 40, 41

Stress inoculation training (SIT) 150–2, 158–9, 161
Stress response 3–4, 58
  central nervous system 82–4
  peripheral nervous system 80–2
  and PTSD 84
Stress theory 57–60
Subconscious 62
Subjective Units of Distress (SUDS) 153
Substance abuse *see* Alcohol abuse/ dependence; Drug abuse/dependence
Suicidal behaviour 20, 104, 120
Symptoms
  aggressive behavior 20, 25
  anxiety 18
  avoidance 14*b*, 15, 18, 24–5, 65
  depersonalization 18, 22
  derealization 18, 66
  dissociation 14*b*, 15–16, 18, 19, 20, 25
  dissociative amnesia 18, 20, 66
  distress, significant 10, 15*b*, 16, 18
  flashbacks 14*b*, 15, 18, 61–2, 72, 90, 91, 92
  foreshortened future 16
  functional impairment 10, 15*b*, 16, 18, 20, 24–6
  impulsivity 22
  numbing 14*b*, 15–16, 18, 25, 143
  persistence of 10, 14*b*, 16, 18
  physiological arousal 14*b*, 16, 18, 84, 142, 143

reduced awareness of surroundings 18
re-experiencing 14*b*, 15, 18, 61–2, 66–7, 72, 74, 142
relationships changes 22
self-mutilation 20, 22, 120
sexual dysfunction 20
stressors, identifiable 10, 13, 14*b*, 18
suicidal behaviour 20, 104, 120
Systematic desensitization (SD) 152, 159–60

TCAs (tricyclic antidepressants) 143
Thought suppression 119, 151
Threats 33*t*, 58, 108, 113
Torture victims 42
Traumatic stress 2–3, 28
  see also Clinical disorders; Post-traumatic stress disorder (PTSD); Prevalence of trauma; Psychological risk factors; Psychophysiological reactivity; Symptoms
  and physical disorders 26–8
recovery 4, 5–9
Treatment of traumatic stress reactions 141
  biological treatments *see* Medication
  therapies *see* Cognitive-behavioral therapies; Crisis intervention; Eye movement desensitization and reprocessing therapy (EMDR); Psychodynamic therapies

Tricyclic antidepressants (TCAs) 143

Uniform Crime Reports (UCR) 30, 31

Victimization
  crime surveys 30–1
  and trauma reactions 100, 101–2, 103–4, 104–5
Vietnam veterans *see also* Psychophysiological reactivity
  age and risk of trauma 96
  anti-social personality disorder (ASPD) 51, 52, 52*t*
  childhood trauma 101
  combat exposure 106
  comorbidity 50
  coping styles 123
  depression 50, 137
  education 99
  peritraumatic dissociation 112
  personality disorders 52, 52*t*
  prior psychological functioning 104
  PTSD 12, 25–6, 40–1, 49–50, 104, 106
  race and risk of trauma 97
  self-reported health problems 27
  shame and guilt 71–2, 131
  and social support 137
  socioeconomic status 99
  substance abuse 50
  treatment 160–1, 165
Violent crime *see also* Domestic violence
  education and risk of trauma 99
  level of violence 107–8

prevalence 35–7, 36*t*
recovery after 7
in trauma victims 26
Vulnerability 125, 127

War *see also* War veterans
neurosis in 60–2
prevalence of trauma
37
PTSD 40, 41
War veterans *see also*
Combat and combat
veterans; Vietnam
veterans
age and risk of trauma
96

coping styles 121
and health care
utilization 27
PTSD 41
race and risk of trauma
98
treatment 160
Witness to serious injury or
death 32, 33*t*
Women *see also* Domestic
violence; Rape and
rape victims; Sexual
assault
coping styles and
strategies 122, 123,
124

effects of physical abuse
on 34, 52–3, 52*t*, 100,
103
prevalence of trauma
among 31, 34, 35–7,
36*t*
PTSD and type of
trauma 105–6
victimization and
trauma reactions 91,
100, 101–2, 103–4,
104–5

Yohimbine 90, 91

Zoloft (sertraline) 143

DATE DUE

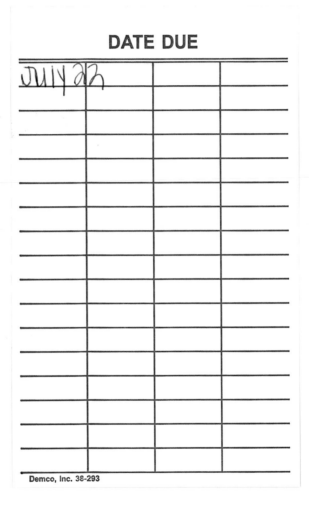

JULY 22			

Demco, Inc. 38-293